BEDTIME WITH BITSY

A CRITICAL READ OF THE CHRONICLES OF NARNIA

ALEXIS RECORD

HYPATIA PRESS

Published in the United States of America by Hypatia Press in 2022

ISBN: 978-1-83919-196-1

www.hypatiapress.org

Dedicated to Linda Record. Thanks for lending me your Narnia series, helping me process my former fundamentalism, and stepping into the mom role on multiple occasions.

Contents

1
The Importance of a Bedtime Story

Magic spells, witches, and children running around without parental supervision? How were my conservative Christian parents okay with this?

I was luckier than some. I had a mother who read to me. Despite a lot of limitations growing up in the eighties and nineties during the height of evangelical culture, I had the world at bedtime. I played with children living in boxcars, raced chariots with champions, made messes with a talking cat, and ate chocolate with golden-ticket winners.

Leaders in my fundamentalist Christian tradition considered many popular books, types of music, and television shows to be influenced by the devil. Anything with witchcraft (Smurfs), otherworldly powers (Power Rangers), or spirits (Ghostbusters) were labeled satanic. The only power allowed in our home was God's and the only spirit was the Holy Spirit. Our church taught an abstain-from-all-appearance-of-evil[1] approach to media which led to substantial restrictions in my early years. If there was any doubt something would not pass the godly sniff test—movies, books, clothing, music, activities, public education—we simply avoided it. It was the Chuckie Finster approach to life. Tommy Pickles was mainstream society and our every response to it was, "Maybe this isn't such a good idea."

---

[1] 1 Thessalonians 5:22

When it came to the culture around us, we were "in it, but not *of* it," as the mantra went. I even proudly wore a shirt that said "Narrowminded" with Matthew 7:14 printed beneath. No influence could touch us beyond what our Baptist church allowed. Yet when it came to *The Chronicles of Narnia*, Christian propaganda in the form of children's stories, suddenly magic and witchcraft were allowed, even encouraged by my pastor! I could finally experience something *new*— journeying to far-away lands, meeting interesting talking creatures, and stumbling upon spellbound adventures. It was incredible!

I was at a friend's house the first time I saw the Teenage Mutant Ninja Turtle live-action movie. Splinter had been kidnaped and the turtles were searching for him. In one scene they all concentrated on their master until he appeared in spirit-form in their midst. My friend's mom grabbed for the remote to pause the movie and sputtered, "I did not remember this part. Please don't tell your mother!" I left thinking I had sinned. Giving Foot Clan soldiers concussions or putting Master Shredder through a garbage compactor was all fine, but the moment those turtle teens used the power of love in a séance, now we were in evil territory!

It makes sense that violence in our media was sanctioned whereas love magic was not, considering brutality is plentiful in the Old Testament stories I grew up with, and magic condemned. If physical violence was truly bad, why would God order so much of it in the Bible and then command his people to teach their children about it?[2] Terrorism and bloodshed were the prescribed methods for dealing with witches, disobedient slaves, or people from countries where God's favorites wanted to take up real estate. It had to be excused then, at least in many cases, from our list of evil things to avoid.

---

[2] Deuteronomy 11:19

I was forbidden to absorb evil content, but what made something wrong or right depended on who did it. Hitting my sister was forbidden, but God could strike people down. A witch's potion used to cure maladies was demonic, but Jesus' magic spit mud[3] was acceptable. It took me a long time to realize the Venn diagram of evil magic and holy miracles is a circle. Or as Aron Ra put it:

> "A boat may be considered a ship if it's big enough. When a rich man is neurotic, we call him eccentric. When a V.I.P. is murdered, it's an assassination. When a god performs magic, he's working miracles."[4]

With definitions this nebulous, I must acknowledge how hard it was for my parents to navigate what exactly was off-limits. The mental gymnastics our family did in order to accommodate *Rainbow Brite* (she's using color "technology"), *Care Bears* (God made them that way; they could be angels), and *The Legend of Zelda* (video game magic beams are just lasers) was baffling. However, I remain dearly indebted for every brain-bending exception to the "no Satanic influence" rule. Each enriched my childhood.

If magic is anything formed in the imagination, then a child must be pure magic. Childhood itself is something precious and wonderous. No wonder we loved *The Chronicles of Narnia*. Sure, C. S. Lewis' tales were stamped and approved Christian fables used to help children understand the weightier parts of the theology they inherited, but they also happened to be fun adventure stories. Many of my friends from similar restrictive religious backgrounds had the same experience with these stories that I did. We felt free to explore magical worlds for the first time. It was a welcomed break from *Foxe's Book of Martyrs* and *The Pilgrim's Progress*, both assigned reading for my limited education.

---

[3] John 9:6
[4] Aron Ra, 2016. *Foundational Falsehoods of Creationism*, (Durham, NC: Pitchstone Publishing).

I must hand it to C. S. Lewis; the man could paint a word picture. I can still imagine transforming into a dragon, falling into a picture frame, and feeling the bottom of a wardrobe turn from wood to snow.

Fast forward a few decades and I find myself with a daughter of my own who loves magical stories. We just finished reading the entire *Harry Potter* series and wondered which magical tale would be next. We read *The Hobbit*, but I often had to stop and explain the extant language or complicated themes. We only got one chapter into the first *Lord of the Rings* book before realizing it was much more of the same and a bit too slow in action for my nine-year old. Then I remembered the first set of children's tales I had really been drawn into when I was around her age. I borrowed the massive novel from my aunt Linda that contained all seven books bound together and we dove into the first tale of thinking trees and a magic wardrobe. It felt like I was coming home to old friends after a long time away and here was my real-life Lucy sitting right next to me!

Even as my heart was pumping with excitement over these stories, my brain was jumping higher and higher hurdles around problematic paragraphs. My daughter, whom I'll call Bitsy for her short stature, stopped me to ask clarifying questions here and there. I realized that she was shocked by some of the material I had simply taken for granted at her age.

One question she asked inspired this book:

"Is Aslan the bad guy?"

Bitsy has been taught how to think critically about what she is reading by her experienced teachers, skeptic mom, and thoughtful dad. When I was her age, I was told *what* to think, but never *how* to think. My reading material was all pre-selected, so I never needed to analyze what I consumed. Since the stories of Narnia were based on the stories of the Bible, a book I was taught never to question, I absorbed my Narnia fare with the same uncritical consumption.

As I read aloud, pausing as Little Bit interrupted with her thoughts, I noticed she was testing the characters by her sense of right and wrong. She found some of the heroes morally lacking when it was clear the author meant to communicate their goodness—*holiness* even. The more I read, the more I began to wonder if Aslan was essentially good. He certainly holds some characteristics that no child should emulate or praise.

It's with a bit of trepidation that I forge into unfamiliar territory by analyzing these books I know so well, grappling with their darker elements of racism, sexism, and prejudice, and confronting their arbitrary code of ethics. While I will always appreciate *The Chronicles of Narnia* for its role in my childhood, it no longer holds a place of inerrant reverence in my heart.

Time to start the adventure with my little guide, but this time with eyes wide open.

2
Going on a Lion Hunt

The Lion, the Witch and the Wardrobe: Chapters 1-4

"Oh, I do not like Edmund."
"No one does, honey."

***

Bitsy has patiently allowed me to explain the air raids of London during World War II before moving past the first paragraph of *The Lion, The Witch and the Wardrobe*.[1] This setting allows the four main characters—Peter, Susan, Edmund, and Lucy—unsupervised access to magical lands away from their parents who are busy with Nazis. It was no real matter to Bits how the children ended up with the "old Professor" out of town. She reads *A Series of Unfortunate Events* with her dad, so children finding themselves in strange living arrangements with bizarre caretakers is old hat to her.

We are only one page in before we get our first taste of misogyny. The *Narnia* series holds to a strong hierarchy of adult men over adult women, older people over younger people, boys over girls, and human

---

[1] Bitsy and I read the original editions of the Narnia books from the 1950s. At some point in the intervening 65 years, it seems minor language edits were made for the modern audience. One example we found while verifying our quotes was "Wer-wolf" became "Werewolf." The quotes in this book will reflect the modern edits.

people over talking animal people. Those not on the top of the hierarchy are rarely given their due which is why women's work is largely undervalued in these stories. Susan, the eldest girl, has been forced into a caretaker role of the other children. Adopting the motherly example she learned at home comes with reviling rather than respect from the others. Susan has the audacity to refer to the professor who took them in as a "dear"—language Edmund finds particularly saccharine—and tells her siblings that they should be in bed when she notices they are tired, thus cementing her unsavory motherly tendencies.

Peter, in contrast, often takes on a fatherly role, but the younger children go along with this without the same lack of respect they show Susan. Edmund is the exception, as he shows a lack of respect to both older siblings, but this is a deliberate effort by Lewis, our author, to highlight Ed's role as the flawed-then-later-redeemed character. In the end, he will change his tune towards Peter, but not towards Susan, and that is considered acceptable.

We have hardly introduced characters or setting when Lucy, the youngest child and Lewis' favorite based on his goddaughter, falls through a wardrobe and is transported to a magical land. If *Lord of the Rings* had found action this quickly, Little Bit may have stuck with it longer!

Lucy finds a talking faun (read: adult male stranger) and, because she is a polite child who does what she's told, goes home with him. In her defense, he does outrank her in terms of age and gender in the hierarchy, so the "right" behavior in Lewis' mind would be to submit to him. I remember being directly taught on numerous occasions, even in my premarital classes, that my duty as a female person was to submit, even to the point of harm, to male persons God put over me. This set up is perfect for predation.

The faun, Mr. Tumnus, is an abuser. Full stop. Narnia fans across the globe may cringe at the suggestion, but the adverse label fits any adult who gives a young girl drugged tea and cake to render her unconscious. The plan was to kill her.

This plot point never bothered me before reading it aloud to my own child. Tumnus is a beloved character and my first reaction to the discomfort I felt during this scene was to make excuses for him. Well, *he* wasn't going to kill the girl; the witch would. If not for the circumstances, he would never do such a thing. *He really is harmless*, I almost said about an adult who drugs children to harm them.

Instead, the bedtime conversation became about how one-dimensional abusers only exist in stories. Abusers are people, and as such, they have emotions, complicated motivations, extenuating circumstances, and they even, on occasion, say they are sorry. None of these things are proof they are safe or good. Tumnus had a change of heart in the story and broke into tears. He laid all his problems on the small child, forcing her to console him. Emotional labor is considered her responsibility as a good girl and she is rewarded when their bond is solidified. Her very next trip to Narnia finds her running straight to his home again.

He said he was sorry. Mr. Tumnus could give lessons in grooming.

The faun greets Lucy as a "Daughter of Eve;" this is our first introduction to human beings being referred to as a binary along with Sons of Adam. Bitsy piped up at this point and said, "Just like in Islam!" I had to chuckle at what I could only assume our Catholic-leaning[2] author's reaction would have been to that! We had just learned about the basic beliefs of Muslims since Little Bit's elementary school is next door to a mosque. According to the Abrahamic religions (Islam, Christianity, and Judaism), Adam and Eve were the first people created by

---

[2] Even though he became the darling of Evangelical Protestants due to his view of women and a literal interpretation of the Bible, Lewis held many distinctly Catholic doctrines. Although he never officially joined the Catholic Church, he was greatly influenced by it.

a creator god, well, arguably "gods" since the language of "us" and "our" are leftovers from the polytheistic Canaanite religion. There was a Canaanite god named El during this time and the Hebrew word for God in Genesis' creation account is Elohim, a plural form of El.

Adam was a mud golem following a long line of traditions from this time and place in which gods formed humans out of clay and made them alive by magic. Eve was created out of Adam, turning the natural order of men coming from women[3] on its head. Eve is also faulted as being naïve, committing the first sin, and bringing about the downfall of the entire human race. Her story has been used for thousands of years to subjugate women and gave my childhood church permission to think of women as weak and subordinate to the men they were supposedly created from. C. S. Lewis bases his Narnia stories on this biblical one, and his view of women throughout the subsequent tales is rooted here.

Lucy returns to find time works differently in Narnia and that she had a whole mini adventure in the space of seconds. She discovers this when she tries to tell her siblings what happened and no one believes her as they just saw her moments before. However, one day Edmund follows Lucy back through the wardrobe and finds himself there as well. He calls out for Lucy to forgive him for teasing her about it, but when she fails to answer, as she's not around, he says, "Just like a girl [...] sulking somewhere, and won't accept an apology." Of course, Edmund is no role model of behavior, but this kind of gender bashing is repeated throughout the series even when the characters are all morally good ones. Soon a giant woman known as the White Witch shows up; named for her white skin, she is the epitome of Lewis' beauty standard. Her looks should be a red flag that she is out to trick unsuspecting boys. She gives Edmund magical food that compels him to

---

[3] Wombs technically, which trans men and nonbinary folk also have.

9

bring his siblings to her since Tumnus failed to do so. While both children found themselves being groomed upon first entering Narnia, their situations are portrayed very differently. I got the impression Edmund was breaking the rule of taking candy from a stranger and is getting some sort of natural consequence for that transgression. Yet when Lucy takes food from a stranger it is considered courteous. Edmund, according to my former church, would be outside God's protection for his actions since victims are blamed for their own victimization. Lucy would be considered obedient, having shown the proper submissive demeaner to an adult man. Lewis can't claim eating treats from a magical creature ten seconds after finding yourself in a magical world is foolish or wrong if it seemingly depends solely on the genders of parties involved!

Lucy does end up running into Edmund after the Witch leaves and they return together to tell the others. For reasons unknown, or simply to prove he is horrid, Edmund decides to lie and say Narnia is all made up. Lucy is considerably upset by this betrayal and enters a period of near-constant crying. The wailing is endless. Susan and Peter start to become concerned. Finally, they decide to do the responsible thing and tell the only adult in charge about their sister losing it. Which leads to one of the worst parts of the book.

The Lion, the Witch and the Wardrobe: Chapter 5

"The professor totally knows about Narnia or he wouldn't be saying this weird stuff, Mom."

"Yep. Just wait until we get to *The Magician's Nephew*."

***

What happens when Susan and Peter, the two oldest children, finally bring their youngest sibling's mental break to the attention of the guy who is supposed to be their guardian? They get summarily reprimanded for a lack of faith. Seriously.

The Professor, as he's called in this book, is here to impart wisdom, not parent brats! His title shows which archetype he is: The wise old teacher, who holds the extra hierarchy cards of being both male and older, and who is supposed to be trusted as an authority. Preferably, without question.

God help him if he ever met Bitsy!

Peter and Susan are worried about Lucy; they can't seem to stem her emotional outbursts. She is the very picture of a distraught believer who must evangelize her siblings into faith in Narnia. When they fail to come around, she wails long and loud. Lucy insists that her fantasy world is real and speaks with such certainty that they can't help but wonder if something is mentally wrong with her. If they were hoping for comfort, sympathy, or even help from the Professor, they're in for disappointment.

I submit that Lewis sees himself as the Professor, and his lessons, mysterious and wise, are meant to wow the children with his intellect. He tells the children that accusing their sister of being untruthful is morally wrong of them despite her claims being outlandish ones, like visiting another world and suspending the passage of time. Why? Lucy is generally a truthful person. The logic goes: Truthful people don't tell lies. Lucy is a truthful person. Therefore, Lucy does not tell lies.

The false premise is clear immediately: All people are capable of lies. Lucy is a person. Lucy is then capable of lies.

The Professor continues with a trilemma, a favorite go-to of Lewis when making a point:

> "There are only three possibilities. Either your sister is telling lies, or she is mad, or she is telling the truth. You know she doesn't tell lies and it is obvious that she is not mad. For the moment then and unless any further evidence turns up, we must assume that she is telling the truth."

Um, no. Who says there are only three options and those are it? Also, what "further evidence" is necessary? The first thing the other children did was go to the wardrobe and check that the back was solid. It was.

The Professor says it is obvious that Lucy is not mad, but obvious in what way? Isn't she extremely emotionally upset? Isn't she unreasonably demanding the laws of physics were suspended for her? When someone's entire mood and sense of reality has changed, isn't that a red flag for mental stress or psychosis? If not, what would be?

For those like me, raised to see Lewis as the epitome of the logical argument, this alone should dispel that notion. The view that Lewis was a great thinker and great man are often very Evangelical in nature, and beyond that, very American. I was in my 30s before I realized that most collegiate philosophers, outside of an evangelical alma mater like mine, laugh at Lewis' arguments. They tend to be one fallacy after the next. The bar for sound reasoning can be pretty low when the only thing that matters is Christian doctrine. This is more evident in Lewis' theological books.

The trilemma of 'mad, lying, or truthful' is disingenuously limited to two positions easily rejected and one that so happens to be the preferred choice of whoever set up the options. Lewis' most famous trilemma in *Mere Christianity* was the assertion that Jesus Christ was either a lunatic, liar, or Lord. This falls under the false dilemma fallacy or the fallacy of false choice. Many other options are available; Christ could be a legend or a lie, keeping with the alliteration. As for Lucy's options, she could be in mental distress due to parental separation, distraught over the war, which is hardly atraumatic, or maybe she was being forced to say things against her will by a bully? Edmund maybe? Or she's simply testing her world as children do. Sorry, Professor, there are way more than three possibilities, and many more reasonable than that of the world's natural laws being completely upended.

Of course, the main fallacy here is the *argument from ignorance*. Just because they cannot prove Narnia is imaginary does not mean they should accept it as true. Or in the words of Hermione Granger, when prompted by Xenophilius to prove something did *not* exist:

> "I'm sorry, but that's completely ridiculous! [...] I mean, you could claim that *anything's* real if the only basis for believing in it is that nobody's *proved* it doesn't exist!"[4]

The world of Harry Potter is also a fantastical and magical one, but it holds a measure of consistency to it without sacrificing critical thinking. Maybe this is an unfair comparison since one set of books does not have the same agenda to spread Christianity to children that the other set does. Dumbledore is graciously spared having to be a stand-in for a major religious deity.

The Professor performs *special pleading*, which is another logical fallacy where certain aspects of the children's arguments are

---

[4] J. K. Rowling, 2007. *Harry Potter and the Deathly Hallows*, (Bloomsbury, London: Bloomsbury Publishing).

deliberately ignored since they are not favorable to the assumption that Narnia exists. The wardrobe is normal, time has never stopped working in known history, young children are known for imaginations— all of these are dismissed without discussion. As a result, our young protagonists are forced to accept an exception to the rules of physics in this one case for no discernable reason. Later we will learn the Professor had been to Narnia himself as a small child. The fact he does not admit this up front is a serious omission.

The philosophic burden of proof requires Lucy to substantiate her claim with evidence. Extraordinary claims require extraordinary evidence, as the saying goes. Furthermore, according to the late Christopher Hitchens,[5] "What can be asserted without evidence can be dismissed without evidence." Lucy fails in this basic first step when the older children test her claim. At this point the other children are under no such obligation to believe her. Yet their *wise* caretaker expects belief in her claims as common decency.

Enter one of the series' biggest themes: Blind faith is a moral responsibility for those of good character.

Belief without evidence is ridiculously presented as essential to goodness. Peter even apologizes for not believing Lucy and it is assumed he was in the wrong for his failure to believe. His initial skepticism, then, was portrayed as foolish. I have so many issues with this, but of course magic is real in the story so the ends (getting to enjoy the magic) justify the means (sacrificing logic).

The Professor starts telling the children that having other worlds hidden "all over the place" is "probable." But is it? When the children push back against this idea, the Professor seems to get angry that his authority is being slightly questioned. When questioning authority is a sin, Professor Botched Logic's response of giving "a very sharp

---

[5] Known as Hitchens' Razor.

14

expression," telling them to mind their own business, and dismissing them abruptly is seen as appropriate. The next paragraph describes the children avoiding the "alarming" subject entirely, never reaching out to another adult, and not dealing with Lucy's crisis at all. That sounds like a *super* healthy response.

That said, this is a fairytale. So naturally all the Professor's pseudo-logic works out. In the real world, which fables like this are supposed to help children navigate, these words of wisdom would lead to disaster. How well would it turn out if a child growing up on these lessons went out to buy their first car sight unseen because of the word of a salesperson? Relying on authority might work out and might not, but it is undeniably an inferior way to make decisions.

After a contrived predicament, all four children find themselves needing to go into the wardrobe and thus into Narnia. Now the story gets interesting.

The Lion, the Witch and the Wardrobe: Chapters 6-7

"Does Mrs. Beaver have a first name? Is she the only girl animal in all of Narnia?"
"No, and, um, no?"

***

All four children find themselves in the wardrobe and wouldn't you know it, it's all real! Peter continues his role as the de facto leader of the group and decides to follow Lucy to Mr. Tumnus' house. Unfortunately they find it ransacked by the White Witch.

Susan remains her *horrible, awful* self by pointing out common-sense things like it doesn't seem safe, it's getting too cold, and they have nothing to eat. (Shut up, Susan!) She must appeal to Peter to let the children wear the coats from the wardrobe and he only relents to her sensible plan once she has persuaded him sufficiently. Yay, the boy decided! Hierarchy at work!

A robin appears to lead the children away from the crime scene and into the woods. Edmund, a hated character by all at this point, tells Peter in a whisper that this may be a foolish plan, but he doesn't mention this to his sisters since "there's no good frightening the girls." Susan is not consulted about the plan even though she is older than Edmund and more mature; she is regretfully the wrong gender for such worries. The boys decide that robins are all "good," so it is fine to be led around by one. Having entire species be good or bad is also a theme of these books.

The robin takes them to a Beaver (always capitalized). This Beaver tells them, "Aslan is on the move—perhaps has already landed." At the very name of Jesus, oh, I mean Aslan (ahem), the children all feel the deepest of feels. Here the character of each child is revealed: Peter felt brave, Susan felt delighted, Lucy felt excited like it was Christmas morning, and Edmund, who was in the throes of the Witch, felt a mysterious horror. I personally felt an eye-roll, and Little Bit, when asked what she felt, shrugged, "I'll wait until I know more about this Aslan guy." Smart girl.

Mr. Beaver takes them home and introduces them to Mrs. Beaver, described as a she-beaver who was both working at a sewing machine but also in the middle of making dinner. The author of this story had no trouble imagining that womenfolk can do these things simultaneously. What stopped her dinner efforts was a lack of fish that she could not retrieve for herself because of gender roles, so she had to wait for her husband to do it for her.

The Beavers' little home is described in detail; the best detail of all is that Mr. and Mrs. Beaver slept in bunk beds. Not kidding. The lack of a sex life was probably one more point in their favor showing their purity. In future books it says there are no more Beavers. Well no kidding! That would take some bed-sharing!

The Lion, the Witch and the Wardrobe: Chapter 8

"Nope to all of this. You can't be both unsafe and good."
"Agreed."

***

The Beavers finally start answering the children's questions and one of their first questions is about Aslan himself. The theology of Aslan is just a bit of a tug and stretch from the original Christian cloth. Aslan was the King of Beasts who had been A.W.O.L. for generations. Sound familiar? He was the son of the Emperor, who had never been seen, and he was prophesized to be coming back. All of Narnia has been buried in endless winter for a hundred years and Aslan had not been bothered about it until now. How did they eat without harvests and why didn't this wreck the ecosystem? I don't know, probably like how a world-wide flood didn't kill all fresh-water fish. It just works out magically with magical magic.

Aslan's people were hurting, being turned to snow, freezing to death, controlled by a dictator, and suffering for generations. But Aslan was busy, okay! He's still super powerful and great, just… you know, *busy*.

Upon learning that Aslan is a lion, like an actual lion, the children are understandably curious if he mauls people. When they ask if he's safe the answer is a clear no. Bitsy piped up at this point and clarified,

"No? So he is dangerous and might eat the children?" I continued reading to where Mr. Beaver assured the kids that even though Aslan was not safe, and was very much dangerous, he was also *good* because he was the king. "What?" countered an incredulous Little Bit.

Peter then says he wants to meet Aslan even though he is frightened of him and Mr. Beaver encourages that kind of self-risking devotion. At this point Little Bit is not having any of this. "Is Aslan the bad guy? Does he make people want to be eaten by him?"

I am relieved to know my girl, who just turned ten, can yank her hand out of an author's grasp if he starts to take her where she does not want to go. I hope it means she'll avoid an abusive relationship one day. She has the good sense to see that someone who makes you feel scared cannot also be good.

When I was her age reading this description of Aslan, I loved it. I interpreted "dangerous" and "unsafe" as powerful. Aslan, like Jesus, would kill other people but not his own followers. Unfortunately, my belief system included the doctrine that all humans were supposedly inherently evil. The Bible verses I was raised on included: "The wages of sin is death," "All have sinned," "The Lord chastises every son," "Folly is bound up in the heart of a child, but the rod of discipline drives it far from him," "I was brought forth in iniquity, and in sin did my mother conceive me," "The human heart is deceitful above all things, and desperately wicked," etc. This leaves children "in the hands of an angry God," as American preacher Jonathan Edwards would say, and not feeling very safe. That right there is why Aslan is scary to the children. Lewis considers this a good thing. Pious readers are supposed to as well.

We also get the prophecy from the Beavers about how Narnia needs to be ruled by humans but not by any of its actual inhabitants. This is because of the hierarchy we've seen previously; Lewis was very clear about it:

"I do not believe that God created an egalitarian world. I believe the authority of parent over child, husband over wife, learned over simple to have been as much a part of the original plan as the authority of man over beast."[6]

It must be nice for Lewis that his place in the hierarchy is at the tippy top. Convenient even.

The Narnian prophecy also says that once humans sit on the throne that the evil time will be over and done. Spoiler: The next book takes place after humans have sat on the throne, but pirates still come into Narnia to kill everyone. This evil act even requires an *additional* second coming of Aslan. Perhaps Lewis didn't have sequels in mind when he wrote that bit.

Eventually endless exposition turns to talk about the White Witch. Her height is explained to be the product of the union between angels and humans that produced the giants—which comes directly from the Bible.[7] Mr. Beaver explains the Witch is a descendent of Lilith, the character believed to be the first wife of Adam until she rebelled against his authority, was replaced by Eve, and became a demon—in that order. Female agency: causing either demonic changes or the downfall of the entire world since men took over religion.

Lewis keeps biblical stories at the heart of his tales and assumes believers would be familiar with this one. I cannot speak for all Protestants, but Lilith was certainly not a character I was ever taught in Sunday School. It's true that Lilith is in the Bible, mentioned by name,[8] but finding her story in the Genesis account takes some creative reading and knowledge of contemporary ancient religions.

Lilith has traditionally been inserted into the Genesis story to smooth the conflicting account between chapters 1 and 2.

---

[6] C. S. Lewis, 1941. *The Weight of Glory*, (San Francisco, CA: HarperOne).
[7] Genesis 6:1-4
[8] Isaiah 34:14

Contradictions in the biblical books are common due to competing oral traditions being written side-by-side. Here, in chapter 1, man and woman are created simultaneously and equally. In chapter 2, man is created, then plants, then animals, and finally woman, but only as a complete afterthought when God sees how lonely man is. She's created *after* beasts. Although some see these two accounts as complimentary—one is the summary of how people came to be and the other explains the details—that does not satisfactorily solve the contradiction. The conflicts are better smoothed if we consider the two accounts as pertaining to two separate women. The first woman was simultaneously created as a golem *with* Adam as an equal to Adam. This eliminates the contradiction in Genesis 1. This woman is Lilith. The second woman, created *from* Adam, tied to him as a submissive replacement once Lilith left, was Eve. Adam was lonely because Lilith left him to pursue her career in demon-ing.

The White Witch's claim to the throne is dependent on her humanity—the idea from Genesis that only humans rule over beasts. Yet her connection to Lilith undermines that claim. She is a demon.

Lilith's name and story predate ancient Israel. The creation story and flood story of the Bible are heavily plagiarized from the Epic of Gilgamesh, a Sumerian poem which preceded Hebrew Scripture by many years. The accounts aren't simply inspired by this poem; they are a blatant copy and paste job with the local Israelite god injected into them. Lilith is a character in the original epic. She was the demon who took over the tree belonging to the goddess Inanna. Gilgamesh had to chase her out into the desert. This is copied into the Bible: "Desert animals will meet hyenas, the goat demon will call to his friends, and there Lilith will lurk and find her resting place."[9]

---

[9] Isaiah 34:14

Eve is the good, submissive woman whom all future women from her line will be. When Mr. Tumnus called Lucy a "Daughter of Eve," he was referring to her goodness evident in her submissive nature. Lilith is the equal of Adam. All women (if you can even call them that) from her are bad.

***

After explaining the history of the White Witch, the Beavers dive deep into xenophobic racism. It's explained that the character of a person is evident by how they look. Anything that looks human, but is not human, is obviously evil. Mrs. Beaver counters with, "I've known good Dwarfs," which prompts Mr. Beaver's retort, "But precious few, and they were the ones least like men." His advice when seeing someone who isn't quite human was to, "Keep your eyes on it and feel for your hatchet."

Little Bit's reaction to all this blatant ignorance was, "Nope."

The Lion, the Witch and the Wardrobe: Chapters 9-13

"Is Father Christmas a bad guy?"
"Him too, huh?"

***

Disgusted by the blatant prejudice of the previous chapter, Edmund sneaks off. Just kidding, he was just going to betray them all. Mr. Beaver says he could tell by Edmund's eyes that he was treacherous and had the look of someone who had been with the Witch and eaten her food. So, to get this straight, Mr. Beaver proceeded to tell him critical information that would benefit the Witch and put their lives in danger because…? What good is judging books by their covers if you have to wait for their actions before condemning them? Prejudice seems like a lot of wasted hate before the fact.

Now Edmund is off to the Witch to get what's coming to him. It's quickly explained that Edmund's motivation for the betrayal was that he was so dumb he believed things he didn't really believe. If this sounds utterly confusing, it is. The book describes a belief "deep down inside him" where "he really knew that the White Witch was bad and cruel." If this does not ring entirely true, it's because cognitive dissonance doesn't quite work this way. Pushing an uncomfortable truth aside to pursue a selfish course of action is a genuine thing people do all the time, but believing a lie you know is false? That's pure lunacy. No cognitively-typical person does that.

There's no conflict within Edmund; he's not struggling with the truth. He acts on his beliefs and those beliefs are supposedly acknowledged lies. How would this work? Lewis failing to understand how human internal processes work would be baffling to me if I didn't already know the Bible falsely claims this is how unbelievers and apostates think. (Because it's easy to write about the motivations of people we disagree with or don't understand.)

Those who aren't convinced that the Abrahamic God is real, according to the New Testament, are actually (surprise!) convinced that the Abrahamic God is for sure real and are just too stupid to confess this.[10] Lamentably, since this is direct from Christian holy text, it's almost impossible to convince a true believer otherwise. To them, atheists don't really exist. Everyone is either a good believer or a stupid, evil one. We are never the arbiter of our own experience.

---

[10] Romans 1:19, 22

Why would atheists claim not to believe when they really do? Rebellion theory would claim it is so they can sin without consequence, but that does not pan out in any simulation. Do people also stop believing in taxes by genuinely buying into the lie that they don't exist? Only to be completely flabbergasted when the consequences come? Is that the level of stupid the Bible is putting on unbelievers?

When I was young, unbelievers baffled me. I only knew their motivation as the strawman I was presented by my church. I had a great deal of pity for them. Of course the point of the biblical author's argument was to convince people to become believers by saying God was obvious, that godlessness was the same as wickedness, and that atheists are "suppressing the truth."[11] Unbelievers are not just dumb, but wicked and deceitful! I'm surprised they didn't say ugly, too.

***

Edmund goes back to the Witch to rat out his family and is treated badly. No reader feels bad for him. Back at the Beaver home, they all make ready to run for it. Everyone gets mad at Mrs. Beaver who slows them down by packing food for the journey that will literally keep them from starving in the next chapter. She does all the mental prep while they stand there lecturing her about how they must leave. When she wonders if she can take her sewing machine—what I imagine is Lewis' way of showing that women are ridiculous instead of practical—Mr. Beaver puts his foot down so they can leave. We're all thankful a man finally put an end to this silliness!

"That's sad. It was like her best thing she owned probably," adds Little Bit compassionately.

---

[11] Romans 1:18-20

They make it to a cave to hide in and Mrs. Beaver gets upset that she didn't pack pillows. She then hands around what is probably hard liquor as it makes the children cough and burns their throats. It works and they are all out like an underage drunken light.

The children wake up the next morning to meet Father Christmas! Because why not! He gives *killer* presents. He gave Peter a sword for stabbing people with, Susan a bow and arrows for piercing people with, and a horn to call for help, Lucy a dagger for, well, you get it. Santa informs the girls, "I don't mean you to fight in the battle." When Lucy protests that she's brave enough (and certainly armed enough) to fight, Father Christmas replies, "That is not the point. Battles are ugly when women fight."

"He did NOT just say that because they are girls! Like, why give them weapons?" Bitsy blurted out in slight shock.

"They took that part out when they made this into a movie," I assured her.

Mrs. Beaver lectures Peter and Mr. Beaver about playing with the new sword, which is "just like men" she sighs, and makes sure everyone knows how wise it was of her to bring the butter knife. Her emphasis on the over importance of kitchenware is a joke. Readers are supposed to know that the realm of womanly responsibility is not really all that important compared to battles.

Meanwhile Edmund and the White Witch set out to kill Edmund's siblings, which horrifies him but also, we're led to believe, is what he truly deep down thought would happen. (Those crazy unbelievers and their incoherence!) On the way, the Witch ends up turning some animal children to stone for celebrating Christmas, which has been illegal since her dictatorship began. Why does Santa give the people of Narnia gifts that makes the Queen furiously kill them? What did he think was going to happen? I assume Aslan did not save those stone creatures as it describes one sitting with "its stone fork fixed for ever half way to its stone mouth." Unless "for ever" is code for "a few days" when the others are turned back to normal by Aslan.

At this point the other three children and Beavers travel to Stone Table, a clearing with a giant stone altar, and meet Aslan.

> "People who have not been in Narnia sometimes think that a thing cannot be good and terrible at the same time."

The narrator repeats this line as if it's not utter baloney. The children were so frightened upon seeing Aslan that they trembled and couldn't look at him. Peter asks Mr. Beaver to go first, but Mr. Beaver answers, "No, sons of Adam before animals." Right, *hierarchy*. Aslan finally welcomes them each by rank and gender, first sons of Adam, then daughters of Eve, and lastly "Welcome, He-Beaver and She-Beaver." We're getting very tired of the ranked order of folks.

Aslan asks where Edmund is, and is disappointed in the children for letting their brother betray them. (Clearly the victims' fault when this happens.) This is the first time I realized that Edmund is Judas. This probably makes Peter, Saint Peter. Is Lewis saying it was Peter's fault Judas made bad choices? I guess the gospels could be interpreted that way. Peter was Disciple #1, in a way, and Judas did get away with a lot under his watch. No time to think about this because wolves are attacking the girls inside the camp with Aslan *right there*.

While in later books Aslan is said to read minds, here he doesn't seem to know what's going on around him. He was the one who sent the girls off directly to the wolves lying in wait to kill them. When Susan calls for help with her horn—which is said to sound like a bugle, but in the next book becomes way more fierce-sounding and awesome in the hands of a boy—Aslan orders the warriors in the party to stay back and let Peter fight alone and earn a knighthood. You know, while Susan is in mortal danger and forced up a tree. (Gee, thanks for that

Aslan. *Girls must be so important to you.*) Peter kills the wolf and gets covered in its blood and fur.

"Is this book appropriate for children?" Bitsy asks at this point which makes me laugh. She is not okay with violence, and I failed to recall just how violent these books were.

While Peter is fighting, the White Witch is making plans to kill Edmund with a knife. She laments not being able to slaughter him on the Stone Table, where our party is, as that is its "proper use." I declined to go into animal sacrifice in the Bible with Little Bit as she detests cruelty to animals, but it's clear this Stone Table is supposed to be the stone altar right out of the Old Testament designed to appease God's bloodlust. It is worse to consider the animals are people in this world, as if sacrificing them to a deity wasn't awful before.

Not to worry since a group of animals save Edmund and bring him to Aslan. The lion and boy have some wonderful conversation no one is to ever know about because it was *that* special. Then Aslan informed the other children that there was no need to bring up the past with Edmund ever again. This was probably an allusion to God's promise to "remember sins no more." I guess never mind the consequences of his actions, or repairing the relationships, or attempting to understand why the betrayal happened in order to prevent it in the future.

The White Witch shows up and meets with Aslan, demanding she get her prisoner back. The law Aslan's father, the Emperor, put in place when he first created magic in the land is on her side. Aslan feigns ignorance of his own father's laws and magical rules. The Witch sets him straight.

At this point Bits has a theory that the White Witch is married to the Emperor. At the very least she works for him. I agreed that they are on the same page as far as evil laws go. The Emperor gave the Witch "a right to a kill" if a person is a traitor. Fun guy, the Emperor. What's next? Letting one of your fallen angels lead people to Hell for all eternity?

"Unless I have blood as the Law says, all Narnia will be overturned and perish in fire…"

The Emperor, or God if we're being literal, decided that one person breaking the law should mean all their neighbors should burn in fire. Gosh, at least the Witch only turns them to stone. She's kind by comparison.

When Susan (*of course* Susan) asks if there is anything that can work against the Emperor's magic, Aslan snaps at her and "nobody ever made that suggestion to him again." Sure, let's not discuss that the Emperor's magic is immoral or unjust. That's off limits apparently.

The White Witch and Aslan haggle over who gets to kill or control Edmund and they come to a secret agreement.

The Lion, the Witch and the Wardrobe: Chapters 14-17

"That's so cool that Aslan was willing to get really hurt for Edmund."
"Yeah, he died."
"But he didn't really die. It doesn't count if he came back to life the next day totally fine like he knew he would."
"What if it took three days?"
"What?"

***

Now we come to the Jesus-esque death of Aslan scene that likely inspired the entire story. Little Bit had been told the Gospel story many times in detail when she was younger, but she had forgotten a lot of it.

I tried to point out the many similarities between the two tales: The death happened on behalf of someone else; it was inspired by the blood laws of God/the Emperor; it appeased the "Deep Magic" (God's bloodlust); evil people jeered, tortured, and humiliated Aslan/Jesus while he remained silent; the Stone Table/Temple Veil is struck in two; and the resurrection was witnessed by grieving women/girls who wondered what had happened to the body and who had taken it.

Aslan even claims to have been around before time began, following a Johannine theology. Aslan's supernatural abilities and credentials will expand as the series continues the same way the biblical god starts out having limitations in knowledge[12] and power[13] that, after enough time and stories, morphs into a being of ultimate omnipotence and omniscience many of us were taught in church. The point is, as in any hyped-up series, the further along we get, the more supernatural abilities get added.

The way Aslan is portrayed as dragging his mane almost to the ground and being very tired and sad as he approached the alter was deeply compelling. His need for comfort from the girls was understandable, but their presence meant they had to witness his murder. Not very selfless of him, but we can never expect that of anyone who desires worship. He even positioned them in a place of "very great danger" to view his death. To test them, he refused to tell them that he would be coming back to life the next morning, leaving the small children grieving all night long. If he is omniscient as the books later imply, all his actions are horrible, self-serving, and particularly cruel.

After the Witch and her minions torture and kill Aslan, they run off to do battle with his army. The lion uses this time to pop back to life. The girls are overjoyed when they realize he is not dead anymore, yet he acts in ways that frighten them. Lucy did not know if she was

---

[12] Genesis 4:9; 18:21; Numbers 22:9; Hosea 8:4
[13] Judges 1:19; Genesis 32:27-30

"playing with a thunderstorm or playing with a kitten" when celebrating his return since he vacillated between fun and terrifying. When Aslan roars, his face is described as so terrible the girls are too frightened to look at it. Fun guy. Why'd we miss him again?

An abuser's mood can be similarly hot and cold causing a lot of unease for the people around them. Aslan has terrifying moments, not only to his enemies, but also to those he loves. This mirrors a Jesus who says to love one another in one passage and to take a sword to one's family if they do not follow him in another.[14] The Lamb of God who gathers children to himself is heartwarming; the Lamb of God who releases the four horsemen of the apocalypse to kill other children, heartbreaking.[15] When thinking of Jesus, most people I know imagine some good or gracious individual, and I can pick out verses to support such a Jesus just as I can pick out choice lines that show a pretty picture of Aslan. Yet it is incomplete. If the Narnia series included a story of Aslan having a sharp sword coming out of his mouth that he used to kill people of every nation (an actual description of Jesus in the Bible[16]), I think some parents might take issue with it.

Jesus' story includes threatening merchants with a whip,[17] lying about attending a party,[18] and calling a woman a dog for being the wrong ethnicity.[19] As a biblical studies student in college, I read whole papers defending Jesus' words and actions. I know the apologetics, and I was motivated by faith to accept them, but it would be dishonest to claim these things were an example of perfect goodness. (The whip thing was kinda cool though.) The popular Western version of Jesus eliminates the darker side of his character by ignoring certain verses

---

[14] Matthew 10:34-37
[15] Revelation 6:1-8
[16] Revelation 19:15
[17] John 2:15
[18] John 7:8-10
[19] Matthew 15:22-27

completely and largely reinterpreting others. I love peacenik Jesus, but Lewis gets it closer to the original.

***

Aslan takes the girls to the White Witch's castle and breathes on all the stone statues, making them animals again. In Luke, Jesus says, "[God] has sent me to proclaim that captives will be released, that the blind will see, that the oppressed will be set free." Breath of life is a reference to the life force that once animated the first human golem. Once more we find ourselves deep in allusions to Lewis' religious traditions.

After the creatures were turned back to normal, the giant among them is asked to smash the gates. It's quickly pointed out that giants are not smart, which Little Bit cannot help but see as a mean thing to say of an entire group of people. Then Aslan and all the others rush to join the huge battle that has been taking place between the White Witch's army of evil creatures and Peter's army of good creatures. First thing Aslan does is pounce the Witch to death. Couldn't he have done that earlier? A hundred years earlier? No?

In the end, lots of creatures are violently slaughtered. At least Edmund was redeemed by being a bit heroic. The book explains how Edmund had "begun to go wrong" after attending a local school, but now he's reborn in glorious battle. We can assume, based on Edmund's cousin's school experience in a subsequent book, that Edmund's school was probably less traditional, didn't rely on the Bible, and did away with corporal punishment. Education and religion are not always harmonious, and this is not the only time this series will vilify progressive education. The old Professor often remarked to Susan and Peter, "What are they teaching you in that school?" How to be bad, apparently, but after happy murder times, Edmund becomes a good guy. The transformative power of killing-for-Jesus will be a theme throughout the series. Onward Christian soldiers!

Aslan magically provides food for the huge company, another allusion to Jesus, and a couple days later the children are crowned kings and queens of Narnia. This is not some equal crowning, oh no, Peter becomes the High King and leader over all the Church, er, I mean Narnia.

After the coronation, Aslan sneaks off and is gone. That's Aslan for you. The four newly-royal-ified children spend the next several years hunting down their enemies and killing them. In the end "all that foul brood was stamped out," says the book that obviously doesn't know those same creatures are back in the very next book. Always assume you'll be writing a sequel, author!

It's icky that entire groups are killed off by our heroes. Sure, we can say those species were "evil" and defend it that way, but it's usually not great practice to justify genocides. When I was a student of the Bible, I remember hearing about how God ordered the murder of children. I was told God knew they would grow up to worship other gods. If I were an all-powerful God, having my followers murder everyone would be a huge failure of ingenuity on my part. I feel like my *God-Brain* would have come up with something better than that. I mean, my *human* brain certainly has several alternatives in mind. But at least it all worked out and there are no people of other religions worshiping other gods in the world today. (Hard look at camera.)

Our royal children are considered good rulers who, "liberated young Dwarfs and young satyrs from being sent to school." School must be stopped! They also took on Libertarian policies by stopping "busybodies and interferers" and letting people "live and let live." No social programs in their kingdom I imagine, just how God wants it.

The children grew up in Narnia and we get a summary of how they turned out. Peter and Edmund are given quality characteristics and said to be wise. Susan and Lucy are simply praised for their looks and marriage prospects. Peter was courageous and noble. Susan? Susan had long hair. Edmund was brave and a warrior. Lucy? She had lots of men who liked to look at her.

Eventually the four protagonists find the original wardrobe and fall back into the real world where they revert to children and find no time has passed since they left. It's fine though; they don't seem overly interested in the lives they abandoned or the friends and suitors they left behind. The Professor finds out they're back and warns them not to talk about Narnia except to others who have been there. (Don't tell your parents, kids!) They ask how they would know who else had been there and the Professor tells them by "their looks," because of course.

The last sentence spoken in the book is the professor saying, "Bless me, what *do* they teach them at these schools?"

3
Prince Murder Boy

Prince Caspian: Chapters 1-5

"Wait, are they going to Hogwarts?!"
"Not all schools in England are Hogwarts, honey."

***

The second book in the series, *Prince Caspian*, opens with four familiar children—Peter, Susan, Edmund, and Lucy—waiting to board trains for their divided-by-gender boarding schools. A year has passed since the last book and they have kept their adventures in Narnia a secret. Well, they did tell one "very wise grown-up"—a proctor for Lewis himself, who distrusts school and bends logic into funny shapes.

Suddenly and without warning, a strong magical pull yanks the children out of the station and into Narnia. They end up on a deserted island with an ancient ruin in its center. That crumbling infrastructure turns out to be their own castle back when they were kings and queens. Untold numbers of years have passed since they have last been here. The first thing they remembered was their old treasure chamber, so they broke into it to find their original gifts from Father Christmas, except for Susan's horn which is missing.

Setting this second adventure so far in the future is perfect; it keeps Narnia from becoming too familiar, too pedestrian, and creates feelings of wonder, mystery, and loss. I've always thought Lewis had some of the most riveting storylines made up of imperfect elements; the details of this newest journey will include all our author's blind spots.

Susan, in true motherly fashion, reminds the others how imprudent it was to break into the chamber without knowing what was inside and without preparing for how dark it was getting. She immediately gets scolded by Lucy and ignored by the boys. I cannot help but think that Lewis meant young readers to identify with the other three children's sense of adventure and be repulsed by faux parenting in their ranks. The effect works more often, however, to cast traditionally feminine roles and responsibilities as inferior or ridiculous. I often get "women are dumb" or "women's work is worthless" vibes while reading certain remarks throughout the series. Susan's downright sensible nature keeps these children from being shoeless this entire book as they were in such a state of excitement that they almost left their shoes behind.

Wow, I really am a boring grown up.

The chamber was filled with riches the royal kids had horded through the years, covered in dust. So much for "do not store up for yourselves treasures on earth."[1] Good thing Narnia didn't go through upheaval and conquest in these intervening years where that treasure would have been the difference between life and death for the creatures forced into hiding. Oh wait. *That all totally happened.*

The next morning the children went down to the beach and saw a small boat with two men holding a Dwarf prisoner. It's clear that the men are about to drown the Dwarf so Susan acts without asking permission and shoots an arrow at one soldier's helmet, knocking him out

---

[1] Matthew 6:19 – As a point of clarity, Jesus' religion depicted in the Gospels is most closely associated with an End Times cult. Instructions to not store wealth, give away your coat, avoid investing in people who disagree with you, and other pieces of advice make more sense in light of the world ending in the disciples' lifetimes. Of course, hoarding wealth is bad for different reasons, but we can forgive 2,000 years' worth of Christians for having savings accounts.

of the boat! (Thank you, Lewis! You owe us more of that!) The other soldier thought ghosts caused this chaos, so he dove overboard out of fear. The Dwarf was thankful for the rescue and explained to the children that he was a messenger from King Caspian. We then launch into Caspian's tale.

Caspian the Tenth, a human child, was raised in a castle where his uncle, Miraz, ruled over Narnia. He loved stories of "Old Narnia"— back when it was inhabited by talking animals before his ancestors slaughtered most of them. Caspian's life changes when a tutor, Doctor Cornelius, is hired for him. Bitsy and I were disappointed in Cornelius' introduction since it marks yet another male character with a compelling backstory, whereas our only female character, Miraz's wife, completes her one job in the story of giving birth to a son and then fades into obscurity. We never find out anything more about her, including her name. Any woman in a C. S. Lewis tale is more a role than a person; they are there to marry a boy, give birth to a boy, or be an evil witch a boy needs to defeat. Mostly, though, they are not in the story at all.

One night, Cornelius takes Caspian to a tower to show him the stars, which are read like tea leaves and interpreted to mean war is coming. Young Caspian has a destiny in front of him. It involves lots of killing!

Caspian is told that his ancestor, Caspian the First, murdered the inhabitants of Narnia and moved in to rule the land. This heinous act of conquering and killing should mean that the current Caspian has no right to a stolen throne, but instead, this book reinforces Caspian's claim, justifying another bloodbath over the throne.

When Cornelius eventually reveals that he is only half human, Caspian's very first thought is, I kid you not, "He's not a real man, not a man at all, he's a Dwarf, and he's brought me up here to kill me." Caspian's reaction is hardly out of place as we learned from Mr. Beaver in the last book that you should mistrust anything that appears to be human. Why? Because such creatures are evil. What was Mr. Beaver's full sentiments? Oh yes, "Keep your eyes on it and feel for your hatchet." Cornelius is not evil, but the lesson is never explicitly redacted.

After Caspian's aunt has a son and heir (and then conveniently disappears forever), it becomes likely Caspian's uncle will kill him to clear the way for his own son to be king. Cornelius kneels before Caspian at this point and declares him the "true King of Narnia" despite what we know about Caspian's ancestors violently murdering their way into power. We literally just read that a few pages ago. A "true" ruler is simply one who completes a hostile take-over, apparently.

Cornelius even gives Caspian a bit of gold before he flees his uncle, but laments, "All the treasure in this castle should be your own by rights." Again, by rights? Really? Are the children of bank robbers the rightful inheritors of plunder? "It should belong to the animals!" cries Bitsy. I agree. I also think the treasure chamber of Cair Paravel filled with unused taxes and plunder should have also gone to the animal people. Just because a murdering monarchy moves in doesn't mean you have to let them keep all the stolen money! Possibly Lewis' love for his chosen home of England, which has a monarchy and a history of colonization, might have made this a blind spot for him. He didn't consider it odd or wrong that kings and queens should cause war and take things for themselves.

Unfortunately, Little Bit and I are not on board with this war from the get-go. It's hard to cheer on the heroes when you're against the book's premise.

***

Dwarves are presented as mostly bad, but the Dwarf telling Caspian's story turns out to be nice and polite. His name is Trumpkin and we'll learn in a parenthetical that he's an exception to the rule when it comes to Dwarves. Having a whole race of bad people with one or two exceptions will be a repeated theme in later books, especially when we get to Calormen, Narnia's version of the Middle East.

Trumpkin continues his story and we learn Caspian had to flee in the night from his uncle. During this escape, our young wannabe-king has an opportune run-in with "Old Narnia" creatures. Out of the three he initially meets, the Black one wants to murder him while the other non-Black ones are kind. Lewis goes out of his way to describe Nikabrik, the "Black Dwarf," with features like coarse hair so the reader can easily envision someone from, say, African descent. These physical descriptions accompany bad character traits so closely that all Lewis needs to do is describe someone's dark appearance and like Disney-villain shorthand the reader intuitively knows the character is bad.

Many things have been written about the racism of C. S. Lewis, but none of it was explained to me when I was handed these near-as-holy books as a child and told they were inspired by God's word itself. Again, we have not even gotten to the people of Calormen who are dark-skinned—described as "Darkies" by one group in the last book—and declared enemies of Aslan.

For Nikabrik, there is no description of him that is flattering to his character. He alone does not join the dance of the fauns; he wants to kill a human; he doesn't immediately buy into Caspian's claim to the throne; he is sympathetic to the White Witch who was nice to his ancestors; he's of dark appearance; and, most loathsome of all, Nikabrik doesn't smoke. Of all the untrustworthy things! (C. S. Lewis was somewhat of a chimney.)

I hope Nikabrik doesn't do something utterly evil like think some species can have good people in them. He does? *Then he's killed by the good guys because of it?* Well, I'll be.

Prince Caspian: Chapter 6

"Why do all the animals have to fight in a war for some human?"
"I'm sure some didn't."
"But they're called traitors."

***

"Narnia was never right except when a Son of Adam was King."

A talking Badger during Caspian's subsequent campaign for allies tells our readers that one must be human and male to rule. Bitsy and I both groaned at this statement. When one of the other creatures asks if Badger is suggesting they give Narnia to humans, he clarifies, "It's not Man's country, but it's a country for a man to be King of." That makes no sense.

Little Bit suggests that maybe the land was magically created that way for some reason we don't yet know about, but she does concede it was rotten to have a human represent animal interests, especially since it comes out that Caspian kills animals for sport. Nikabrik is incensed about this hunting revelation, but it is quickly dismissed as clearly not the same thing as murder. The animals Caspian killed were dumb, and talking animals are smart after all. By this logic, could they rightfully kill those with intellectual disabilities? With Caspian the First and subsequent kings hunting down all talking animals, many played dumb to survive. Just how many of them were possibly pretending to be regular animals when they found themselves in our Caspian's hunting scope? Is it possible that some of the creatures Caspian had fun killing were sentient and intelligent people? I'm not sure. Narnians tend to be bigger than average so they'd make better hunting trophies.

I get that Lewis seemingly abhors vegetarianism, so in his world a real king would eat meat and do *manly* things like killing animals. I admit I have a few furry obligate carnivores at home, and it's not like animals don't eat other animals, but why create a world of talking animals where killing animals for sport is ever okay? This left Bits and I with a lot of questions. Best not think about it too much.

On the campaign trail, Caspian meets more Black Dwarves and it is made clear that they are also all bad. Like Nikabrik, they are slow to take up Caspian's cause and only relent, not because of any noble reason, but because of their hatred of Miraz. They also helpfully suggest getting an ogre or a Hag to join the cause. To be clear, a Hag is an old woman who does magic. There are plenty of old men who do magic, like Cornelius, but when a woman does it it's bad. At this suggestion, Caspian and his cohorts (except Nikabrik), clutch their pearls and shut that business right down.

"We want none of that sort on our side."

Caspian is shocked that those kinds of "horrible creatures" had descendants in Narnia. Maybe he was confused because the last book said they were all hunted down and killed by the adult versions of Peter, Susan, Edmund, and Lucy.

Aslan does not want the wrong kinds of allies, but what makes them right or wrong seems to be their race, species, or country of origin. Aslan's alter ego, a certain Jewish messiah, had the same thinking when he claimed God sent him only for the Jews[2] and ordered his disciples to initially avoid Gentiles[3] as he wouldn't want any

---

[2] Matthew 15:24
[3] Matthew 10:5-6

of *those people* in his new kingdom before the better people had the chance to get in. There's "us" and there's "them." Don't mix the two. At least he was a step above his predecessor, Yahweh, whose xenophobia easily became genocidal. I would not want to be a Canaanite or Amalekite in those stories.

Trumpkin's tale has finally caught up to the present day, where Caspian is at war with his uncle. His army's strategy up until this point consisted of raiding and pillaging innocent farmers. All is fair in war, I guess. Even if the farmers don't know you're at war because everything you're doing is in secret. Caspian's efforts are painted in the book as righteous when they are arguably the opposite. Lewis portrays morality as being on the right *side* instead of having the right *actions*, determined independently of side. One side is considered good and holy, therefore their deeds naturally inherit that goodness and holiness without critical evaluation. When God's people burn down a city, it's a holy act, but when the other side does it, it's an evil war crime.

To prove our heroes are on the right side, a Centaur prophet tells Caspian that a Son of Adam has "arisen to rule and name the creatures," which is a reference to the Genesis passage where Adam was put in charge of naming the animals. Caspian does not do any naming of any creatures as they obviously already have names, so I assume Lewis just wanted to make another biblical reference but not follow through on it. As is often the case, prophetic wisdom is not to be taken literally.

As we meet more creatures, and they are invited to join the war party, we get descriptions of them based on their species. The giants are all stupid—we only meet one and he's referred to later as a "true giant" referring to his poor intelligence, not his height. The squirrels are all impulsive. The mice are all brave. I was less offended at these physical generalizations based on species than I was at the moral generalizations. I'd rather a characteristic like sleepiness be applied to all bears than something like evilness be applied to all wolves.

Here we meet Reepicheep for the first time, the fierce mouse who is a descendant of the mice who cut the ropes off Aslan after the White Witch momentarily killed him. Reepicheep is described as a foot tall at what is assumed full grown, but in the next book is described as two feet tall. Racism, misogyny, bloodshed, *and* contradictions? Wow, my Christian school was right! *The Chronicles of Narnia* are a spot-on way to introduce the Bible to children! (Haha, fight me.)

Prince Caspian: Chapters 7-9

"Mommy? Why did you laugh when they said they were going to wind Susan's horn?"
"Ummmmmmm…"

***

Caspian's army was discovered by Miraz's army and they engaged in battle. Caspian is now losing so it is time for Susan's *deus ex machina* magic horn to call for otherworldly help. Yes, the horn the children couldn't find in the treasure chamber has been with Caspian this whole time. It had a weak bugle sound in the first book, but now it's described as "loud as thunder" and "strong enough to shake the woods" but also paradoxically "cool and sweet as music over water." It's had some sort of awesomeness upgrade now that a boy is using it.

Our storytelling Dwarf, Trumpkin, was one of the first creatures Caspian met after fleeing Miraz. (Not the Black one who tried to kill him, obviously.) He became a messenger for Caspian and has come to retrieve the children so they can fight Caspian's war. Susan's horn was the magic that ripped the children out of the train station and into Narnia.

As we've seen, anyone who doesn't believe in Aslan is lying to themselves and believes "deep down." We saw this with Edmund when he took the White Witch's side. In this book we were informed that the humans who claimed to be afraid of ghosts in the woods were *actually* afraid of Aslan, who everyone knows is said to come from the east and would have to cut across those woods. Never mind that the first two humans we see at the beginning of this book are terrified of Susan's arrow when they think it came from a spirit. *No, no*, people are *actually* afraid of Aslan. Who they don't believe in. But really do. Deep down.

Trumpkin seems to defy this general rule for unbelievers and be an actual, legitimate skeptic. Of course he's allowed to be because he will convert into a true believer soon enough and needs that sweet transformative testimony. I suppose it's hard to lump all nameless, faceless non-believers into one general category and then have to write about one's origin story without humanizing them a bit. He's no true skeptic in every sense since he believes in the ghosts that turn out to be make-believe, for example, but what I like about Trumpkin is that he does seem to need evidence to accept claims. This is in line with the tradition of Saint Thomas, who, admittedly, is scolded by Jesus and told he's not blessed like blind-faith believers.[4] At one point Caspian and the others are talking of magic rather than strategy so Trumpkin complains, "I wish our leaders would think less about these old wives' tales and more about victuals and arms." In this way, Trumpkin is every rational person trying to fix a problem while their friends' solution is to pray about it.

---

[4] John 20:29

It's almost as if Trumpkin is retroactively bathed in the privilege of being Aslan's elect. He's going to believe in Aslan later in the story, so his character qualities can be appreciated before the fact. Every goodness is bestowed upon him except the "goodness" of faith, so he was never so rotten that he did not deserve a correct belief system. For one thing, he's got blind obedience working for him. Although Aslan does scare our Dwarf friend as a punishment for his skepticism, Trumpkin is still considered a good guy because he was primed and ready to accept Aslan into his heart.

It's not like he's got Black features or anything disqualifying.

Trumpkin mirrors the language of Isaiah 6:8 to be the willing vessel to be used by God (or Caspian) in a religious task, "Send me, Sire, I'll go," he says.

"But I thought you didn't believe in the Horn, Trumpkin," says Caspian in return.

"No more I do," Trumpkin confirms before blindly following bizarre orders while his comrades are dying.

Trumpkin's reward for obedience is becoming a believer. Then the reader can enjoy Trumpkin's continuous reliance on reason getting pummeled every time faith is warranted. "I've made as big a fool of myself as ever a Dwarf did," Trumpkin will conclude of his questioning, slow-to-be-fooled, evidence-dependent rational thought.

Once the children have heard Trumpkin's entire tale, the four feel as if they got pulled out of their lives just to go into their second war for Aslan in as many years. Lucy responds to this with, "But we want to be here, don't we, if Aslan wants us?" Yes, no matter what you personally feel or want, if Aslan wants it then you want it, too. Even if it means killing a bunch of people. *Again.*

I was told that I should want what God wants. "Not my will, but yours be done,"[5] was the mantra modeled by Jesus himself. The trick was to not want my own things or think my own thoughts, but to follow, submit, and be obedient. God knows best. Or rather, those appointed by God do since God is conveniently silent. When Peter gives an order to be fitted for battle, Edmund hesitates, but Lucy corrects him, "Hadn't we better do what Peter says? He is the High King, you know."

Reminds me of the children's song:

"Always submit to the church administration. For they were placed by Lord God to lead His nation. If we obey then we will receive salvation! Sing along with me!"[6]

Because Trumpkin is the kind of damned skeptic who won't just let magical savior children jump into battle, the kids have to go about proving themselves and embarrassing him. Edmund beats him in a sword fight, Susan beats him in archery, and Lucy heals his wound even though it's "not a sight for little girls." Susan, of course, is female so did not enjoy her match because she was "tender-hearted" and didn't want to emasculate him. She immediately makes excuses for her victory to spare the guy's feelings, which is seen as the correct way for girls to behave. She may be capable, but she's a proper lady who knows her place. Queen Susan: Protector of the Man Feels.

The party sets sail to meet Caspian. Susan thinks they should have gone by the river, and her reasoning is sound, but she was told no and thus they end up lost in the woods. Does she think at this point that anyone values her opinion? She reminds them again they should have taken the river and Edmund replies, "Oh, don't take any notice of her.

---

[5] Luke 22:42
[6] Available at: https://youtu.be/3nmYOQIidqo

She always is a wet blanket." A very correct, nearly always right *wet blanket.*

The boys hash out a plan to get to their destination. Susan says she can't remember it all and Edmund strikes back, "That's the worst of girls. They never carry a map in their heads." Lucy responds, "That's because our heads have something inside them." It's a nice zinger, and made Little Bit chuckle, but it reinforces rather than denies the idea that girls' brains are inferior to boys' when it comes to geography.

Suddenly a bear attacks! Susan hesitates to shoot an arrow because she ~~is a girl~~ is afraid of killing it, so Trumpkin must save her. Her reasoning was that it could have been a talking bear. The others assure her that she was foolish since it didn't look sentient. Already she is a better person than Caspian. The boys skin and cut up the bear for meat while the girls go off to save their dainty eyes from watching. Even though they are headed directly into a battle where much worse will occur, but whatever.

Trumpkin is a new believer and the children are solid ones, so what better test of all of them than a test of faith! We get this test when our most valiant believer of all, Lucy, sees Aslan and wants to follow him onto the steeper path. So far Bits and I have had issues with this book, but that was nothing compared to the confusion and frustration these next chapters inspire.

Prince Caspian: Chapters 10-11

"Aslan is a horrible jerk."

"Agreed."

"What's a worse word than jerk, Mom?"

"What do they teach you in these schools?"

***

Lucy's experience with Aslan is every Christian's wet dream. She's described as having a changed face with eyes that shone similar to Moses after seeing God's face.[7] She says Aslan wants them to follow him, but she can't say why or how she knows. She just knows, y'all. She *knows*. Like when anyone asks for evidence of someone's personal belief system and they talk about their feelings and inner confirmations. All those contradictory religions who claim the exact same feelings and knowledge are wrong though. Truly epistemology at its finest.

Lucy's path is by far the hardest, so they take a vote. Only Lucy and Edmund vote to follow Jesus. I mean *Aslan*. They start on the easier path while Lucy cries like a banshee as per usual.

I sang, "I have decided to follow Jesus" in church all growing up. "Though I may wander, still I will follow. Though none go with me, still I will follow. No turning back, no turning back." Now I know you can always turn back, especially before going over a cliff!

Aslan, as we will learn, is a dick and watches them in a rage while playing hide-and-seek. Not only is he not communicating to Lucy in

---

[7] The Bible states that Moses both **did** and absolutely **did not** see God's face. "And the LORD spoke to Moses face to face..." Exodus 33:11. "[...] Moses, whom the LORD knew face to face..." Deuteronomy 34:10. "You cannot see my face, for no one can see my face and live." God to Moses in Exodus 33:20. "No one has ever seen God." John 1:18. Biblical contradictions make it difficult for me to claim that the story includes Moses seeing God's face, but Moses' face shining like a scary beacon after being with God is not in dispute.

a way that makes sense to her, but he's also freaking invisible to everyone except Lucy, and then only briefly visible to her. His instructions and his intentions are cryptic as crap. He couldn't just appear and say, "Hey kids, this way." Oh no. He must toy with them like, well, like a cat I suppose. When they follow logic instead of Lucy's hallucinatory insanity they are punished with paragraph after paragraph of horrible struggles on their journey. The Bible not only says to trust that the LORD knows what's best for you, but specifically *not* to trust your own understanding of what's best.[8] There's even a biblical promise that if you submit to God your path will be made straight (aka easier). The children's path was nothing good so it's proof they did not submit to Aslan's vagueness. I'm sure they knew what he wanted "deep down."

They get back where they started with no progress made and go to sleep sore and frustrated. Time for Aslan to mess with Lucy again! Lucy is called by name in the middle of the night. With no witnesses. In the dark. (She's how old?) She obediently follows the voice calling her name and discovers it's Aslan. She runs to him without thinking through if he is safe. *Thinking*, of course, is not how this works.

Lucy tells Aslan that she wanted to follow him earlier, but her siblings were stubborn. He starts to growl at her for her remark, and since she "understood some of his moods" she apologizes immediately. That kind of emotional labor sounds exhausting, but she's basking in his glory and doesn't seem to mind these controlling and awkward emotional manipulations.

Aslan is extremely capricious. He confirms it was all her fault for not abandoning her family from the beginning and following him alone.

---

[8] Proverbs 3:5-6

"What is Aslan thinking? It's her family! That's mean!" says Bits who is outraged at this point. She's the type of person who wants to please adults and follow the rules, so this is driving her up the wall on Lucy's behalf. Turning her against her family would have been taking things too far for Bitsy. Yet since he's based on the biblical Jesus, Aslan must divide and conquer to be true to character. To quote everyone's favorite Christian messiah:

> "Whoever is not with me is against me, and whoever is not working with me is working against me."[9]

Or this gem:

> "Do you think I came to bring peace on earth? No, I tell you, but division. From now on there will be five in one family divided against each other, three against two and two against three. They will be divided, father against son... mother against daughter..."[10]

For followers of Jesus, they can look forward to their "enemies" being "members of their own household."[11] I know I was prepared for as much as a child.

Aslan tells Lucy to go back to her family and wake them up from sleep and tell them to follow him.

"Will the others see you too?" asks Lucy.

"Certainly not at first," says Aslan. "Later on, it depends."

"But they won't believe me!" says Lucy.

"It doesn't matter," says Aslan.

She apologizes and obeys even though she thinks the idea is horrid. And it is. Her siblings are about to get very cross with her. *This is like every evangelism effort, y'all.*

---

[9] Matthew 12:30
[10] Luke 12:51-53
[11] Matthew 10:36

Aslan says to tell the others to follow, and, "If they will not, then you at least must follow me alone."

Lucy's response is, "I mustn't think about it, I must just do it."

"No!" says Little Bit, "You should always think about it. You shouldn't just follow orders you know are wrong." She's right. **This is how cults work:** Follow the leader and not your own reasoning. Trust the leaders before they prove their trustworthiness to you. You will be tested until you can do this without effort.

My Accelerated Christian Education school system took this to an extreme. If an adult in charge told us to do something absolutely ridiculous, we were expected to obey without hesitation. We even had to submit to physical punishment. My examples are on the extreme end of fundamentalism, but all those little manipulative religious steps in the middle led up to this abuse.

When Lucy tries to wake Susan, Susan tells her that she's dreaming and to go back to sleep. Edmund is the closest to having true faith and believes her initially when she says she sees Aslan, but the sneaky lion goes invisible when Edmund looks that direction. They wake the others and Susan is just not having it: "She's been dreaming. Do lie down and go to sleep, Lucy."

Trumpkin predictably has no use for talking lions that don't talk and can't be seen, but he obeys without question as a matter of duty. His mindless obedience will be rewarded, but his wise crack about having no use for invisible lions gets punished by Aslan later.

Peter finally gives the okay to follow Lucy's invisible lion, who has started to get impatient and is beating his paw on the ground for them to hurry up. Susan, however, was the worst. That's not editorializing, the book says, "Susan was the worst." She asks the group what would happen if she behaved like Lucy and is told to just obey. Seriously, Trumpkin tells her off for not shutting up and obeying Peter, the boy authority. Susan continues to mumble as the journey becomes a

49

difficult descent so Peter says, "Why, a baby could get down here. And do stop grousing."

Very slowly Edmund begins to see Aslan. Peter sees him next, and then finally Susan. Seeing is not believing because supposedly Susan always believed it was Aslan, wait for it, "deep down." Holy hell, not this again!

Susan admits as much:

> "I really believed it was him—he, I mean—yesterday. When he warned us not to go down to the fir wood. And I really believed it was him tonight, when you woke us up. I mean, deep down inside."

Is Lewis for real right now? I guess only the fool says in their heart there is no Aslan. What could Susan's motivation possibly be? Lewis has her saying: "I just wanted to get out of the woods and—and—oh, I don't know." That's her entire defense! She was just willfully wrong for no reason and doesn't know why. Who does that? (Spoiler: We're supposed to think atheists do that.)

This would be like if I made a claim that Caspian is a Werewolf and then assumed everyone who disagreed with me was simply suppressing a secret belief in the Werewolf king. I could claim people know my lupine doctrines are true "deep down." See? Not at all completely self-serving or offensive. All bow to the wolf! Tax exemption status to the pack! (I'm planting the seeds now so unbelievers are "without excuse" when his Werewolfness is clearly revealed later.)

Aslan has shown himself to be a huge bully so it's no surprise that he would toy with poor Trumpkin upon becoming visible to him. The lion uses a loud voice with a roar in it when speaking to him for the first time in order to terrify the poor Dwarf. The book clarifies that the children "knew Aslan well enough" to know he was only messing with him. Aslan was not going to rip him apart but Trumpkin didn't know that. He was greatly disturbed when Aslan pounced him, picked him up to where he was "hunched up in a little, miserable ball," shook him until his armor rattled, and then threw him up in the air. Just to add madness to the mix, Aslan says out of nowhere, "Shall we be friends?" See, all a game. Trumpkin was too upset to respond so Aslan ignored him and started ordering the boys off to kill humans with Caspian. They didn't dare ask him what the plan was and instead just obeyed as they had been conditioned to do.

What does Aslan do with the girls once he's sent the guys away? Two words: drunken orgy. (No really. I'm not joking.)

Prince Caspian: Chapters 12-15

"Hey Mom, Aslan should have had the fighters come party instead of fighting."
"Some of the party seems just as scary though."
"Yeah, Aslan is having fun hurting people."

***

We left off the night before with the girls in a wild party centering around Aslan. It turned out to be a bacchanalian orgy with none other than Bacchus himself, surrounded by "wild women," whom Lucy admits she wouldn't have felt safe around without Aslan there. The party got out of control and people were drunk. Everyone was laughing and "behaved as if they were blindfolded." It would have been fun times if there weren't people dying just off camera. Silenus, servant to the god of wine I discovered when we looked him up, starts magically calling vines to grow from the ground. The grapes formed on them were eaten by everyone with "no table-manners at all." Then everyone flopped down breathless on the ground to admire Aslan.

I knew these books contained bloody violence, murder, and the like, but drunkenness was a whole new conversation to have with my curious kid. On the other hand, I've got to hand it to Lewis. He may not have liked women, dark-skinned people, foreigners, vegetarians, or nonsmokers, but he loved him a drunken dance party! Many upstanding believers have been, and continue to be, in an uproar over all the pagan imagery in these chapters. When I was little, my pastor told me to skip these pages when reading through the series. (I didn't.)

While Aslan is partying, the army he was begged to help is dying. Badger, Caspian's friend, says he has faith that Aslan will come save them. Imagine if poor Badger could have seen his lion god at that exact moment partying with the god of wine and sex.

Oh wow. It just hit me what Aslan was doing during the 100-year winter in the previous book. Busy lion!

Nikabrik reports that a fifth of his Black Dwarves have died, but no one cares. He then brings in two "friends" to help turn the battle around: a Werewolf and a Hag. These are the wrong kind of creatures for pure Aslan to accept. Nikabrik doesn't hide them; he brings them into the chamber where Caspian, Badger, and the animal generals plan battle stuff so he can suggest a plan to bring back the White Witch using the Hag's powers. I mean, the last book says the White Witch was nice to the Dwarves and, hey, his friends and family are dying. The least Caspian and company could do is not immediately attack and kill him over it.

It's obvious I'm not the one writing this children's book since that's exactly what they do.

Caspian gets bitten by the Werewolf during the fight. Little Bit and I have concluded this clearly means Caspian is a Werewolf now. Maybe this is not how it works, but I would argue that everyone secretly believes this is *totally* how it works *deep down*.

When the Werewolf, Hag, and Black Dwarf are dead, Peter then kisses Badger who helped him fight. The reader is assured that: "it wasn't a girlish thing for him to do, because he was the High King." Yes, that's a pull quote.

Peter, Edmund, and Trumpkin come in and devise a plan to invite Caspian's uncle to a David-and-Goliath-style combat to decide the war. They send Edmund to carry the message to the enemy. Edmund could walk across enemy lines without fear because he was glowing with Aslan breath. The lion had previously breathed on the children and given them courage and "greatness" and other vague attributes we're not supposed to think about too hard. Slaughter times are about to feel happier.

Miraz's advisors want to kill their own king and take his place, so they tricked Miraz into taking up Peter's challenge. When Miraz trips during combat, those same advisors rush in and kill their own king. "The blade went home" was a fun sentence I got to explain to my daughter. The battle then continues with lots of death and killing.

Peter calls Reepicheep a "little ass" for the crime of fighting in battle while small. This adds a level of "big" to the hierarchy. Reep had the right gender, rank, and age, but the wrong height, apparently.

Then the freaking trees all rush into battle! Victory is assured at this point. Try fighting trees! Where were they earlier?

Meanwhile Aslan is off somewhere with the girls saying things like, "We will make holiday." What he meant by this was terrorizing a small town of people while his army was being killed. First Aslan has his buddy, Bacchus, destroy a bridge to release a water god. Next, the whole group of dancing, partying "wild people" visit a school for girls. They scare away all the fat girls, likely described that way to justify their abuse. In one case Aslan asks another schoolgirl, "You'll stay with us, sweetheart?" I think we're supposed to assume she's the only skinny one as she's not described as fat, and that equates to attractive by book logic. Bacchus' wild women help this girl out of her restrictive clothing so she can join in the fun! I can't make this stuff up! They repeated this act in every town by terrorizing people while collecting the (pretty? skinny?) ones they want.

During this time, the group comes upon a man beating a boy. Aslan kills the man by turning him into a tree. The boy then "burst out laughing and joined them." Yeah, that's a bit psycho. You definitely want psycho boy on your team. He'll fit right in. Being joyfully happy while watching or committing murder is not healthy. (Looking at you, Bible.[12])

The fun continues! They come to another school where a girl is teaching a class. She declines the offer to join Aslan, saying she doesn't want to scare her students. What does Aslan do? He respects her decision and moves on. *Nah*, of course he terrifies the students so badly they jump out of windows to escape, turns them into pigs, and then orders the girl to follow him. This time, rather under threat, she joins him. (Enthusiastic consent is not a thing with Aslan.)

It just keeps going! They come upon a child crying because his aunt is dying. Aslan goes into the house to see the aunt and ends up crashing through it and destroying the whole thing. (Whoops, broke your house.) The old woman asks if the lion has come to take her away and he replies it's "not the long journey yet." Wait, Aslan is also the grim reaper? Okay. At least he does end up healing her, even though he doesn't heal anyone falling by the hundreds in the battle going on a short way away.

Aslan may go missing for hundreds of years, but when he does show up, it's chaos! He just murdered, terrified, and violated the bodily autonomy of so many folks not involved in the battle, and did so while laughing and dancing like a drunken loon. (The fact he attacked schools and school children will make more sense when we learn about Lewis' history.) Bitsy was especially disturbed about people getting

---

[12] Psalm 137:9

changed into animals or things. She was born with some severe physical differences and has needed surgeries to help her function better. She knows how difficult a changed body is to deal with emotionally as well as practically, and that consent is needed before any change to a body is made. Aslan doesn't seem to understand this concept. Or even care.

In the end, our party meets up with Peter and the menfolk who were just finishing up in the battle. The human soldiers fear Aslan because "they had not believed in lions," so in other words they were scared for no reason because they really believe in them "deep down," right? Right?!

Aslan asks Caspian if he's ready to be king. Caspian says he doesn't think so.

> "Good. If you had felt yourself sufficient, it would have been a proof that you were not."

That's right, humans are garbage and should know their place. What if Caspian had been feeling confident? Then he's no good as a leader? He needs to recognize how lowly and dirty he is. There's my childhood indoctrination in a nutshell.

Next, Reepicheep is brought before the king near death. Lucy's magic bottle heals him but fails to regrow his tail. Reepicheep is horrified since his tail is his honor, not to mention his balance. Aslan simply says he looks good that way. I baulked at this pretty hard. *For real, Aslan?* Reepicheep asks for his tail to be restored because he lost it in Aslan's service and the lion is clearly powerful enough to do it, plus it's culturally and personally important to him. The Jesus lion (who has a tail, mind you) does not feel compelled at all to help his people. It seems he was waiting until all the other mice got out their swords to take their own tails before he is willing to restore it. He made sure everyone knew he didn't do it "for the sake of [Reepicheep's] dignity." He just liked that others were willing to mutilate themselves.

Lastly, we get a weird explanation from Aslan about where all these humans in Narnia came from. They all come from six pirates and their captured wives (that's rape, just to be clear) who found a magic cave that catapulted them to Narnia. That's not a lot of genetic diversity, but it did the trick. Boom! Humans in Narnia! No matter if you're a thieving, raping, possibly inbred human, it's all good since "you could be no true King of Narnia unless, like the Kings of old, you were a Son of Adam."

Chanting time! *Humans! Humans!*

When Caspian learns his origins, he becomes rather ashamed. Aslan clarifies:

> "You come of the Lord Adam and the Lady Eve. And that is both honour enough to erect the head of the poorest beggar, and shame enough to bow the shoulders of the greatest emperor on earth."

This is the lesson I received as a Christian. I was a child of God but also a horrible, wretched sinner. Which was it? Yes! Both! Humans are the best-worst! Yay Christian worldview!

Aslan sends all the humans, the ones who want to go anyway, back to Earth. This includes Peter, Susan, Edmund and Lucy. Aslan tells Peter and Susan that they won't be returning to Narnia because they are "getting too old" so this is their last trip before they are boring grown-ups who he couldn't care less about.

The book ends when the children get back to their train station as if they had never been away.

"They're probably going back to Hogwarts," says Bits.

If they were, they'd get a proper story.

4
Treading Water

The Voyage of the Dawn Treader is the third installation in the Narnia series, going in the order of original publication. If a Narnian theologian was writing a systematic theology text, she could skip over the first two books as reference material and go straight to this one. While always heavy with allegory, Lewis' messaging will start to become more clunky. What started as a wink to Christian children—a story of a lion that mirrored a familiar resurrection tale—will now contain character statements, motivations, and situations that will occasionally create mild confusion for the biblically uninitiated. I would argue that the main focus of *Dawn Treader* is the spiritual salvation of a new character, Eustace. Children who do not understand the original biblical directive of propitiation to God by appeasing his bloodlust with a murdered sacrifice[1] and the need to be saved from their own God's desire to torture them for all eternity by accepting and obeying that sacrifice,[2] will fail to understand why Aslan is so scary, why Eustace needs Aslan to be pleased, why his interactions with Aslan are physically painful, or why discussions about Aslan with his followers are so abnormal.

This is not your lovey-dovey Sunday School Christianity; this is hard core.

At the end of the last book, we learned that Aslan takes people's souls after they die. In this book it's revealed he takes them to "Aslan's

---

[1] A practice that evolved from the blood cults of Bronze Age people who sought to appease their own wrathful gods.
[2] Jesus is also God in many traditions.

Country," the afterlife named for him. Like his biblical counterpart once did, Aslan is undergoing a deification process; there will be so many new revelations and abilities added to our feline god in this adventure it will seem as if the author could not pile the superpowers upon him quickly enough to meet demand. Biblical scholars will find this escalation familiar.

The Voyage of the Dawn Treader: Chapter 1

"So Eustace is bad even though his parents are good?"
"Oh sweetie, the book is trying to describe bad parents."
"What! How?"

***

We begin our adventure with Edmund and Lucy finally getting a last name, Pevensie! They go to live for sixteen weeks with their cousin, Eustace. I'm fairly certain the Pevensies got their last name so that Lewis could give Eustace a terrible surname, Scrubb, and readers wouldn't assume it also belonged to our beloved characters as well.

We left off last bedtime with Aslan telling Peter and Susan they were "too old" for Narnia and would not be returning with their younger siblings in the future. Being too old for Aslan is a bit disturbing to me. I mean, this lion is literally a predator and he's only interested in young children. Ew.

My cynical side sees this aging out plot as a condemnation of mature rationality. Jesus commands his followers to have faith like a child and warns they will never enter his kingdom otherwise.[3] Following suit, Aslan requires the same childlike surrender to get to his heavenly "Country." Believers in any religion are more likely to be

---

[3] Matthew 18:3

indoctrinated as children; it is more difficult to make converts out of folks who have reached full brain maturation. Most of us don't get the opportunity to think critically through our options before signing up for a religion. That's how I found myself reverently celebrating an act of human sacrifice that would normally be abhorrent to me. It was normalized by the culture and community around me when I was young.

As a missionary, I was trained to target children in my evangelism efforts. Children must comply with adults since they rely on them for survival. For this reason, God requires perpetual children. "Children of God" are what the adults in my fundamentalist church called each other. They had a Father God who could control them or mess with them in a power dynamic from the Old Testament when patriarchs ruled over their children and grandchildren. A patriarch had ultimate power and could force a son to marry his brother's widow, a daughter to marry her rapist, or a grandchild to be sold into slavery to pay family debts. Absolute obedience was required of everyone under hierarchy rule.

The biblical god "scourges every son whom he receives"[4] which includes scaring and hurting them as part of the salvation process. One biblical writer encouraged continued obedience of the faithful in order to secure their salvation through "fear and trembling."[5] Why does Aslan toy with Trumpkin when he suddenly pounces and throws the trembling Dwarf up in the air? Because he can. Because testing obedience and submission is seen as beneficial to the powerless. We will see even worse done to Eustace in this story that will be rather disturbing to the modern reader.

I may be especially sensitive to compulsory obedience and indoctrination because my powerless and vulnerable years were filled with

---

[4] Hebrews 12:6
[5] Philippians 2:12

non-stop religious propaganda. I was given a false binary choice between adhering to Christianity and rejecting my parents, family, and only community I had ever known—not exactly a valid option for a dependent child. Additionally, nonparticipation in religious school and nonadherence to Christian principles came with physical punishments. Unfortunately, this method of coercion works. I was a believer in a fundamentalist faith for almost twenty-five years before I questioned any of it. It would take me several additional years in a Christian belief system before deconstructing it completely, and only after it had failed me at some crucial times, leaving me to handle the real-world consequences. It was still hard to leave, even then. Childhood indoctrination has a powerful effect on the brain, which is something I write about in detail in Karen Garst's anthology, *Women v. Religion: The Case Against Faith and for Freedom.*[6]

After Narnia rejected them for growing up, Peter went off to live with the "wise" Professor (yeah, *that* guy) and Susan traveled to America because she was so bad at school her parents decided to give her a social experience instead. This is code, I assume, for introducing her to boys who might take her off their hands. From all accounts, she was *all about* this plan. Get it, girl.

Due to adherence to strict masculinity rules regarding displays of emotion, Lewis had to have at least one female character to carry the emotional load every good story requires. The first two books seemed gender-balanced at first blush but never felt that way to Bitsy and me since the girls did not seem to have as much agency as the boys and most all NPC characters were male. It was disappointing that this newest adventure eliminated all female characters but one, Lucy—an incongruous addition to three boys, multiple seamen, several lords, and

---

[6] Alexis Record, 2018. "Women v. Indoctrination." In *Women v. Religion: The Case Against Faith and for Freedom*, (Durham, NC: Pitchstone Publishing), pp. 73-98.

male-dominated cities. At least since Lucy is Lewis' ideal vision of what girls *should* be there will be fewer opportunities to mock traditional female concerns. Fewer, but not none. She will mostly be molded into a paragon of female supportiveness of male heroics.

Our story opens in Eustace's home, which took Little Bit a while to realize was supposed to be bad in every way. She initially thought these were very good yet quirky people. We're from Southern California so we're used to families of all kinds. Several things Lewis presented as marks against Eustace's parents were not actually bad things. For example, they were nonsmokers. Lewis, being an avid smoker, could think of nothing worse. Who else was a nonsmoker in Narnia? Freaking evil Nikabrik the Black Dwarf. All the good guys smoke.

These awful parents gave their son the wrong kind of books—those nonfiction textbooks of educated adults. Why? Because he loved them. Repeatedly throughout *Dawn Treader* the author laments Eustace's taste in books. He must overcome this academic mindset in order to thrive in Narnia. He must be more simple, *childlike*.

Eustace's family is described as "very up-to-date and advanced people." If the modern reader does not catch this at first, it's a slight. One way this is illustrated is by Eustace calling his parents by their first names. While that's odd, it's not the disrespectful slap that Lewis seems to think it is, especially when the parents themselves have encouraged it. Bitsy and I have noticed Lewis likes to assign good or evil attributes to simple societal or cultural differences.

The condemnation grows as we learn the Scrubb family had a severe diet: They were vegetarians who did not drink alcohol. (*Gasp and faint.*) Lewis often describes both eating meat and drinking wine in relished detail, so teetotaling vegetarians would be extra ridiculous to him, suspicious even. Like smoking, these things are pleasures straight from God's hand, and whoever would forego them must be *wrong* somehow. To understand Lewis' view of underage drinking, recall the time Mrs. Beaver gave the children what I can only assume was hard liquor to get them to sleep. Or, you know, the entire Bacchus storyline!

Speaking of unnatural, this weirdo family wore special underwear. Initially I assumed this was a knock against Latter-day Saints, but it seems instead to be a reference to those who go with current fashion fads even when others couldn't see it. Again, nothing noted here made it obvious to Bits that this wasn't just a nice family with different values or tastes. If different is bad then the Scrubbs are the worst kind of people. As proof of how bad they are, Eustace's character will be ascribed every malice.

Little Bit was not prepared to have Eustace turn out so rotten. "It doesn't make sense," she would often remark as Eustace's actions seemed to defy explanation. Eustace is hardly a three-dimensional character, and rarely has compelling motivations for anything he does. Yet we can intuit the real reason Eustace is so terrible: sin. It's his nature.[7] This is the first lesson in the Christian salvation message: All people are dirty[8] rotten sinners.[9] Religious readers may pick up on these dog whistles more quickly and realize Eustace's home life is one that does not reflect the proper Christian values of obedience, piety, humility, and authoritarian respect.

The lack of violence in Eustace's home is supposed to explain his violent tendencies. Lewis does not present a child who is innately violent either, but one who is violent *because* he had not known violence. His parents failed to follow the biblical command to hit their child with a rod[10] and now he will beat up others due to lack of correction. We know children who have received corporal punishment are more

---

[7] Romans 5:12

[8] Isaiah 64:6 compares righteous human deeds to menstrual rags.

[9] Romans 3:23; 1 John 1:10

[10] Proverbs 13:24; 22:15; 29:15

likely to be violent, not less,[11] but since "scourging sons" is a biblical principle, it would take an act of rebellion against God for fundamentalist parents to do otherwise. Eustace won't learn his lesson about hurting others until he is assaulted in Narnia.

To sum it all up, Eustace is annoying, smart, loves advanced technical books, isn't subjected to drunkenness, eats a healthy diet, isn't around smokers, and isn't beaten at school. The horror! Only Aslan can bring salvation to this lost cause!

When Lucy and Edmund notice a painting of a Narnian ship in the Scrubb home, Eustace teases them about their make-believe world. He did this because "he was far too stupid" to make up a fantastic story like Narnia himself, but apparently he's smart enough to know what assonance is when defending why the poem he made up to tease them didn't rhyme. I found the label of "stupid" to be more the taunt of a bully author than a fitting description for this young boy. Back off, Lewis!

I'll admit I'm protective of Eustace. Maybe it's due to being a foster-and-adoptive parent, but I do have a soft spot for kids who have a tough time fitting in.

Suddenly the three children are pulled into the painting. Lewis masterfully describes the scene so that Bitsy and I could picture it as if we were experiencing it. Lewis can create imagery in our minds with such flourish and detail. We get a good introduction of the character qualities of each child during their chaotic fall into the picture as well: Edmund is knowledgeable about magic and keeps his head, Lucy is pragmatic and ditches her shoes upon finding herself in the sea, and Eustace is reactive and destructive, almost drowning others in his panic. They are rescued by a familiar character, Caspian, who was on the ship they saw in the picture.

---

[11] Jeff R. Temple, 2018. "Childhood Corporal Punishment and Future Perpetration of Physical Dating Violence," *Journal of Pediatrics* 194: 233-237.

Important note: Caspian is also a secret Werewolf. Those who claim this isn't the case actually believe it is *deep down*. This has nothing to do with any plot point whatsoever but makes Bitsy and I giddy to think about.

Not long after the children reach the ship do we get our first clue of how boring the sailing portions of the subsequent chapters are going to be. Lewis stops the story to explain the difference between port and starboard and how we need to know these things if we "are going to read this story at all." If the reader isn't in love with sailing, large sections of this book will be horribly dull. Spoiler: Large sections of this book are horribly dull.

Upon being rescued, Eustace starts crying "harder than any boy of his age has a right to." Boys don't have "a right to" express strong emotions, apparently; even boys who are kidnapped by magic, taken from their home and parents, and almost drowned. Eustace is even more scared when he meets Reepicheep onboard. The talking mouse immediately suggests violence towards him because Reep is "the most valiant" so of course wants to hurt people who are upset by the presence of magical creatures.

Caspian gives the children alcohol to warm them up and the wine makes teetotaling and sea-sick Eustace miserable, causing him to cry even harder. Aren't non-drinking children the worst?

Life in Narnia is going to be rough for this little guy.

The Voyage of the Dawn Treader: Chapters 2- 4

"This is soooooooooooooo boring. Why is sailing so boring? You'd think it'd be fun!"
"If we suffer through this there are dragons later."
"There'd better be. When do we get to the dragons?"

"Um, shoot, not until chapter six."
"Uggggggggggggggggghhhh!"

***

Lucy has a special place in Lewis' heart and does not fall prey to the same witless nonsense as any of the other female characters, which admittedly has only really been Susan and Mrs. Beaver as Lewis doesn't have a lot of womenfolk in his worlds. It does seem that Lucy's good qualities are often the most pronounced when she is avoiding traditionally feminine trappings. Lucy goes shoeless, joins in on adventures, wears boys' clothing,[12] and is "as good as any boy"[13] at least up to the point her gender demands a different course of action like getting her hand kissed. Lucy is also described here as loving every single aspect of this ship—a sentiment not shared by Bitsy or myself.

Three years have passed in Narnia and one year in London since the last book. Caspian has been busy beating up giants ("they pay us tribute now"), almost marrying a child bride but didn't for, er, gallant reasons ("[she] squints, and has freckles"), running into pirates who they didn't get to murder ("we ought to have […] hanged every mother's son of them"), and has now, with Aslan's approval, set off to find the seven lords the former king sent out to sea years before. Reepicheep joined the trip in order to be sacrificed to Aslan as part of a prophecy he was given as a child. (*Yep, that's not a misprint.*) Once Aslan's name is evoked this adventure becomes more of a holy quest.

Little Bit had trouble with every ship being given female pronouns or called "lady," usually a complement for having perfect lines and

---

[12] Or I should say what Lewis would consider boys' clothing. If it's on a girl then it's girls' clothing.

[13] This quote is anachronistic as it comes from another book in the series, *A Horse and His Boy*, where Lucy is being favorably compared to boys as an adult woman.

being visually beautiful. Bits would hear a "she" or "her" and get excited for a new character, only to be disappointed that an object was being described. She made a small groan *each and every time this happened* so we were forced to notice *each and every time this happened.* She also had a habit of repeating the word "presently" after I read it aloud because it is over-used and foreign to her vocabulary. Add in a giggle at mention of the ship's poop and let's just say it took longer than necessary to get through these chapters.

At one point the ship reached a couple of islands named Felimath and Doorn. They were not feminine-sounding names and got the pronoun "it." Little Bit asked, "Is that because only women are objects and not men?" Aww, my little girl already knows the rules for objectification! Adorbs!

Lewis goes on to describe the differences between this ship and other Narnian ships, or even steam ships of London, and we suffered through these long pages. Ship navigation is only agreeable for so many paragraphs before we were tired of it.

Eustace starts keeping a diary because he liked getting good marks in school so he decided to do a kind of book report on his adventure. We're supposed to roll our eyes at the very thought of finding writing reports enjoyable. (Hey! I was this kid!) Eustace is said to always keep a notebook with him (which is not soaked when they ended up in the sea, how?) as if that was the most priggish thing ever. This part of the narration displays the same distain for education we've seen before, but it's more vicious somehow. Before it was about hatred of the school *system* and now it's an attack on children who would thrive in such a system. Eustace will only stop journaling when he becomes a better person.

During these diary entries we learn a bit more of Eustace's horrible liberal parents. His father had warned him not to shut his eyes to facts, and that is mocked as bad advice because Eustace is a liar by nature.

When Eustace writes about how unfair it is that Lucy gets a cabin to herself, he is told it's "because she's a girl" so he baulks at this. (They seem to have mispronounced "Freaking Queen of Narnia" here and instead said "girl.") Eustace recalls his mother's warning that benevolent sexism "is really lowering girls." No one in Narnia seems to agree and we're supposed to think the male characters are honoring Lucy by treating her differently. When, for example, Reepicheep interrupts dinner and says, "I ask your pardons all, and especially her Majesty's," it works to show how removed Lucy is from the rest of the company. She's considered above it, but even as a queen she's not seen fit to lead it. The same reason works for both her supposed elevation and essential subjugation: "because she's a girl."

Why was Reepicheep interrupting dinner? It was because Eustace had, without cause, decided to grab the giant mouse's tail and swing him around. Reepicheep responds by stabbing Eustace's hand and beating him repeatedly with the side of his rapier. When explaining himself, Eustace claims he is a pacifist, even though his actions show he's clearly not. This may be how we're meant to think pacifists secretly act.

We finally reach the island of Felimath where the children and Reepicheep run into a group of men led by a "black-haired fellow." If you didn't catch that ethnic clue, this is code for men who are evil. In fact, they are slavers who kidnap the whole party. No worries, though, since a good guy named Lord Bern, one of the seven lords Caspian is there to find, runs into them on the way back to their slaver ship. The children are saved! No, just kidding. Bern buys Caspian and leaves the others to be chained up and sold off. What a good guy.

Lord Bern does not give a second thought to buying slaves, but only considers selling them to be immoral. Even though he literally just participated in the slave trade, and by the economic principle of supply and demand has actually made the problem of slavery *worse*, he immediately starts virtue signaling by saying, "I have moved his Sufficiency the Governor a hundred times to crush this vile traffic in man's flesh." Like, he says this directly after HE JUST BOUGHT A SLAVE. It's not like he was planning on releasing Caspian either, but merely promises to treat Caspian well, and explains the purchase was impulsive, "I bought you for your face." (Creepiest sentence ever.)

We'll later learn slavery is only bad when people of color do it, but just fine when Aslan or White people do it, especially if they use a different word for it.

Caspian tells Bern that he's the king of Narnia, so Bern invites him to dinner where Bern's nameless prop-piece wife and nameless proppiece daughters greet him. The next day the men execute a plan to save the others by making a great procession to the governor. This spectacle will make it look like they have more men than they do and they'll be more likely to gain entrance. During this grand march to the governor's front door, crowds gather in gendered groups by age to watch. You know, as they do. Lewis describes each group in stereotypical ways: All the young men cheered to add to the disturbance because boys will be boys and all the young women cheered because they had a vested interest in the governance of their city. Just joking. It was because, "Caspian and Drinian and the rest were so handsome."

The "handsome" men take over the castle, overthrow the governor, and march down on the slave markets. Who are these horrible slave masters? The Calormen. Literally colored men. They are described as having "dark faces" as well as "long beards" and "orange-coloured turbans." Just to sum them up in the worst kinds of stereotypes, our not-xenophobic-at-all author tacks on the characteristics of "wise, wealthy, courteous, cruel and ancient." This is how Lewis views the Middle East.

Novelist Philip Pullman inspired the wrath of many ardent C. S. Lewis defenders when he called the author "blatantly racist."[14] Pullman notes that in Narnia, "light-colored people are better than dark-colored people." Even theologian Paul F. Ford, a longtime fan of Lewis, condemns him as being "unsympathetic to things and people Middle Eastern" and using "exaggerated stereotyping in contrasting things Narnian and thing Calormene."[15] So we'll need to get used to that.

Bern ends this chapter by noting, "This closing the slave market might make a new world; war with Calormen is what I foresee."

Yes, dark-colored people are *that* evil.

The Voyage of the Dawn Treader: Chapters 5-6

"Lucy never complains. Is that because she's a girl?"
"What do you think?"
"I don't mean real girls, Mom, but Narnia has rules or something for what girls can feel."

***

Lucy is consistently painted as cheerful and loves every aspect of sailing. She wakes up each glorious morning charmed by the violent seas, the heat, the rocking, and the nearly dying of dehydration. They lose a lot of their water during one particularly tumultuous storm and it gets so bad the whole crew gets fevers. Lucy's reaction to this is not

---

[14] Philip Pullman, 1998. "The Dark Side of Narnia." *The Guardian*, October 1.
[15] Paul F. Ford, 2005. *Companion to Narnia*, Rev Ed. (New York, NY: HarperCollins Publishers).

normal. In miserable times it is somehow okay for the men to complain, but Lucy is struck silent.

If you can't say something nice, let the men do all the talking I guess.

Eustace tries to steal some water during rationing and is caught. Caspian threatens "two dozen" to anyone who does it again. It was a meaningless threat to Eustace who didn't know what "two dozen" meant as he'd never been whipped before. Little Bit didn't get what it meant either as the author never explains it, so she guessed push-ups. Understanding about beatings "comes in the sort of books those Pevensie kids read" we're told, which doesn't help Eustace (or Bitsy) who, we're repeatedly reminded, reads the "wrong" kinds of books. Lewis' right kind of books, however, would say things like, "Whoever spares the rod, hates their son,"[16] and, "Endure suffering, God is treating you as sons."[17]

Lucy gives some of her water to Eustace and claims it's because "girls don't get as thirsty as boys." Here we see where gendered othering is harmful. It's clear by the context she is just being nice, but notice she used her status as a girl—a foreign thing outside the typical human experience—to convince Eustace to take the water. He was more than happy to accept that her body worked differently.

Lucy almost has no choice in her actions since deviating from selfless subservience would place her outside of good femininity, which is seen as her natural state. Dying from dehydration with less water than everyone else is something Lucy does without fuss. She really is saintly and gracious and cheerful and [insert any other stereotype about what a "good" girl should be that is never equally expected of male humans here].

---

16 Proverbs 13:24
17 Hebrews 12:7

Eventually the sailors find land and water. Eustace decides to sneak away to nap while the others start the hard work of repairing and restocking their ship. He climbs up a mountain and finds a freaking dragon!

"Finally," pipes Bitsy who is sick of all the sea travel.

This is my favorite part of the entire book, maybe the entire series! While Caspian and the other children were busy (underage) drinking the "strong wine of Archenland" fresh off their bout of dehydration, Eustace is off on the best adventure yet! He doesn't know he's seeing a dragon at first, because, once again, "Eustace had read none of the right books." (Don't read, kids!) The dragon conveniently dies right in front of him at that very moment and Eustace now has a free dragon cave to sleep in filled with treasure! The only tiny little down side is that apparently this cave turns people into dragons. Eustace falls asleep only to wake up and discover he's more lizard than boy.

It was not cursed treasure nor the pool of water he drank from, which was what Bits and I had initially guessed, that turned Eustace into a dragon, but it was his bad thoughts. Eustace never cared about treasure before, but immediately starts thinking that with enough of it he could move to Calormen, "the least phoney of these countries." In other words, the worst, beastly character wants the worst, beastly country. Calormen is a land of dark-skinned people, after all, so who would want to live there unless they were horrid like Eustace? It was these thoughts he was cursed for.

Eustace has this dawning awareness of his transformation that is completely relatable. He is in shock initially and can't believe what's happening. After a while, though, he accepts the fact of his transformation and grieves deeply. His first act as a dragon, after sobbing, oh and with full human awareness I might add, is to eat the other dead dragon. It was a little horrifying to read.

71

Eustace recognizes his wretched state and misses his human companions. He realizes they were not the fiends he made himself believe they were. In the Christian fantasy, this is when sinners see the superior believers around them and want to know their secret. *Please, tell us trash people about your Jesus that makes you so so special.*

Meanwhile the sailors are out looking for Eustace (sans Lucy) with no luck. Later that night all the menfolk (sans Lucy again) start speaking to each other about the dragon they have noticed on the beach. For the second remarkable time in this series, fear of causing female worry has led to female exclusion of important problems. This time it was not simply one or two important menfolk discussing an issue, it was "the whole company gathered close together and talking in whispers." The only talk was of dragons, and the only ears excluded were Lucy's, so it was only a matter of time before she found out.

After a breakfast that included even more wine, they all march against the dragon, with Lucy protected in the middle of the group. They approach the dragon to fight it, but it backs away crying. It's up to Lucy, the only one with emotional super powers, to have pity. (Girls are truly otherworldly.) Lucy notices a golden bracelet Eustace had previously put on his upper human arm that was now digging painfully into his large dragon arm. Lucy runs towards it and applies her cordial which brings down the swelling. They ask the dragon questions and figure out by his nodding and head shaking that it's Eustace. Eustace becomes emotional at this point and thumps his tail making everyone jump. Some of the sailors reacted "with ejaculations" and I want some sort of credit for not giggling when I read that part out loud.

To make him feel better, Lucy kisses the dragon in the opening paragraphs of the next chapter. She had to muster up her courage to do it. Upon hearing this, Little Bit pipes up, "You don't have to kiss anyone you don't want to, especially if they are gross or scare you."

Yeah, I think Little Bit will do just fine in life.

The Voyage of the Dawn Treader: Chapters 7-8

[Content warning: Some weird imagery that may trigger those who were physically or sexually abused as children.]

"Aslan wants to hurt people, but only to save them?"
"What do you think about that?"
"Oh, um, well, it makes him seem bad, but he's the good guy."
"Would you want Aslan's help if you were a dragon?"
"No, but I'd need it, right? If I didn't obey him he might hurt me worse. It *is* Aslan."

***

I've argued that this story is ultimately about the salvation of Eustice. Once he is a monster, and hates himself properly, there's a sense in which he transforms into a better person. The sailors notice and appreciate the change in Eustice as he becomes a useful worker for the first time. He enjoys his new Christian, er, I mean *Aslan-following* community and enjoys the benefits of being part of the in-group.

During my missionary training years, we were taught all the ways we could help show someone just how much they deserved, simply by being born,[18] to be labeled horrible sinners. Recall that the first step in the salvation process is to recognize one's own wretchedness. We thought people would somehow be inspired to greatness by the knowledge that God would sacrifice his son for awful sinners like us. The result of that kind of thinking can be ugly. For one thing, try loving your neighbor as yourself when you consider yourself every sort of evil.

---

[18] Psalm 51:5

After accepting one's monstrous nature, complete with self-loathing, the next step in the Christian salvation plan I learned growing up is to accept and follow Jesus. Our Jesus in this book is Aslan and Aslan appears to Eustice in the mysterious and vague way his counterpart is said to appear to believers today. I used to quote Scripture and talk about my intangible God-inspired emotions, but I couldn't pony up satisfactory, demonstrable evidence for what I believed. Remember when Lucy *just knew* to follow Aslan in the last book? It's all very spiritual and mysterious. Religious experiences feel special and real, even if there's nothing more than brain chemistry behind them.

Eustice has a "Come to Lion" moment when Aslan tells the boy to follow him. Not that he asked Eustice with *words*, because it hasn't worked that way in a while, but Eustice somehow got the message while experiencing *all the feels*. His most overwhelming feeling is fear, and with good reason: Aslan is constantly described as unsafe. At least the biblical God doesn't eat little children. (He sends bears to do that.[19])

Aslan leads the boy dragon to a magical well, like a mikvah, for a kind of baptism. Eustice can't fit his huge dragon body down into the well so Aslan orders Eustace to undress. "You should *not* get undressed for strangers!" Little Bit interjects, but, unable to hear my daughter, Eustace starts to do as he's told. Aslan then orders him to "let me undress you." Eustice was afraid, but tells his cousins, "So I just lay flat down on my back to let him do it."

Here is where Aslan cut him so deeply and painfully that it "hurt worse than anything [Eustice] ever felt."

I must stop to point out that this is a children's book advocating total submission to authority by having children lie down and let that authority physically abuse them. Additionally, it reads like sexual

---

[19] 2 Kings 2:23-24

abuse. Not that Lewis, or any believer I know, would advocate child sexual abuse, but when the overall lessons are "submit to authority" and "obey God and those he put over you without question," it can create a perfect environment for it.

Afterwards Aslan grabbed Eustace ("I didn't like that much") and threw him in the well ("it started like anything") and afterwards took him out again and dressed him with his paws. That last bit feels like the hug so many victims of childhood violence were taught to give our abusers after a "correction" (read: beating). It works to normalize domestic violence and violence against children.[20]

Eustace gets summarily dumped back near camp where he was found lurching and near fainting. I guess his experience had been pretty horrific. The treasure he had once had in his pockets had also disappeared and Bitsy helpfully suggested Aslan took it as payment. As George Carlin would say, "God loves you, and he needs money!"

I hated how the others treated Eustace's pain as a good thing because Aslan had done it. We're led to believe Aslan is powerful enough to do whatever he wants, including changing an eleven-year-old back into a boy without any suffering, but he chose instead to be sadistic. But why though? What pathological reason was behind that? It was completely unnecessary since Eustace had already learned his lesson while he was a dragon and had already changed for the better before this. The effects of this trauma changed Eustace, *even his laugh*. This is clearly meant to be a redemption story, but it's just *sad*.

When Eustace asked if Edmund knew who Aslan was, his cousin replied, "Well—he knows me." Oh come *on*! Edmund has talked to Aslan, fought two wars for him, and fear-loves him, but claims he

---

[20] Christian books on biblical parenting that I was exposed to growing up often advocated violence against children followed by a hug. "To Train Up a Child" by Michael and Debi Pearlman was one. This resulted in many deaths, including 4-year-old Sean Paddock, 7-year-old Lydia Schatz, and 13-year-old Hana Williams. For survivors, it taught us that love included pain and fear.

doesn't know him? I get that the biblical deity is supposedly incomprehensible,[21] and therefore logic conveniently slides right off him, but applying this same characteristic to a known figure in our book is confusing. Edmund could have easily said, "*Yep, he's the Narnian deity and we have literally met. Multiple times.*" How hard is that?

Christians are told that upon conversion they become a "new creature" and their old self is gone.[22] While transformative experiences are universal and have many catalysts, they do not change one's fundamental personality, which tends to be generally stable over time.[23] Your "new creature" self is still you, so to make Scripture work with what we know of people, we must treat this idea more *flexibly*. In Eustace's case he "was a different boy," but, "to be strictly accurate" he only "began to be a different boy." Also, he was the same exact boy who still had "many days when he could be very tiresome." Eustace is a new creature in Aslan, but also *not* a new creature—good now, but also the same. Belief in Aslan cured him, but not really. I found this description of conversion honest, relatable, and wonderfully counter to Scripture.

Inspiration can motivate large changes in people's behavior, yet it seems the power of a supportive community is the key for sustaining that positive change. Believers find this in church just as Eustace found it in *Dawn Treader*. My evangelical pastors would have us believe that transformation stories are unique to Christianity; in fact, they are a quotidian human experience. A dear friend of mine has been sober for decades, changing her life without any religious influence. I would consider my own experience leaving fundamentalism and eventually deconstructing my faith as positively transformative. A natural view of

---

[21] Isaiah 55:8-9

[22] 2 Corinthians 5:17

[23] Dan P. McAdams, Rebecca L. Shiner, Jennifer L. Tackett (Eds.), 2019. *Handbook of Personality Development*, (New York, NY: The Guilford Press).

the world inspired me to become more involved with making my community a better place for my children since I could no longer rely on a higher power to step in. I also learned to love my body, support LGBTQ folks, and accept people from different backgrounds. I had been raised under the harsh words of Jesus that "apart from Me you can do nothing"[24] and instead found myself doing quite a lot of good in my corner of the world. It was like leaving an abusive relationship. Turns out, there are a whole bunch of communities out there for people just like me.

It's hard to put good out into the world and get my efforts credited back to the religion I left. I do a lot of volunteer work that sometimes gets labeled as "Christlike." I always say thank you, but honestly, the biblical version of Christ is not entirely moral, and I don't want to be too closely associated with the guy who invented the idea of eternal torture. Plus, without faith in Jesus it's impossible to please him,[25] and he considers good deeds done by unbelievers "filthy rags,"[26] so I couldn't say definitively if my work counts as Christlike or not. It's like I am Schrodinger's ex-Christian: I exist simultaneously as a tool of Christ and as a worthless apostate, but this box doesn't open until the Christian I'm with decides how I fit properly into their theology.

***

Back at sea, a giant serpent wrapped its body around *Dawn Treader*, and everyone "except Lucy" (because girls can't participate in their own survival) pushed the snake off the deck to save their lives. Since Eustace joined the group in this effort, it's evident he is a brand-new boy. As he must be.

---

[24] John 15:5
[25] Hebrews 11:6
[26] Isaiah 64:6

The next island they came to, Deathwater, was my second favorite plot line. It had a pool that turned anything it touched into gold. They discovered this rather accidentally by getting a spear and the toes of their boots wet. They also found the corpse of Lord Restimar, one of the lords Caspian was there to find, turned into a golden statue. That's somewhat horrifying, but whatever, they're rich!

Caspian tries to claim the pool, Edmund challenges him, and they almost start fighting despite Lucy's protests of "that's the worst of doing anything with boys." Finally, a ghost-like Aslan steps in and does his whole not saying anything or doing anything shtick. Once again "nobody ever saw how or where he went" but later it all felt like a dream and their memories were foggy. They all left rather befuddled.

All the gold belongs to Aslan.

The Voyage of the Dawn Treader: Chapter 9

"No one is allowed to just change my body! I would tell them no way!"
"What if they made you stronger?"
"Then I would think about it, but they would have to ask me first!"

***

To fully understand why Bitsy would be horrified by magical modifications once again done to unwitting creatures in the following chapters, I think it's important to know that Bitsy was born with a condition called arthrogryposis multiplex congenita caused by an amyoplasia diagnosis making all the joints in her limbs fixed in place, her range of motion severely limited, and her muscles poorly developed or non-existent in some parts of her body. It's why she's a *Little Bit* shorter than the typical kid her age. Short, of course, is not a bad thing as Lewis presents it as; it does not place her lower on some ridiculous hierarchy of human value. Short is simply a beautiful difference.

While multiple surgeries did improve her functionality, they also caused her some grief due to the loss of her former body. Our bodies are personal and precious. For those of us who can only imagine what it would be like to have all our arms and legs surgically cut and rotated—Bitsy *knows*. And trust her, bodily autonomy is sacrosanct.

Our party comes to an island full of invisible people called Duffers who have had their legs fused together by a magician. At first the Duffers surround Caspian and company demanding, "We want something that little girl can do for us." Since Lucy is literally the only female character it's obvious who they want. Reepicheep threatens to kill the Duffers if their request violates Lucy's honor, but he doesn't seem to much care if they merely mean to jeopardize her safety. So chivalrous. Good thing her lady cred won't be tarnished, just her well-being!

The Duffers explain that they used to be Dwarves, but the magician who enslaved them got mad at them and warped their bodies in "a great rage." Now even their children are all "monopod" with one leg instead of two, altering their ambulation into a bounce. They made themselves invisible to hide their shameful looks, but that spell has become somewhat inconvenient, as one could imagine, so they'd appreciate the spell getting broken. Since a little Duffer girl cast the invisibility spell in the first place, another little girl, Lucy, would need to break it. To do so, she needs to sneak into the magician's house and read the counter spell from his grimoire.

This may seem like a clear-cut situation where the helpless townsfolk need relief from an evil, slave-driving, magical-wielding fiend who is violating their bodies with unnecessary amputations. We didn't like it when the White Witch changed bodies to stone, now did we? And slavery of all things! This must be evil! Well, supposedly it's not. The magician will turn out to be a ruler appointed by Aslan. (Only women are evil for changing bodies, enslaving the masses, and doing witch-craft, remember?) Also, no one is supposed to care one lick about the Duffers because they are dumb. The definition of a duffer is an incompetent or stupid person. That's why Aslan gave them as slaves to his magician follower in the first place.

But, wait! Aslan gave a guy slaves? Isn't slavery wrong?

(*Blows dust off Bible.*) Actually kids, Scripture not only condones slavery, it includes rules for buying[27] and beating[28] your slaves! Since Lewis was a follower of a biblical religion, although not as strict as my denomination, these awful verses held some sway over his thinking in an otherwise open and shut moral case. In Lewis' essays collected between 1940-1945 he opined, "Aristotle said that some people were only fit to be slaves. I do not contradict him."[29] Lewis does go on to say he ultimately rejects slavery since people are sinners and therefore cannot be perfect masters, but this puts the failures of slavery on human error, implying there could be a perfect version of slavery, perhaps in Heaven. Lewis must make allowances for slavery since it's got God's stamp of approval. In the holy texts, God blesses his favorites by increasing their number of slaves[30] and specifically orders Joshua, David, and Solomon to take loads of slaves.[31] If Aslan gives a magician with a bad temper a bunch of slaves against their will, that must also be fine. This can be confusing for a young reader to hear a story of slavery so normalized.

When I first read the Duffer story as a child, I didn't see an issue with slavery because I grew up in a fundamentalist church that didn't shy away from the worst of biblical passages. The Ten

---

[27] Leviticus 25:44
[28] Exodus 21
[29] C. S. Lewis, 1986. *Present Concerns: Journalistic Essays*, (Glasgow: HarperCollins Publishers).
[30] Genesis 24:35
[31] Joshua 9:23, 1 Kings 8:2-6 and 9:20-21

Commandments mention slavery twice, but neither time as a sin! One commandment even considers women possessions. In a particularly distasteful Bible story, the Lord orders Moses to take 16,000 virgins as slaves to rape.[32] Yes, to rape. When Moses' slaves were gifted to the men of Israel, the Bible says this was "just as the Lord had commanded." It's not as if they were into sex trafficking for plain old human reasons; this was the Lord's work! The Lord himself received 32 of the girls as tribute since that's the way the tithing system worked. The chief priest, Eleazar, accepted those girls on God's behalf.[33] It's likely he raped them or gave them to his sons to rape. It's also clear that these are pre-pubescent girls to assure they were virgins, and their mothers were all slaughtered before they were taken.[34] If you're out of Sunday School Bible story ideas, this one's a real winner.

Not many Christians I know had a Bible teacher or pastor defend this passage. I did though. I was told women didn't have the same expectations or feelings back then, and as a result of these lessons I truly believed my own gender was less human. I've also been told sexual slavery somehow protected the girls. Would I rather they be murdered like their older sisters or mothers? See, this was an act of God's mercy! I'm a monster for thinking otherwise! Plus, God would make these girls bearers of children who would be called his own people! They would be blessed!

I wonder just how "blessed" those apologists would feel if they were a young girl getting used by an older man to give birth to children who would belong to a foreign people. How blessed would they feel if those men were allowed by God's holy law to beat them without

---

[32] Numbers 31:15-54
[33] Numbers 31:41
[34] Numbers 31:15-17

consequence until they were bedridden for a couple days for not pleasing their owners sexually?[35]

It's not like slavery is just an Old Testament thing. The New Testament has an entire book named after a slave master, Philemon. Paul was writing to Philemon about his slave, Onesimus, whom Paul was returning after the slave ran away. Paul says in verse 13 that he would have liked to keep Onesimus, but that was obviously up to his owner. While reading the summary of this biblical letter online, I ran into so many disgusting defenses of slavery it made me physically ill.

The *good book*, gentlefolk.

Our main characters do not consider the Duffers' bodily violation or enslavement as all that horrifying. We've been down this road before when Aslan turned boys into pigs and the reader is supposed to think it serves them right. We know the Duffers hated what was done to them since they turned themselves invisible to hide their shame, yet their plight is considered inconsequential, even *funny*.

I want to point out that I'm not against stories that have magical elements or even stories that transmogrify people; we got a kick out of Eustace becoming a dragon. There's an important distinction, however: When the good guys are the ones doing it—and the story is advocating for it to be considered acceptable behavior as long as our guys do it—then it's problematic. When the story is justifying it based on a master/slave relationship that is ordained by what we are supposed to consider the deity of goodness, Aslan himself, then it has the potential for real harm.

But it's all okay because these creatures are intellectually inferior so who cares, right?

As an aside, it's implied that Duffer girls can read and are intelligent which is why a girl performed the spell and a girl must undo it.

---

[35] Exodus 21:20-21

In a group of people whose men cannot perform most tasks due to lack of knowhow, it's only because of a firm belief in the hierarchy that the most limited and ignorant of male persons holds control over intelligent and competent non-male ones. It's sad that Lewis lacked the mental flexibility to invent a world where positions of power would be decided based on ability instead of gender.

The Duffers threaten to slice all of Caspian's party's throats if Lucy, or Caspian I guess, since the menfolk get a say in Lucy's decision, declines her mission. Lucy later says the Duffers "are not treacherous" so they can be throat-slitters and still good somehow. This was probably just a way for Lucy to come across as gracious, as her gender role demands. Although, threatening violence to get one's way does seem to be acceptable behavior as we see with Caspian, Reepicheep, and later in the series, Prince Corin.

I don't get the Lucy subplot here. It would be one thing if our heroes really feared the Duffers' threats, but they don't seem to. Until now Lucy has been protected to the point she's been robbed of agency. Weird how now the men around her argue for her to perform a risky B&E on their behalf. It's clear that Lewis has a future scene in mind between Lucy and Aslan, but he can't quite get her into that situation alone without contradictions in the personalities and beliefs of our protagonists. Even Reepicheep gets a character transplant. When else in history would he be advocating a young girl go alone into danger?

Reepicheep pulls out an *ignoratio elenchi* argument, which is a fallacy where one fails to address the actual issue at hand; he changes the subject to one of her honor instead of her safety. He implies her life is not more important to the group than her moral purity.

It would seem that protecting and sacrificing women are two sides of the same coin. It's only wrong if the woman doesn't submit. Lucy heads off alone into the magician's lair as it would go against her good girl nature to disobey the men's consensus.

The Voyage of the Dawn Treader: Chapters 10-11

"Aslan didn't make the magician change the Duffers back? What?!"
"He should have, I agree."
"It's wrong! Mom, I really don't like this."

***

As they prepare to send Lucy into danger, Edmund and Caspian idly wonder if the Duffers are giant grasshopper creatures since they jump around. This is before they know the whole story and the Duffers are still invisible. Edmund warns Caspian not to tell Lucy about this grasshopper hypothesis to protect her from yucky information due to her femaleness. Girls and bugs go together about as well as girls and critical information. It's sad that the Duffers have been dehumanized to the point our main characters wonder, "Do you think they're human at all?" The physical differences put upon them have effectively excused their treatment. In Lewis' world, funny looks deserve funny treatment. No one seems particularly sympathetic to the Duffers. It's fine to do something to, say, a grasshopper that you wouldn't do to a person.

The Duffers treat the party to a feast that night. Eustace, being from a teetotaler family, is said to be "sorry afterwards" that he had drunk too much alcohol. His cousins and Caspian hold their liquor better, apparently. Eustace is barely out of elementary school.

The next morning, jumpy and scared, Lucy goes into the magician's house. She finds the magic book in a room upstairs and tries to shut the door behind her, but it's blocked somehow. This leaves her exposed from behind and even more scared. It turns out invisible Aslan is there holding the door open so he could watch her be tested. He doesn't care about her fear, as we should know by now. She's not actually in danger since the magician is a good guy by Lewis' standards, but she doesn't know that yet, so she's understandably terrified.

Lucy flips the pages and finds a spell that would make her super appealing to men. The spell book makes it clear that this beautification process will lead to war since men will not be able to keep from killing each other over her. (Men are beasts and we must control them with our modesty, ladies.) All this talk of death didn't dissuade her because she's a girl and MUST BE PRETTY. Aslan had to step in and growl before she turned the freaking page. Once again, her deity lion made her "horribly afraid." He remained invisible.

Lucy ends up being tempted by a spell that lets her eavesdrop on her friend. The friend betrays her to another girl and their friendship, it's implied, is ruined forever. I was disappointed that only spells of beauty and social gossip appealed to our only girl character. Lucy was supposed to be better than this.

The grimoire also contains a story described as the loveliest story in the world. It was about "a cup and a sword and a tree and a green hill." She immediately forgets the story upon reading it and the book won't let her go back. Some Narnia fans believe this story is the crucifixion of Christ: The tree could be the wooden cross, the hill could be where the crucifixion took place, the cup could be the holy grail or maybe the cup at the last supper, and the sword could be what Jesus returns with to slaughter people who have done him wrong.[36] Bloody and macabre, or in other words, the lovely Christian gospel story.

Lucy finally finds the spell she was hunting for to make invisible things visible. She chants the magic words, because magic chants are only bad when witches do it, and it works! Thankfully the Duffers are not grasshoppers as Lucy would have had no warning about that

---

[36] Matthew 10:34; Revelation 19:11-16

shock. Not only are the Duffers visible again, but Aslan appears in that doorway he was blocking!

Aslan explains he's been watching the whole time, but only became visible because he was obeying his own rules. I have heard religious folks attempt to explain why bad things happen when an omnipotent benevolent god exists, and one weak argument is that God follows his own rules of nature. Putting aside the fact that this makes an all-powerful being limited, making God an oxymoron, the bigger issue is that the end result is a universe that functions just as it would without a god in it. A pastor once told me that we wouldn't want God to intervene by changing the laws of physics even when a child is about to be killed because the consequences would be getting hit by a bus as gravity goes sideways or drowning because we now float "down." Is God so incompetent he can't just save one child without messing up the whole world, Pastor Ron?

This obviously doesn't explain miracles, which are throughout the Bible messing up the physical world, or so we're told.[37] Clearly my former pastor was just trying to help believers accept the world for how it was without having to discard faith to do it. This got me thinking. If God's actions were not measurable in any way, what practical thing was this god good for? Christians seem to think he's good for a lot, particularly after death where no one can prove otherwise, but reality doesn't seem to bear that out. Saying the physical world plus God equals reality is like saying $1+0=1$. The math works out the same with or without the addition of a deity. I learned this lesson almost seven years ago when I attempted to pray to a fork and got the same results as years of praying to my all-powerful Heavenly Father.

---

[37] Hard to find a certified miracle since the invention of video cameras.

***

The first thing our newly-visible Aslan does is lecture Lucy for using the eavesdropping spell as he sat back and watched. He even lectures her for wanting to know the consequences of doing so. He then introduces her to Coriakin, the magician. Aslan shows gross support of the magician's treatment of the Duffers:

> "Do you grow weary, Coriakin, of ruling such foolish subjects as I have given you here?"

Aslan is sympathetic to the magician's anger that caused him to rashly curse all his slaves' bodies, but totally apathetic for the Duffers' plight as he considers them too stupid to warrant his favor. As punishment for the Duffers' mental limitations, Aslan says he will not show himself to them for centuries. In addition to older kids, neurodiverse people seem to not be on Aslan's favorites list.

I once cared for a child with a mental disability whose family was worried that he didn't understand the right steps to get into Heaven by accepting Jesus. We had him learning songs about Jesus and were constantly talking about Jesus hoping it would sink in. "My people are destroyed for lack of knowledge,"[38] the Bible says, so I knew ignorance or mental inability would not be acceptable excuses when this little guy found himself before the holy throne. My brand of Christianity held the doctrine of biblical inerrancy with an unhealthy dose of literal interpretation, so when God didn't allow those with physical disabilities in his Temple,[39] for example, I could be forgiven some confusion when it came to figuring out their place in his Kingdom. People with disabilities made me really uncomfortable as a result.

Then my daughter was born.

---

[38] Hosea 4:6
[39] Leviticus 21:16-21

Aslan promises Lucy he'll be back soon, but not for the Duffers of course. Now before we could praise him for trying to comfort her with his quick return, he clarifies that his definition of soon is utterly meaningless. A biblical writer, trying to explain why Jesus failed to return in the timeframe he gave his disciples, once wrote, "With the Lord a day is like a thousand years, and a thousand years are like a day."[40] It can't be that Jesus lied or his promises failed, and it *definitely* can't be that his story is complete fiction. Nope, it must be because his understanding of time is different than ours. Maybe Jesus just isn't that great at considering human perception.

After Aslan disappears, the magician treats Lucy to a leisurely lunch while her family waits anxiously for her return. (Kind of serves them right.) This slaver dude explains that he thinks he's improved upon the Duffers' looks; he even claims non-Duffer people would agree. The opinion of the Duffers themselves over their own looks is of no importance. Since Lucy finds the new shapes of the Duffers "funny," she is delighted to hatch a plan to get them to stop whining and just be fine with it already, *geez*.

In the end our group sails away from the Duffers who are forever stuck in their monopod shapes, never to walk again. Bitsy has been furious on behalf of the Duffers for the last two chapters and feels they have been grievously wronged. We had to take a break to talk through her feelings.

The Voyage of the Dawn Treader: Chapters 12-16

"ASLAN WAS JESUS THE WHOLE TIME!"
"THE WHOLE TIME!"
"A bit on the nose, right?"

---

[40] 2 Peter 3:8

"I thought it was… what's it called when something is used to teach you about something else?"

"An allegory?"

"Yeah, an allegory."

"But nope."

"Nope!"

"The whole time!"

"The whole time!!"

***

Dawn Treader comes upon a weird blanket of unnatural darkness. They almost do not sail through it until Reepicheep calls them cowards. Caspian looks to Lucy as their last excuse for not going, "I suppose we shall have to go on. Unless Lucy would rather not?" Nice try, pal. You're all going. Lewis makes a mistake here when he says, "how long this voyage into the darkness lasted, nobody knew," making it seem like some unknowable amount of time had passed. However, later he says it was around "five minutes." That changes how I picture it, but either way at some point they arrive at a dark island in the center of the black fog.

Lord Rhoop, another of the lords Caspian is searching for, has been tortured on this island for years. It's a magical island that makes nightmares come to life. They discover Rhoop screaming and traumatized so they grab him and hightail it out of there. Lucy is scared as they flee so she prays to Aslan; nothing changes, but she feels better. I was initially impressed with such a realistic description of prayer, but it turned out that Aslan was just stalling to test her before appearing in the shape of an albatross to guide them through the darkness. I keep forgetting he's a sadist who loves when kids are terrified. Everyone sees the albatross, but only true-believer Lucy gets the revelation that it's really Aslan. Here's where we learn that Aslan can take different shapes, which is important in the last chapter.

Once safe, Aslan, we assume, destroys the island. He couldn't do this before it tortured and traumatized Lord Rhoop for years, because reasons.

The very next island they come to contains all the last remaining lords. They are in an enchanted sleep at a very large table covered with food. Our heroes dare not eat the food thinking this will make them sleep, too. Eventually Lord Rhoop gets to join the other lords in their dreamless sleep because he is literally too traumatized to be conscious. Guess he didn't pray to Aslan.

While our heroes are sitting at the enchanted table, a girl who was so pretty that when they saw her "they had never before known what beauty meant" approached them. She explained that one of the lords had touched the White Witch's stone knife which happened to be kept at this island. This caused him and his buddies to fall into a magical sleep.

This beautiful girl is described down to her long hair and bare arms because her looks are the most important thing about her. What's not important, however, is her name. She is only ever called "the girl" or "the daughter of Ramandu." Her purpose is to be nice to look at, be a prize won at the end of Caspian's journey, and eventually, as the only fitting thing women are good for in this series, to give birth to a male child. That's it.

Caspian tells "the girl" the story of Sleeping Beauty where the guy had to kiss the beauty to wake the kingdom. (Nice and subtle there, teen wolf.) "The girl" informs Caspian that he will have to break the spell before he can claim his prize. She is talking about herself. *She* is the prize. What do these sleeping dudes have to do with her? Nothing. Why would she then give herself to a guy to save them? No reason. It's just assumed women are only good for this. Bitsy and I decided to name her Trophyna, since we couldn't stand that she didn't have a name and she's literally a human trophy.

Trophyna doesn't have a mother because that would be way too many adult women in a world created by C. S. Lewis. She does have a father who, unlike her, is an actual person with a name, Ramandu. He comes out next and explains that the only way to break the curse on the sleeping lords is to sacrifice Reepicheep, who is along for just that purpose. The adults in Reep's life prophesied over him when he was a child and told him this was his duty. "So messed up," says Bitsy. Thankfully, this sacrifice includes leaving the world and joining the afterlife. It is closer to robbing someone of life than gruesomely hurting them. It still ends with him dead though. I realize that Christianity literally revolves around a human sacrifice but *really*?

Ramandu turns out to be a former star. The Book of Revelation, the last of the biblical books, teaches that at least some stars are really principalities. There's even a biblical prophecy that a third of the stars in the sky will be cast down to Earth.[41] Obviously, ancient writers didn't know just how big those suckers were. Eustace tells Ramandu that in the real world a star is "a huge ball of flaming gas" and is informed, "in your world, my son, that is not what a star is but only what it is made of." Lewis is trying to blend science and Scripture and the result is a magical mess. It's a mess I enjoyed, though. Probably because it reminded me of Mufasa appearing in the stars in The Lion King.

Aslan sends Ramandu magical birds that go pick berries from the sun every day to feed him. These make him younger, even though he's old enough to have retired from being a star. Eventually if he eats enough hot coals he gets to return to the sky. It's rather random, unless

---

[41] Revelation 12:4

you know the story of the purification of Isaiah who has a coal brought to his lips from seraphim. (Thanks Bible school!)

The details of Ramandu's life are not important, nor do they have any bearing on future stories or plotlines, but what's remarkable is that his history is thoroughly and unnecessarily fleshed out while his daughter—the young lady who becomes queen of all of Narnia—IS NOT EVEN GIVEN A NAME. The fact she needed a father figure at all was just so Lewis had a man to give the exposition. These books rely on a character giving a ton of backstory at some point in every story, and that character, being an authority, must be male.

Caspian says his mission is over as they've found all the lords. Somehow waking up the lords will be a *brand-new* mission. This is ridiculous since it's all technically the same mission, but Caspian is setting up some weird testing of the crew. In a strange story promoting the idea that those in authority get to make unreasonable demands to test those beneath them, Caspian decides to have his men volunteer for the next task just so he can punish the last one to sign up for not doing what Caspian wanted fast enough. Too bad that last sailor guy thought Caspian was honorable and took his time to think over his answer. Since the slowest sailor's biggest fear was being left behind, this was extra traumatic for him. This abandonment ruined his life. (Don't think through things, kids! Just obey quickly!)

Sailing this last bit towards Aslan's Country is described as a surreal experience in a spirit land. Everything becomes too bright, the sun gets bigger, and the crew finds they no longer need to sleep, eat, or talk. The older members of the crew even start to become younger! The scene has every imaginative element Lewis could pour into it. They sail past fierce-looking merpeople who I think only exist to get Reepicheep to dive into the sea looking for a fight and inadvertently discover that the water is actually drinkable light. Little Bit loved the merpeople.

They finally reached the last leg of their journey where lilies covered the entire surface of the ocean and the ship could go no further. Caspian tries to go on and leave the *Dawn Treader* crew behind, but when this is met with resistance, the king stomps off back to his quarters in a tantrum. He's only a teenage (Werewolf) boy, after all. In his room a lion head statue on the wall morphs into a decapitated Aslan. "It was terrible," he says of the horror show when the others ask about it later. Aslan tells Caspian that the other children and Reepicheep will get to go on ahead, but he must endure a Moses-can't-go-into-the-Promised-Land-style punishment for stomping off. These deity guys are big into punishments that do not fit the crime. This marks the end of Caspian's adventure and leaves him a crying mess.

Lucy, Edmund, Eustace, and Reepicheep get into a couple small boats and continue to the end of the world without Caspian. The entrance to the afterlife is not a drop off a waterfall into nothingness, but a lift *up* a rainbow wall of water into the sky. Reep sails his little ship straight up that rainbow like some sort of furry Enoch, and that's the end of him. The children get a glimpse of Heaven, like the Apostle Paul claims happened to *a guy he knew*,[42] but they can't go in without dying. Instead they find land and go for a walk. They reach the edge of the world, and because this planet is a flat circle like it is in the Bible, the sky touches the ground like a dome.

Who do they meet there? The Lamb, who was said to be so white it hurt to look at him. He invites them to a meal of fish like the post-resurrected Jesus did with his disciples. Then the Lamb turns back into a very familiar lion with an important task for the children: They must go into the real world, find out his real name, and figure out who he really is. We learn that the only reason the children were ever brought

---

[42] 2 Corinthians 12:2

to Narnia in the first place was to get to know Aslan enough to recognize his alter-ego, the Lamb,[43] in church sermons.

It was important they learn Aslan's true name as calling on it is required for salvation.[44] My Baptist church was very intentional about saying the name Jesus during our salvation prayer since the Bible promised that all those who call on the name of the Lord will be saved.[45] This is directly and awkwardly refuted by another New Testament passage that promises not all who call on the name of the Lord will be saved.[46] One of my closest friends during my missionary training in Papua New Guinea believed 99% of the same exact doctrines I did, but belonged to an entirely different Christian denomination due to this one contradiction in Scripture. This meant we were not allowed to work together. It would have caused confusion to those tribes we were sent to colonize, er I mean, "reach with the Gospel."

The Bible failing to be the cohesive collection evangelicals claim it to be has caused many believers deep psychological scars. Story after story has emerged online of exvies, or ex-evangelicals, having endured sleepless nights as young children due to the contradictions and obscurity around salvation passages; fear of eternal torment became their constant companion until they fully deconstructed their faith. Going to their parents or pastors did nothing to end the cycle of abuse as the only advice they were given was to call out to Jesus, something they were already staying up late doing! I had a few of these nights myself, but my experience pales in comparison with most of the ones I've read.

Little Bit was utterly confused by Aslan, his cryptic instructions, and why he had to be a lamb now. None of this is spelled out for non-Christians. I explained that this meant the children will only get to

---

[43] John 1:29
[44] Romans 10:13
[45] Acts 2:21
[46] Matthew 7:21

Aslan's country by dying, but only if they figure out to believe in Jesus first. *You know,* because Jesus is the Lamb of God who gets slaughtered just like the lambs they used to sacrifice to appease their God's barbaric requirements for... *on second thought, go play with your dolls.*

"Aslan was Jesus the whole time!" she finally confirmed.

"THE WHOLE TIME!"

These stories went from creative allegory to blunt-force apocrypha in the space of one chapter.

Lucy asks Aslan when she and her brother can return to Narnia and is informed they are both too old now! (Sailing for months on end was your last ever adventure. You're welcome!)

Aslan/Jesus then tears a hole in reality and dumps the three of them back at Eustace's house. Sadly, Eustace has been changed into the kind of person who fits in more with his Christian cousins and less with his parents, so things get awkward. His mother now finds him tiresome and boring. It's what you'd expect if you sent your kids to Vacation Bible School and they came back constantly wanting to tell you about the Good News.

Caspian goes back to fetch his human trophy and they return to Narnia to get married. Caspian was thirteen years old in the last book, and three years have passed since then, so he's really ready to start a family. Trophyna "became a great queen and the mother and grand-mother of great kings." No daughters are mentioned. Do daughters become kings? I don't think so. Also, Trophyna's personal accomplishments tap out at "mother" and "grandmother." Technically she dies before she has any grandkids, but Lewis didn't know that as he hadn't written that book yet. Her legacy is merely that which advances the stories of the men in her life.

We left an entire race of people disfigured and enslaved, sacrificed a person to our god, took a nameless human trophy, lost two of our friends who are too old to ever return, ruined a sailor's life for no reason, and made Eustace into someone his parents can't stand. Happy ending!

5
The Simpleminded Signs

The Silver Chair: Chapters 1 and 16

"Why didn't Eustace tell Jill everything before making her believe in
Aslan?"
"Why do you think?"
"So he could be in charge and she'd have to follow him."

***

Bitsy and I had a bit of a rough ride on the *Treader* and took some
time recovering our land legs. We enjoyed several literary palate cleans-
ers until Bits saw *A Horse and His Boy* when flipping through our Narnia collection. "I want to read the book on horses!" she said innocently.

I quickly explained to her that despite the *Chronicles of Narnia* om-
nibus being in (*gag*) chronological order, also known as HarperCollins
order named for the publisher who started producing the series in
1994, we were an original **publication order** household. If Bitsy
wanted the horsey book, we'd have to finish *The Silver Chair* first. Her
daddy backed me up on this and when the Christian parent and the
atheist parent both come together on anything this strongly, there's no
arguing.

The Silver Chair opens in the most hellish of landscapes: a co-edu-
cational school. Yes, where boys *and* girls are educated *together*. At the

same time! In the same buildings! The horror. Eustace's liberal parents must be stopped; they have no business making decisions for children.

Not only was this the natural order on its head, but Lewis adds that this kind of school "used to be called a 'mixed' school" but "was not nearly so mixed as the minds of the people who ran it." How did they run it? A-freaking-mok. For one thing, they didn't beat the children. Like at all. So, naturally, without corporal discipline, the worst of human behavior emerged. The school flouted the biblical command for dealing with unruly children:

"Hit your kid with a rod, come on, do it! It's not like he'll *die*."[1]

A 2014 study recorded parents correcting their children and found that most who resorted to corporal punishment saw their children resuming the same behavior within ten minutes.[2] Yet the *magical beating* trope will pop up more than once in this series: One good assault will be a panacea for all societal ills, guaranteed to knock the sin right out of any child's heart.

Instead of beatings, Eustace's school's reaction to troublesome kids was to attend to the struggling ones as if they needed extra care and correction. The Head, the equivalent of a dean, saw children as psychologically fascinating and spoke with them for hours. What place does child development or psychology have in the correction of young people I ask you? The American Academy of Pediatrics concludes that the Head's approach would be best since spanking children as a form of discipline makes them more aggressive and raises their risk of mental health issues.[3] True believers know that's not right because

---

[1] Proverbs 13:24, ever so lightly paraphrased.

[2] G. W. Holden, P. A. Williamson, G. W. Holland, 2014. "Eavesdropping on the family: a pilot investigation of corporal punishment in the home," *J. Fam. Psychol.* 28(3): 401–406.

[3] Sege RD, Siegel BS; Council on Child Abuse and Neglect; Committee on Psychosocial Aspects of Child and Family Health. Effective Discipline to Raise Healthy Children. Pediatrics. 2018;142(6):e20183112.

mental illness is really internal demons that can be beaten out *wackity smackity*!

The nail in the coffin for this school: "Bibles were not encouraged." Excuse me while I faint.

The school had the most fitting name of Experiment House and by all accounts it was a failed one. No grander example would sum this up than the fact it was run by a woman. Lewis points this out in a sexist "by the way" parenthetical so we would know we weren't reading about a man doing all these silly things. Women in power without male oversight in the Narnia series are always portrayed as evil and their outcome is always destruction. This will be no less true here. Does she have a name, this Head? Well, if you followed along on the last journey, you'd know the answer to that. Girls sometimes get names. Sometimes. But why name women? Are they individuals or something? Because I always thought they were unknowable and mysterious aliens that we hid from at University of Oxford clubs.[4]

Lewis seems to go out of his way to name several random child bullies, giving them first and last names like Adela Pennyfather and Edith Winterblott. He even gives other students nicknames like "Spotty" Sorner or "big" Bannister. Do these characters get one iota of development? Nope. They are only blips in the story. What about the Head, who is a woman ("by the way"), and has lines of dialog, bookends the plot, and has her entire career path described? Nothing. No name. Little Bit and I are going to call her Hedy, like Hedy Lamarr. Or, as Bitsy put it, "Hedy the Head-y."

The worlds Lewis created are largely androcentric, so any non-protagonist we come upon with a role in the story will usually be a man, boy, or male animal. When we started to pay attention to who was speaking in these books, we realized that women were part of the

---

[4] I'm mocking Lewis here.

background scenery, like silent painted figures on a stage. Other times it will just be taken for granted that whole crowds of people, like the Earthmen, will all be men. *Lonely, lonely bros.* A contemporary of Lewis and author I admire, J. R. R. Tolkien, does the same. Men enjoy society and make up its core, but women are supposed to, even keen to, stay home. Hobbits stay in the Shire, but lady Hobbits stay in the Shire's kitchens.

Girls have adventures in Lewis' stories, which is part of why his books are so popular, yet when they grow up, they become *less*. He reduces them to the ornamentation of men as we saw when Lucy and Susan hit puberty. Lewis' Bible teaches that Christian women ought to be "discreet, chaste, keepers at home, good, obedient to their own husbands, that the word of God be not blasphemed."[5] That means no heading schools or running around like they're people.

The Bible primarily celebrates the stories of men, including their birth stories. But women? Not a single birth story of a single woman or girl is found anywhere in its 66 books.[6] If the Bible were a movie, you'd have a crowd of men surrounded by another crowd of men. The casting call would include 1,181 parts for men with names, and thousands of men with minor yet important roles after that. Men would talk and act most of the movie, while women would only get a whopping 1.1% of the lines.[7] In the credits at the end, of those 93 women who did get to speak, only 49 would have names. The rest would be listed as "Woman, Woman, Woman, Woman, Woman."

Lack of female representation is not a glitch in the Bible; it's a feature. Having a woman in a position of "Head" goes against the Bible's

---

[5] Titus 2:5

[6] This is the number of books in the protestant Bible. I should point out that, although not a birth, one origin story is included: the creation of an animated rib woman as an afterthought. So checkmate, atheists. I guess.

[7] Lindsay Hardin Freeman, 2014. *Bible Women: All Their Words and Why They Matter*, (Cincinnati, OH: Forward Movement).

teachings that "the head of every woman is man."[8] These verses don't say *some* women are ruled by men, but *every* one of them. That is not an idea limited to the Old Testament, either; that verse is from the Jesus-y half of the Bible! Aren't women in positions of power the worst? When is Aslan going to violently save us from all these uppity women ruining society and our children?

It turns out, soon!

***

The Silver Chair opens with a girl named Jill Pole crying over her treatment at school. A familiar bully from this awful school by the name of Eustace Scrubb will attempt to comfort her. It's all good now, though, because Eustace had, as of the last book, become a follower of Aslan (not a cult) and was a somewhat changed boy. Eustace doesn't let her finish crying before self-reporting his list of recent good deeds as a result of Aslan (not a cult leader) converting him (not in a cult-y way).

The two seem to bond quickly in their very first ever real conversation, especially considering Eustace bullied her up until this moment. When she asks why he is being so nice, he responds, "A lot of queer things happened to me." When she asks what queer things happened, *like he hoped she would* (ugh, evangelicals), he gets quiet and "mysterious" to build suspense. Then he asks her to believe what he's about to tell her before she can know what it is. Oh, and he *may* also be taking advantage of her emotional state. (Totally not a cult.)

The opening paragraphs seem to present a girl so emotional she lashes out at our poor Christian hero who must suffer through her moods. She went by herself to cry and was interrupted by a boy who physically crashed into her. When she said to watch where he was

---

[8] 1 Corinthians 11:3

101

going, he tone-policed her. Then instead of getting some time to herself, she had to listen to the boy give her a lecture and was ignored when she demanded he go away. The whole interaction is a lesson in disrespect. However, that's not the most problematic part of chapter one. As a former believer-turned-skeptic, I think the worst thing Eustace said has got to be:

"Pole, I say, are you good at believing things?"

Faith in these pages is presented as a test of her good character, and it is strongly implied that disbelief would be wrong on her part. This is followed up by Jill responding, "I think I would be," and even promising not to tell anyone else the secret he is entrusting to her. Eustace can only trust her, however, if she is *able* to believe the secret before hearing what it is. He even says that most people would laugh, but she's not *most people*, right? She's special. Faith is an *ability* and if she were to baulk at his outlandish claim, that would be a failure on her part.

Faith is not a pathway to truth. No amount of belief makes something a fact. Anything and everything can be believed by faith. Faith does not produce knowledge; on the contrary, it gives up the pursuit of knowledge in favor of a prepacked explanation. When faith is considered a moral good that special people can hone with practice, it follows that Jill, as a good girl, will swallow without chewing whatever nonsense Eustace feeds her. In this case the nonsense is a place, to quote him, "where animals can talk and where there are—er—enchantments and dragons—and—well, all the sorts of things you have in fairy tales."

Isn't that ridiculous! Now excuse me while I read my former holy book where animals can talk[9] and where there are—er—

enchantments[10] and dragons[11]—and—well, all the sorts of things you have in fairy tales.

I do believe the book with all those elements was not encouraged in that school!

Jill isn't supposed to come across as completely childish or hopelessly naïve in her introduction—on the contrary, she's supposed to be exhibiting the traits of a Narnian heroine. In the ensuing chapters, Jill will be rewarded the harder she works to believe. Gathering evidence would cheapen or negate her faith, risking her reward. Recall the story where Jesus told Thomas that belief is rewarded with blessing only if it is without evidence.[12] To get this blessing, Jill tends to act in ways that promote faith, like speaking in whispers, which helped her find it "easier to believe"—adding an artificial gravity to the secret and giving it unearned weight.

When "a horrible suspicion came over her" that it was all made up, Jill worked hard to bury that cognitive dissonance deep down. In response, Eustace simply promised that he wasn't lying, which was all that was required of him to prove his claim's veracity. When I was a missionary spreading my claims to the world, all I had to be was a "sincere Christian" to make my claims feel more valid. "Sincere," I would learn, is a modifier that can be applied to any position without changing a single thing about the validity of that position. Sincerity is the stuff of every religion, every position, every political stance; it's not proof any one of these things is best.

---

[10] 2 Kings 21:6

[11] The word for dragon or dragons appears 21 times in the Old Testament. It's often translated as sea monsters (Psalm 148:7) or jackals (Isaiah 43:20) even though jackals aren't in the sea and the same word is used. In the New Testament no translation trick was used so we get a big red dragon in Revelation 12. Fun!

[12] John 20:29

The fact is, belief is absolutely required of believers, both in Narnia and in traditional Christendom, to avoid ultimate punishments in both cases. Therefore, belief must be conjured this way, almost magically, despite how human minds typically function. Sometimes belief is possible, but other times it's absolutely not. I could not make myself believe again, no matter how hard I tried. Deconstructing my faith meant risking, not only my only worldview, but an entire community I was motivated not to lose. Yet believing is not a switch one flips. It is like knowing someone's dark secrets and being asked to interpret their actions the same innocent way again. Or seeing the hidden image in one of those Magic Eye 3D paintings and then pretending it's not there. Lewis might have seen this as a failure on my part to gain the Lord's favor, but I could never see lobotomizing away my rational enquiry as a measure of success.

Once Jill agreed to believe, the belief took hold fast! It took the space of a few sentences for Jill to go from horrified at the prospect of being suckered, to adopting several fanciful ideas into her knowledge base. Even when I truly believed in Heaven, and a very specific way to get there, it took much more than that for me to calm my doubts! Jill has what my church would have called "strong faith." Yet zero multiplied by a million still leaves us with zero; all the faith in the world does not make something true.

The children's initial idea on how to reach Narnia, which they were calling "That Place," was to perform witchcraft by drawing a circle on the ground with "queer letters" in it and reciting "charms and spells." When Eustace rather abruptly decides this would not please Aslan, or Lewis' Christian audience for that matter (because magic is bad), they decide to instead petition Aslan in prayer (because magic *thoughts* are good). Jill asks about Aslan but Eustace evades her and keeps changing the subject by saying, "But let's get on." Before we know too much about the ominous lion, it's time to summon him! Don't think about it too much! NO QUESTIONING. What could go wrong?

Eustace decides to chant Aslan's name and direct Jill to repeat after him while facing east. This is considered prayer and *not* witchcraft, just so we're clear. Eustace berates Jill for not immediately knowing which way east was because of her gender:

> "It's an extraordinary thing about girls that they never know the points of the compass."

At this point Bitsy got quieter than usual. Usually she pipes up if some generalization about girls is uttered. I catch her eye and she admits in a quiet voice that she doesn't know what points of a compass were. Once she understood, she was quick to say, "That's just Google Maps!"

With Little Bit's confidence back up, we return to the "praying" (*wink wink*) children. Suddenly they are set upon by bullies, forcing them to climb a hill behind the gym. Lewis mentions here that students at this school were not taught "much French or Maths or Latin" but were experts at getting away from bullies quickly. Probably because a woman is in charge.

At the top of the hill was a tall wall with a gate leading outside the school grounds. It was usually always locked, but the knob turned in Eustace's hand and they went through.

> And before she quite knew what was happening, he had grabbed her hand and pulled her through the door, out of the school grounds, out of England, out of our whole world into That Place.

The voice of another girl behind them turned off as if someone had turned off the radio. Everything around them is described in bright colors, beautiful nature scenes, and by the repeated word "lonely." Turns out this place wasn't quite Narnia; it was Aslan's Country, the afterlife.

Before we went on with the adventure, Bits and I thought it would be fun to return to London and see what happened next from the other students' perspective at the very end of the book. Eustace and Jill had just disappeared through the gate as the bullies were looking for Jill. Without warning the 30-foot-high stones around the gate crumble to the ground as Aslan gives a roar that shakes the sun. Thankfully, messing with the sun has no cosmic ramifications just like when Joshua does it in the Bible,[13] as I was taught in my *history curriculum* at my Christian middle school.

Eustace and Jill then come bursting out of the gate. Jill has a switch that Aslan directed her to take for this moment and "with the strength of Aslan in them, Jill plied her crop on the girls." Eustace has been informed by Aslan to draw his sword and use the broad side for beating the others. We won't just get violence against children, but Aslan-approved violence *with weapons* against unarmed children.

In the end, our dear heroes leave all the bullies crying, bloody, or concussed. Hedy the Head (a freaking woman "by the way") goes into hysterics. When Hedy calls the police for help with the escaped lion, Aslan magically fixes what he destroyed and sneaks away. Seeing that Hedy is mentally unstable and "no use as a Head," the nebulous powers that be promote her to Inspector in order to "interfere with other Heads." When she "wasn't much good even at that," she gets placed into Parliament! This is the level of power an ill-equipped and useless woman can attain if we let them out of the house!

Experiment House was over, and what replaced it "became quite a good school." Because of violence. Violence is good. The end.

I guess we are forced to read the whole book to know how these children went from scared victims to savage monsters. What kind of

---

[13] Joshua 10:13

messed up land is "This Place" they went to anyway? That's for next bedtime.

The Silver Chair: Chapters 1-2

"Mom, we already know Aslan is a jerk. I don't even have to say it."
We continue reading.
"Ugh! Jerk!"
Reading some more.
"What a total jerk!"
Two seconds later.
"Aslan is a real jerk!"

***

In this next section Aslan will be (*spoiler*) a jerk. I know, shocking. We left Jill and Eustace in another world that was bright, beautiful, and eerie. It was filled with birds and bugs, trees and rivers, "blue shadows and emptiness." It will also often be described as very lonely; Jill would even call it "dreadful." This was Heaven.[14] This was Aslan's Country.

In all my years as a believer in a Christian afterlife, I never felt brave enough to sit down and describe it. My best guesses seemed empty of all the wonders it must contain. I was wary of religious authors who attempted it, but Lewis does a fantastic job painting an incredible scene. Although his version of the land of the dead seems horrifying if anyone were to actually live there longer than a few days. I mean, it may be a wonderful sight to stumble upon, but it was monotonous and pedestrian—sparse with no undergrowth, level turf, and nothing

---

[14] Heaven is my protestant interpretation of this afterlife, but purgatory may be closer to Lewis' vision. Either way, it is presented as the place people go after they die.

moving on the ground. Lewis updates and expands Aslan's Country in the last book to avoid a white torture eternity.

Even though this is paradise, Jill is about to suffer immense emotional turmoil here that would haunt her dreams and interrupt her sleep for years to come. She'll cry through most of her time here while lion Jesus watches pitilessly and, later, even threatens her life. Not exactly the Sunday School version of things.

The children arrive on the edge of a cliff because, just like Aslan, his place is regrettably and unnecessarily dangerous. Eustace notices the cliff and tries to pull Jill away, but she won't be handled by a former bully. She purposely walks to the edge to show how tough she is and then predictably starts to faint. So far, our token girl character has been ignorant, careless, a damsel in distress, blubbering, and constitutionally weak. Anyway, Eustace falls off the cliff in an attempt to save her. His last words were a deserved insult of "blithering little idiot." Okay, bye Eustace.

Jill is destroyed by the knowledge that she has just seen someone die. While Jill is still grieving, Aslan, the creeper jerk, comes out from the bushes and blows Eustace to Narnia on lion's breath. He allows Jill to continue to sob and mourn Eustace's death for quite some time without telling her that he just saved the boy. Is it just me or does he seem to get off on children's pain?

Jill calms down enough to realize she has been given a supernatural thirst. She heads towards the sounds of a stream, terrified that the lion she spotted earlier would get her. Aslan decides to stand right between her and the water because he's a giant dingledick. Once she hears Aslan's voice, she was "frightened in rather a different way." Oh for crap's sake. Little Bit and I are sick of hearing how fear is *different* and somehow hallowed when it comes to this powerful deity. It's rather deranged that the Bible commands believers to both love *and* fear God at the same time.[15] God is scary. We get it. I wish the faithful would stop acting like that's a good thing when it's not.

Jill asks Aslan to promise not to eat her if she approaches to drink from the stream. Remember, she's now literally dying of thirst. What would a total dick say in this situation?

"I make no promise."

Yep, that.

Agreeing to not kill her would diminish his power over her. He can't have that. Jill implored him to at least move, but he wouldn't even consider it. She "realized she might as well have asked the whole mountain to move aside for her convenience." As if trying to save herself from death is an inconvenience! Jill gets right to the point and asks Aslan if he eats girls. Turns out, yep.

"I have swallowed up girls and boys, women and men, [whole] cities…"

Aslan just admitted he was a mass murderer! (And all God's people shrugged.) If anyone tells children to love a god, can we at least make sure it's not a genocidal one? Aslan comes off as a psychopath who doesn't feel sorry or angry about eating folks just as his biblical counterpart doesn't feel bad about drowning, stabbing, or starving folks. It would be even closer to the self-proclaimed God's Word if Jill were then told to praise Aslan for being so powerful and fear-inspiring. Ooh and ahh and *barf noise*.

After hearing her odds at survival, Jill says, "I daren't come and drink," prompting Aslan to taunt, "Then you will die of thirst." It's a thirst he supposedly gave her, to be clear. He wants her to know he can kill her either way. When Jill finally approached, it was "the worst thing she had ever had to do."

---

[15] Deuteronomy 10:12

We also get yet another taste of warped epistemology when a facial expression becomes proof of honesty.

> It never occurred to Jill to disbelieve the Lion—no one who had seen his stern face could do that.

Threats, control, and violence being justified as righteous is bad enough, but so is the message that a severe tone is trustworthy. Children may not come upon lions with magic powers, but they will absolutely meet tricky individuals. They will not be able to tell for sure if someone is lying based on their face, their claims alone, or their tone, yet all three of these have been used thus far as evidence of truthfulness—from Eustace's weak yet passionate assurances, to Aslan's furrowed brow, to the children's whispers. Baseless faith is repeatedly confused with actual truth, and Lewis props up his pseudo-truth with the flimsiest of supports that fall well below the threshold for evidence.

After Jill finally gets a drink, Aslan tells her to come close. The book says she "had to." This is really problematic, especially for kids with trauma backgrounds. This power dynamic is giving Bitsy and me gross feelings, especially when Aslan makes Jill stand between his paws in a show of forced intimacy as he intimidates her. He makes her admit she was showing off when she stood near the cliff as if that is a crime worthy of punishment and she hadn't suffered enough already. I get the impression "showing off" is doubly bad when girls do it as they really have nothing to boast about. Consider that Jill's false show of bravery led to her immediate near-fainting spell.

Jill also gets 100% of the blame for what she did near a cliff Aslan purposely set her on. Who is the all-powerful, omniscient adult in this situation again? If someone kidnapped my daughter from school and transported her to a nearby cliff, I'd be livid! The power-tripping lion can't be blamed, apparently, and decides to punish Jill for the newly-confessed (under duress) act of "showing off" by making a task he's about to give her unduly difficult. She gets no say in having a task in the first place, either, especially one she must either accomplish or "[die] in the attempt." Her life is literally worthless, and that lesson is hammered into young readers.

Jill randomly brings up the way they got there, which seems awkward and forced. This is obviously just so Lewis could have Aslan say, "You would not have called to me unless I had been calling to you." If we had any delusions that praying (not witchcraft) caused Aslan to do jack diddly, he set us straight. Oh, okay, *whew*. Good to know the lion is in charge and humans are still powerless garbage.

Why did Aslan bring them here? To complete a task that involves steps or "signs." He made Jill memorize the four signs word perfect. They are unnecessarily wordy so I've summarized them below:

Eustace needs to immediately greet an old friend in order to get help.

They must leave Narnia and go north to a ruined city of ancient giants.

They must find writing on a stone in that city and do what it says.

They must find a lost prince who utters Aslan's name.

The signs, when cut to their meat, are literally, "Go to here. Find thing. Meet guy." It's brain-numbingly simple. Jill is instructed to repeat these signs "when you wake in the morning and when you lie down at night," identical to Scripture's order to repeat God's commandments "when you lie down and when you get up."[16] It's one thing when you have to learn a list of complicated instructions, interpreted by different religious men, and handed down by oral tradition, but making these signs on par with that biblical mess is an unfair comparison.

---

[16] Deuteronomy 6:7

Aslan warns that "whatever strange things may happen to you, let nothing turn your mind from following the signs." I recognized this as my own forced obedience to the teachings of the Bible as a child. It's like a hymn we used to sing in church:

"Trust and obey, For there's no other way, To be happy in Jesus, But to trust and obey."[17]

If you're not catching the master/slave dynamic here, the hymn is calling for slave-like obedience to Jesus. Translating that over to our story, Jill is in the slave role while this deadly Jesus animal is the master. Aslan gets to punish her, order her, torture her, scare her, inform her how to think, and task her with a quest that puts her life at risk. She has no equal power, even to just ask him anything "inconvenient" like not mauling her please and thank you.

Since consent is not a thing, Aslan has the authority to do what he wants. He sends her over the cliff into Narnia on the same lion's breath as Eustace, but this time we get to experience the journey. The sun got in her eyes at one point, and because she was so directionally challenged just like every single girl in this entire series to date, she didn't know that meant she was heading west. Even though Lewis brings up the directional ineptness of girls constantly, he does concede in a helpful parenthetical that he's not sure this is a problem of girls in general. So #NotAllGirls #Maybe #IDontKnow #JustEveryOneIHaveWrittenAbout #LewisOut

Aslan's blow job (couldn't help it) is described in detail, with reasons given why Jill didn't feel the rush of wind at the thousands of miles per hour she was traveling because she was encapsulated inside the breath. Rather than a completely comfortable ride which no one should expect from Aslan, Jill is driven into a cloud and flown too

[17] First appeared in Hymns Old and New (1887), Words by John H. Sammis, Music by Daniel B. Towner.

close to crashing waves, so she arrives completely drenched. It wasn't until writing that out just now that I realized the whole explanation for fast travel is negated by the fact she could be driven into a wave at—what?—a thousand miles an hour? And get wet but not die?

She lands a few feet away from Scrubb! Best sentence in this chapter: "He must have blown you quicker than me." (These things go over the head of my young audience.) The kids immediately miss the first sign, the one about meeting up with a friend who will help them. Time ran out and the friend sailed off. Maybe Aslan shouldn't have had her sit there between his paws so long.

The familiar friend Eustace misses, by the way, is Caspian.[18]

The Silver Chair: Chapters 3-4

"They're telling the queen's story! Now we'll finally learn her name!"
"Nope. She'll be referred to as the dead Queen or Caspian's bride."
"You know, she is part star. Maybe some women aren't real people."
"Was the man who was a former star a real person?"
"Yeah, so maybe just women aren't real people? In Narnia I mean…
You know what I mean, Mom!"

***

We are finally back in Narnia and the scene is magical. Creatures of all descriptions are gathered wearing royal colors. The sights are so awesome that Jill temporarily thinks about something other than the signs. My Sunday School teacher would call this being distracted by the things of the world and failing to focus on God's Word. I call it normal human brain function. Either way, this will be the book's theme: Jill doesn't constantly have the signs repeating in her head like

---

[18] Who is a werewolf! You know it's true because it's written in a footnote.

some sort of obsessive psychological compulsion and things go wrong as a result. This same mindset was why my family had me constantly memorizing the Bible as soon as I was around five years old and big enough to rattle off entire King James chapters.

The same book of the Bible that tells believers not to be friends with atheists whom God will destroy,[19] also instructs the pious to meditate "day and night" on God's words. As someone who has genuinely attempted this, let me just say it doesn't lead to a healthy, well-rounded life! When I finally gave up prayer and Bible study, my life got so much better! Maybe in part because I was finally getting good sleep and creating healthy boundaries.

When I was in elementary school, I was encouraged to memorize all 176 verses of Psalm 119. I also memorized six books of the Bible by the time I was 12 years old, and later, thousands of other verses, including all the ones required to earn the highest award in AWANA. I didn't really have a childhood education thanks to the Accelerated Christian Education system that has failed every academic study to ever scrutinize it,[20] but I did save all that brain space where logic, science, real history, and higher math would usually go to make room for more Bible study! I even graduated valedictorian of my Christian college with an interdisciplinary degree that included Biblical Studies. (Maybe my ex-Christian butt can get a career in… church? Damn it!)

Anyway, Psalm 119 was pushed on us as Bible-thumped kids since it's a chapter about constantly thinking about the words of God, similar to how Jill is instructed to think about the signs. Here's how effed up this passage is. It starts out innocently enough:

"You have commanded us
To keep Your precepts diligently.

---

[19] Psalm 1
[20] J. Scaramanga, 2017. "Systems of Indoctrination: Accelerated Christian Education in England." Doctoral thesis, UCL (University College London).

Your word I have hidden in my heart."

Much of it reads to modern eyes like a man desperate and in pain. He's hoping the words of God can revive him:

"I opened my mouth and panted, For I longed for Your commandments.
My soul clings to the dust; Revive me according to Your word.
My soul melts from heaviness; Strengthen me according to Your word."

He fills his belly with the holy words in an Ouroboros-like fashion, causing the very pain he's trying to relieve. He claims to love these words, yet confesses they are not enough for him. Very quickly this turns into an unhealthy obsession. When he fills his day with anything else, he considers it worthless and feels guilty:

"Turn away my eyes from looking at worthless things."

And almost every other sentence is this biblical chapter contains all-consuming fear of punishment for forsaking the words of God:

"I cling to Your testimonies;
O Lord, do not put me to shame!
I will keep Your statutes;
Oh, do not forsake me utterly!
My flesh trembles for fear of You,
And I am afraid of Your judgments."

He even thinks being tortured over this is appropriate:

"It is good for me that I have been afflicted,
That I may learn Your statutes."

Jill's proper reaction to Aslan is supposed to be like this emotionally abusive relationship between the psalmist and his god. Even when he's doing it all right—waking in the middle of the night to repeat the holy words as Jill was instructed to do—he is still miserable. His faithfulness does not prevent real world harm to befall him.

"Princes also sit and speak against me.
The cords of the wicked have bound me.
The wicked wait for me to destroy me.
They persecute me wrongfully; Help me!"

But his fear of these dangers is nothing compared to his fear of what his deity would do to him if he didn't repeat the signs:

"I am a companion of all who fear You.
Turn away my reproach which I dread."

In the end, he will stick to the Scriptures since it's the only way he believes he will receive help in his afflictions someday. Maybe. His impatience is clear:

"Let Your hand become my help,
For I have chosen Your precepts.
It is time for You to act, O Lord."

This Psalm is absolutely tragic, yet many parts of it are found in modern worship songs. The overall context is the gross injustice of a limited and capricious god. To quote early twentieth century author Zora Neale Hurston, "Gods always behave like the people who make them." This biblical god acted just like the human kings who failed to provide justice but still demanded tribute. Coincidentally,[21] many ancient gods of this exact nature were worshiped around the time this was written.

Now Back to Narnia with a similarly limited and capricious lion who doesn't seem to care about children's suffering.

---

[21] By "coincidentally" I do realize large parts of the Bible are blatantly plagiarized from the religions of the Assyrians and Canaanites.

Like the Psalmist, Jill has realized her sin of not constantly repeating the signs, and immediately becomes desperate to communicate to Eustace about them before they are punished. Time works differently in Narnia so Eustace's friend has aged by 70 years, making him unrecognizable. Not that the signs would even hint at this turn of events. The children find themselves among many Narnian animals all gathered to send this elderly king off on some adventure at sea which he's too old to return from. He's going off to die seeking Aslan's assistance. The ship sails off just as Eustace learns the king was Caspian.

I have trouble imagining one of my dear friends coming back over summer break having turned into an octogenarian. It would be pretty traumatic. That's the kind of shock Eustace starts feeling once he realizes who the king was. Jill shuts his grieving right down by reminding him, "It's far worse than you think. We've muffed the first sign." How is that worse than his friend going on a death journey? No time for human emotion in the face of not pleasing Aslan, I guess.

Before they can contemplate just how bad things are, they get invited to a feast at Cair Paravel. Trumpkin, now very old, is there and allows them to eat dinner and stay the night at the castle. During the feast, a blind bard told them the story of *The Horse and His Boy*. Little Bit threw me some shade here. "We're reading the horsey book next!" I assured her. **Publication order!**

The punishment for missing the first sign is not being allowed to sleep that night as they rush to play catch up with their quest. Also, absolutely everything about their journey will be harder without proper tools, clothing, transportation, and food that the king could have provided. A new owl friend goes to Jill's window and asks if she's serious about finding the lost prince. She "remembered the Lion's voice and face" and replies she must do it as she's afraid of what Aslan will do to her otherwise. That's totally a journey with her enthusiastic consent right there.

The owl takes her and Eustace to an owl meeting where all the other owls give Jill a ton of crap about missing the first sign. She is shamed as if she is reasonably responsible. Ugh. The all-male owl parliament will be our exposition device à la Mr. Beaver, Trumpkin, or Ramandu in previous books, so Bitsy and I strapped in for a lot of backstory. We learned that Caspian's son, Rilian, was missing. Hey, it's the lost prince from the signs! Out of the large field of **no other princes**, he's the only one. Rilian's mother, whom we are calling Trophyna since she is *still* without a name in this book, was killed by a snake "as green as poison." Rilian went off to avenge her but became enchanted by a "thing" (Lewis meant woman) who wore a dress "as green as poison." Suspicious color descriptions aside, the nameless woman in the dress also just happened to hang out in the same place Trophyna was killed. The menfolk were ridiculously slow to pick up on the red flags.

Lord Drinian, who was captain of *Dawn Treader* in the last book, heard about "the most beautiful thing that was ever made" (the unnamed adult woman) and asked Rilian if he could go with him and "see this fair thing" (again, a *human woman*). Drinian put two and two together with the color clues but didn't tell anyone since he didn't want to be a little tattletale. After Rilian disappears the next day, Drinian tells the king his suspicions to help find the boy. Caspian responds super reasonably by trying to kill Drinian with a battle axe. The king only stops trying to kill his buddy because he had just lost his wife and now his son and didn't want to lose his friend, too. Aww, friendship. (I'm real tight with people who try to battle axe me.)

The owls confirm that magical women are evil just like the White Witch. We've already gone over how women with powers are never good while men with powers are just fine. The owls make this lesson more explicit.

Jill is the first to make the connection between the snake and the woman while the story is being told, but we're supposed to believe that she fell asleep a few sentences after being engaged in conversation. (Girls are such weak-willed creatures.) Now Eustace must arrange travel north by himself.

The owls offer to fly the children north and the quest is finished almost immediately. The end.

Or wait, they fly them to the king's ship which only took off literally that afternoon! He turns the ship around and gives them horses and supplies. Also, now the king doesn't have to die at sea. Then the quest is finished in comfort and style. The end!

Fine, none of that happens. Instead, the owls fly the children to a random swamp to find a nihilistic Marsh-wiggle and they continue the long and arduous quest on foot for no reason.

The Silver Chair: Chapters 5-6

"Ohhh, PuddleGLUM. I get it now."
"Yeah, he's depressing, but he's going to help them on their adventure."
"Unless they die first or get eaten by a lobster or choke on their gum…"
"Cute. You sound just like him."

***

Jill is whiny and tired—a delicate flower of need. Yet Eustace is made of tougher stuff (like a penis!) which keeps him from such frailties.

"Oh, come on, Pole, buck up. After all, it is an adventure."
"I'm sick of adventures."

Wow, I am exactly this extra by default, so I get it. Jill goes on being "even less pleased" throughout the flight on owl's back to meet our next primary character: Puddleglum the Marsh-wiggle.

"What's a *mashed* wiggle?" adorable Bitsy wanted to know. The Internet says Marsh-wiggles are human-like creatures, so we can assume they are more than talking frog animals. They have long limbs and webbed fingers and toes since they evolved to survive in the swamp lands. Despite being beloved by my former tribe of evangelicals who tend to hold a creationism bent, C. S. Lewis accepted the discoveries of evolutionary science—at least in so far as he understood them and strained that understanding through a biblical filter. For example, he saw that scientific evidence backed evolutionary theory, yet he rejected the parts of it which conflicted with the Bible, calling those parts "Evolutionism." [22] As if drawing scientific conclusions Christians didn't like was itself a belief system. He often mixed scientific findings with his religious beliefs in an attempt to make them compatible. Many believers retain their own faith by inserting magical interference into the evolutionary story. Did we evolve from ape creatures? Sure. God zapped the last of the *homo sapiens* with souls, named them Adam and Eve, and placed them in the Garden of Eden. See? It all works if you don't get Biblical Studies degrees! (Which, honestly, I do not recommend.) In the same way the Marsh-wiggle people could have evolved to handle the wetlands and then were magically given souls, language, and personalities by Aslan.

My own Christian denomination treated scientific discoveries— those painstakingly and meticulously collected bits of data used to make predictions and save lives (also known as "made-up Satan garbage")—as a giant atheist conspiracy. The Accelerated Christian Education's science curriculum taught me facts such as: dinosaurs existed

---

[22] C. S. Lewis, 1967. "The Funeral of a Great Myth," *Christian Reflections*, (William B. Eerdmans Publishing Company), p. 85.

at the same time as people, snow created electricity, scientists are malicious liars who know God's truth and purposely suppress it, the sky used to be pink, homosexuality is unnatural, our planet is clearly only a few thousand years old, the Loch Ness Monster is real, a world-wide flood created the Grand Canyon, and mathematics prove the sun stood still in the sky for a whole day as the Bible claims.[23] All of these claims have evidence *against them* and are patently untrue. (At the time of this writing, my country's current secretary of education advocated strongly to give taxpayer money to these schools.[24]) Research papers or peer-reviewed studies were presented as merely religious faith in something called scientism.

At least my church leaders didn't have to do the intellectual bludgeoning Lewis and others had to do. What do creationists do when grappling with fossils of prehistoric predators who had sharp, flesh-tearing teeth during the time of Eden when they were all supposedly vegetarian and huggable? Or the sheer number of transitional humanoid fossils? Or macroevolution seen in bacteria? Or the new species of flies and mice that have evolved in isolation?[25] Or how all our strata layers confirm a progression of simple to complex? They just rejected it all as fake news. It's much easier to deny all scientific discoveries than to make the Bible fit with what we know.

Do biblical Christianity and science fit together? If they did, my former faith group wasted a lot of time teaching us that the zoo was infiltrated by Satan and the posted signs about extinct species or

---

[23] J. Scaramanga, 2017. *Systems of Indoctrination: Accelerated Christian Education in England*. Doctoral thesis, UCL (University College London).
[24] Rebecca Klein, 2017. "Voucher Schools Championed By Betsy DeVos Can Teach Whatever They Want. Turns Out They Teach Lies," Huffington Post. Retrieved 13 December 2017.
[25] Aron Ra, 2016. *Fundamental Falsehoods of Creationism*, (Durham, NC: Pitchstone Publishing), pp. 313-316.

evolutionary ancestors were lies. I felt weird about going to the zoo well into adulthood.

There are some solid reasons my church rejected reality for the sake of their Bible. Evolution involves death on a grand scale as species reproduce, mix their genetics about, and make way for the next generations, but the Bible claims death entered the world only after human sin,[26] not millions of years before it. Adam, who was considered a real person by at least one New Testament writer, is said to have brought death through sin, and Jesus is said to have come specifically to end what Adam started.[27] If sin didn't introduce death, then how does Jesus' promise to free us from death by forgiveness of sin make sense? It doesn't. It only works when the tale is real and the science is false.

An old Ken Ham video I had to watch during my missionary training warned that scientific "attacks" on the Genesis creation account would lead to the undermining of Christianity. He wasn't wrong. Yet Christianity didn't disappear, it, ahem, dare I say, *evolved.*

Another reason to reject evolution, from the mouth of one evening service pastor during my teen years, is that evolution would be one of the most brutal systems of killing, maiming, and mutating that a loving god could ever have invented. (No one introduce him to the Old Testament.)

***

Jill and Eustace arrived at the swamp to meet their evolved-to-his-environment host. Jill made a nasty remark to Eustace about not bathing under these conditions. Adventures are gross, right? Best leave them to boys.

---

[26] Romans 5:12
[27] 1 Corinthians 15:21-22

Puddleglum is very pessimistic and everything out of his mouth assumes the worst, but we have some real clues that he's one of our heroes. He smokes, so as we've previously learned, this is meant to communicate that he's one of the good guys. He offered the kids sips out of his nasty "square black bottle"—alcoholism being another sign of goodness. He also served them eel meat to show he wasn't a vegetarian. Smoking, drinking, and meat-eating—the qualifying trinity of what makes a decent chap in Lewis' view.

Puddleglum joins the party and they set off on foot (thanks to lazy owls) into giant country. Jill sees the giants and is understandably afraid. Is Eustace equally afraid? Well, who knows. He's not a girl so we don't mention his emotional state. The giants are the same as in *The Lion, The Witch and The Wardrobe* and especially stupid. They ignore the humans while throwing "cock-shies" at a pile of stones as part of a game. Little Bit and I had to look up what cock-shies were and found out they are hard sticks people in England used to throw at a rooster tied to a fence until the rooster died. (Fun game, psychos.) Maybe the simplicity of the game or its bloody roots are supposed to speak to the giants' character. The giants all end up fighting and then crying like babies as the humans walk past them.

Then our small group comes to a giant bridge—literally a bridge built by giants. Since giants are too stupid to build anything, our party assumes it was built long ago when the giants were "far cleverer than the modern kind." This regression could be a nod to the idea I grew up with that people used to be smarter the closer they were to God's initial creation; we have declined with each subsequent generation removed from that divine intervention. This is compounded by the idea that sin has a cumulative effect passed down through our ancestors. It's like if the sentiment "it was better in the old days" were turned into a doctrinal position. I know I was taught humans were getting worse, allegedly both morally and intellectually, even as crime rates were clearly going down, women's rights were on the rise, and technological discoveries were skyrocketing.

Once across the bridge the kids see two people approaching them. The first was a silent knight with his visor down to conceal his identity, and next to him, a woman in a gorgeous green dress riding a white horse. The horse is described as beautiful, and the woman atop it, "lovelier still." Did she just get compared to a horse? Yes. Yes, she did.

This is our main villain in the story: The Lady of the Green Kirtle. Lewis has a wonderfully rich vocabulary for describing characters up until that character has a vagina. Then he can only muster up either positive or negative physical attributes. This woman also rolls her Rs "delightfully" so there's that taste of something pleasing and foreign about her—the perfect addition to a British collection. This accent assumes that everyone else has an English accent, or what Bitty and I call a "BBC accent." Lewis' xenophobia was well known and this was his subtle way of saying, "Beware of foreigners. They could be snakes."

"Should we be naming this woman?" Little Bit asks me.

I couldn't remember if her name was revealed once they got to her underground kingdom so I suggested she would get named later because I am an idiot who has never read a Lewis story with women in it. This all but guaranteed a groan from my daughter each time this character gets called variations of "female wearing dress."

The children ask this woman where the ruined ancient city of the giants is located and she tells them to ask over at Harfang, a modern giant city. She then describes how wonderful Harfang is with all its warm baths and free food. When they asked if the giants would take strangers, she assures them.

> "Only tell them that She of the Green Kirtle salutes them by you, and has sent them two fair Southern children for the Autumn Feast."

I swear, the green dress should have been a clear warning, or the fact that there's an adult woman in Lewis' world who seems to be in charge and has a speaking part while the man next to her does not. (Danger danger!)

"*She* better get a name later," Little Bits said with a frown.

She doesn't.

The children went on about how beautiful she was after she left. They guessed the knight was silent because "perhaps he just wants to look at her." That's the best thing about those lady folks: lookin' at 'em!

They believed the giants at Harfang would be nice because a stranger with a nice voice and face told them they were. Don't they know only lions with stern voices and faces can be trusted? It seems the rules for verifying claims by faces and voices are ever-changing.

For the rest of the journey all the children could talk about was hot baths and warm rooms like *she* had promised. Because, you know, they're freezing, dirty, tired, and hungry. During talk of Harfang, Jill stopped repeating the signs to herself every night and morning.

> She said to herself, at first, that she was too tired, but she soon forgot all about it.

I'd like to point out that meditating on any one thing day and night is an obsessive fixation. (Can we say psychiatric disorder, anyone?) We've already been over how God, er, Aslan punishes Jill when she is not constantly exerting mental focus on the Bible, um, *signs*. For you heathens who have already forgotten them, they are:

~~Eustace needs to immediately greet an old friend in order to get help.~~

They must leave Narnia and go north to a ruined city of ancient giants.

They must find writing on a stone in that city and do what it says.

They must find a lost prince who utters Aslan's name.

They spot Harfang in the distance.

If you have never been in the wild wilderness, day and night, for weeks, you will hardly understand how they felt.

Lewis really thinks his audience is spoiled rotten. That night it was so cold their blankets were covered in frost. The moral of this whole story is not to be tempted by the temporary things of this world, no matter how legitimate they are. Wanting to stay alive, keep warm, be safe, keep from getting sick, keep from starving, keep from losing toes, avoid extreme pain and discomfort, and keep healthy is nothing more than some worldly pleasure trip—something a biblical psalmist might flippantly deem "worthless things."

Nevermind this life! Psh! Follow the signs!

The Silver Chair: Chapters 7-8

"She got the order of the signs wrong? Wait, what were the signs again, Mom?"

"Hold on, let me flip back."

"You think Aslan will punish us for forgetting?"

***

Chapter seven opens in a snowy torture land. The children's feet are in great pain, their ears ache, they can't see more than a foot in front of them, they can't hear each other even while shouting, the wind is whipping up sheets of snow directly into their faces, and everything hurts. They are heading towards warm baths and relief, but their guide, Puddleglum, reminds them about the signs once more. Jill Pole is not having it.

"Oh, come on! Bother the signs,' said Pole. 'Something about some-one mentioning Aslan's name, I think. But I'm jolly well not going to give a recitation here."

Narrator Lewis explains:

As you see, she had got the order wrong. That was because she had given up saying the signs over every night. She still really knew them, if she troubled to think: but she was no longer so 'pat' in her lesson as to be sure of reeling them off in the right order at a moment's notice and without thinking.

"Without thinking" is the primary way I memorized the Bible. I may have used my brain for the task, but never critically. This was a problem since God's word was violent, problematic, had inaccuracies about the physical world, made up large sections of history out of whole cloth, and was a steaming pile of sexism. While following the Bible gave me a sense of accomplishment, and endless bragging rights in a religious context, it did nothing for me beyond those concocted gold stars. I no longer have my Bible memory down "pat," and thanks to the Internet, I'll never have to, yet my life continues to improve without that added weight. Go figure.

I keep harping on about how following God's word and meditating on it day and night is simply bad advice, especially when it comes at the expense of improving one's situation in real life. That said, *from the story's perspective* it would be *very important* to remember the signs. I realize my childhood of memorizing large chunks of Elizabethan English doesn't help put me in the typical preadolescent's brain space, but these signs don't seem particularly hard. Plus, they only need to know three of the four at this point. The only reason Jill—and let's face it, this is only expected of Jill—would not have the signs "pat" by now is if Lewis is trying to make a ham-fisted comparison between relying on Aslan's words and Christians relying on the Bible. But come on! The Bible is not intuitive for modern life, and rarely cohesive.

Signs from a magical lion on the other hand? Ones in your original language that are directly useful for your exact situation? Ones you'd been reciting nightly (if not recently), and *still* can't rattle off? That makes zero sense. The only reason Jill would forget the next sign that she's supposedly hiking towards is if we're pushing the false equivalence between signs and Scripture. Or because girls are dumb. Either way, I'm not buying it.

Also, does Puddleglum not have a working brain? Why is he pestering Jill about signs he could easily memorize himself? Hell, write the damn things on three sheets of paper and then they're all set! Puddleglum asks because he *doesn't know*. He's **not expected to know**. Knowing is female work. Jill gets constantly ragged on throughout this book as if she is the only one who should be saddled with these signs when all of them are on the same quest!

The other advantage of writing the signs down would be that Jill could shove them down the throat of the next lazy male character who demanded an immediate recitation from her during a snowstorm.

Jill worries out loud that they are about to die because that is a real possibility here. She has known this mission could cause her death since standing between the lion's paws. Despite this, Puddleglum, the only true follower of Aslan at the moment, is solely focused on the signs. He gets rewarded by noticing one. It's the ruined ancient giant city! He starts to mention it, but Eustace rudely shuts him up and Jill spots Harfang. They all race towards earthly pleasures, you know, those things that make up the bedrock of Maslow's hierarchy: food, shelter, warmth—those boring fleeting pleasures of this world that don't come close to the amazing heavenly rewards for dying of frostbite in Aslan's service.

When they arrive at Harfang, the giant at the gate remarks that he didn't realize children were blue. Jill explains that their faces are blue because they are so cold. To warm them up the giant offers

Puddleglum some hard liquor. When Puddleglum downs it all, the giant says, "Why, Froggy, you're a man. See him put it away!" That is pretty toxic and assumes real men get drunk. Puddleglum took issue with a different aspect of these words:

"Not a man... Marsh-wiggle." And later as the liquor took effect, "Marsh-wiggle. Marsh-wiggle. Very respectable Marsh-wiggle. Re-spectowiggle."

These books have provided so many opportunities to explain drunkenness to my child.

The three are taken (carried in Puddleglum's case) before the king and queen of the giants. Now giants are all supposed to be ugly, but there's an extra emphasis on the queen's looks. Since women are visual props, it seems to be especially wrong if they're ugly and Lewis must comment upon it at length. The king was alright, for a giant, but the queen was downright failing at existing in the visual range of men.

[She was] dreadfully fat and had a double chin and a fat, powdered face—which isn't a very nice thing at the best of times, and of course looks much worse when it is ten times too big.

The children explain to the king and queen that the Green Dress Woman said Harfang would "have us for your Autumn Feast." That wording is a bit of foreshadowing. Jill then starts crying from hunger and the trauma she's been through, so the queen orders them to be bathed and fed. Jill slept fifteen hours that night. It restored her body enough to feel healthy again. Of course, Aslan haunts her dreams as punishment for her failure to prioritize the signs over sleep. (I think he just likes making Jill cry.) He predictably left the boys alone to rest.

When the storm was calmer, the children could see an ancient city out the guest room window. It was the same one Puddleglum had spotted earlier. Upon further inspection they realize the words "UNDER ME" are carved into its stones. Perfect, all that's left to do is some spelunking! This knocks out the second and third signs. Boom and boom.

Sign refresher:

~~Eustace needs to immediately greet an old friend in order to get help.~~

~~They must leave Narnia and go north to a ruined city of ancient giants.~~

~~They must find writing on a stone in that city and do what it says.~~

They must find a lost prince who utters Aslan's name.

Instead of rejoicing at this discovery, they are all upset. Why? Because Jill didn't have the signs memorized well enough to spot it *faster*.

Bits thinks it worked out well since they can now start fresh, but for some reason they are all feeling terribly guilty that they failed Aslan. (Feeling guilty for no reason? Insert religious joke here.) Jill takes most of the blame and all of the guilt:

"I've spoilt everything ever since you brought me here."

It reminds me of a time in my Christian elementary school where I was fighting with a certain boy and I got in more trouble because "a young lady should know better." He overpowered me and sexually assaulted me, but I was the only one who got in trouble for being immodest. The Jills of the world almost always end up taking responsibility for the Eustaces of the world.

Next a weird conversation takes place where our party tries to work out what "UNDER ME" could *possibly* mean. Bitsy hollers from her bed, "Go under the city. Duh." But for this merry band, the instructions are just *indiscernible*. It's okay though, because they have faith!

"Aslan's instructions always work: there are no exceptions."

Any comparison to the Bible at this point has become officially laughable.

"'We've brought the anger of Aslan on us,' he said. 'That's what comes of not attending to the signs. We're under a curse, I expect. If it was allowed, it would be the best thing we could do, to take these knives and drive them into our own hearts.'"
"Stop it, Mom. You made that up. Puddleglum did NOT just say that."
"I'm just reading what it says."
"Is he secretly a bad guy?"
"Actually, he's supposed to be the wisest one."
"What?"

***

Our heroes need to leave Harfang, but they want to sneak out. Little Bit figured out right away that the giants are going to eat them, but these geniuses haven't yet, so why the sneaking around? Who knows? Jill is put to work in a very gendered way for this chapter. She acts very silly, adopts a baby voice, and giggles and whips her curls around. Her job was to get information, and her foolishness was so they would not suspect her of working them over. Some of the giants reacted in a bizarre way to her cuteness; they would dab at their eyes or look sad for no reason. (Pssst! Because she's going to be dinner!)

> "She made love to everyone—the grooms, the porters, the house-maids, the ladies-in-waiting, and the elderly giant lords whose hunting days were past. She submitted to being kissed and pawed about by any number of giantesses..."

Female labor is often draining, and this work even came with giving up bodily autonomy. It wasn't something she wanted to do, in fact, "it made her hot all over when she remembered it afterwards."

Embarrassing and degrading work is often expected of women. Lewis explains:

> Scrubb and Puddleglum both did their best, but girls do that kind of thing better than boys.

What is the one thing girls finally do better than boys? Degrade themselves.

The information Jill obtains is useful: A door in the kitchen is left open for the cat. They can use this to sneak away. During lunch, Puddleglum overhears that the protein in that day's meal was a Talking Deer, meaning they ate a person. This is horrifying. Puddleglum says this is Aslan's punishment for not sticking to the signs better. So, Aslan punished them with cannibalism? (What in the world did the sentient deer do to piss him off?) Then our Marsh-wiggle suggests it would be better if they killed themselves than follow the signs halfheartedly. Since he is the mature one of the group, Aslan's best follower, we're supposed to take this as wise advice. We are entering religious fanatism territory. I have to hope it wasn't a real suggestion and more of a "if your right eye offends you, pluck it out"[28] nonsense that Jesus commands believers to do. No one sane takes that suggestion seriously either.

Upon finding they had eaten someone, it was now more important than ever to escape the giants who were capable of such evil. While in the kitchen waiting for the service staff to leave, the three discover an Autumn Feast cookbook open to a page on how to cook men with the crusts for making "man-pies" already laid out. I explained to Bitsy that they would be eating Jill as well, and that thanks to androcentric language, she was considered a (lesser form of) "man." They wait for the giant in the kitchen to fall asleep and then they make their way out. Unfortunately, the king and queen are returning from a hunting party

---

[28] Matthew 5:29

at that very moment, which forces the children to make a run for it as the king shouts to not let their meal get away. They hide in a crack in the rocks and accidentally slide a mile downwards on the loose stones. Congrats! They made it under the city! Easy.

"Now to find the prince!" said Little Bit excitedly.

A stranger greets our cut and bruised heroes, but it's not the prince to Bitsy's disappointment. It's just a dude who takes the children and Marsh-wiggle to the underworld queen. On their way, they see giant dragons and weird creatures who are sleeping until the end of the world. They also see Father Time who is waiting for the apocalypse. Are these things explained at all? Nope. Moving on then.

Getting on a boat they row endlessly towards a city of depressed underground dwellers who keep repeating, "Many sink down to the Underworld and few return to the sunlit lands." These guys are called Earthmen because they are men who live under the earth and Lewis takes only ten seconds and one shot of whiskey before naming things.

At the queen's palace they discover she's not available, but her fiancé tells the guards to bring the children to his room instead of the dungeon to wait for her return. This fellow is the same silent knight who was with the Green Dress Woman who told them the giants would "have them" for the Autumn Feast. The no-longer-silent knight laughs that off. He tells them that the queen is great and she's going to marry him and make him king in the overworld. All he is expected to do is follow her instructions and surprise attack a random city they are currently burrowing under. He is downright flippant when talking about murdering the city's inhabitants.

"Where I come from," said Jill, who was disliking him more every minute, "they don't think much of men who are bossed about by their wives."

That's the official response from our party after learning about a plot to kill innocent people. *That's* what they focus on. It turns out that a queen can't rule the overworld without a man. Why? No one ever explains; it's just universally accepted and unquestioned that that is how it works. How sad for her. This is one elaborate plot on her end just so she can have a kingdom to rule.

As the evening progresses, the knight tells them he is under an affliction where he briefly turns into a beast and attacks people at a certain time each night. Then he wakes up slightly weary with no memory of it. The hour is nigh, so he asks them to stick around because he's scared to go through such an ordeal alone with his queen away. Our boy is cowed *and* cowardly, so the worst kind of man to Lewis. No one in the room likes him due to this, but they do agree to stick around. They hide in the other chamber while Earthmen tie the cursed dude to a silver chair. (Hey, the book's title!)

After the guards leave, the children and Marsh-wiggle come back to keep him company. The knight tells them not to release him from his bonds for any reason, no matter what he says. The beast in him would kill them if they did. They all agree, and then naturally, mere moments later, our heroes sit there debating releasing him since he used Aslan's name while frothing at the mouth. I mean, they are *pretty* sure that's the fourth sign. Now they had to do it.

I feel weird harping on these signs *again*, but they really do make up so much of this storyline and they teach children all the wrong lessons. For instance, when they hear Aslan's name, which they interpret as the fourth sign, coming from a madman who has told them he would kill them if freed, they decide they must follow Aslan and die.

> "That fellow will be the death of us once he's up, I shouldn't wonder. But that doesn't let us off following the sign."

Of course it lets you off following the sign!

People I trusted when I was very young told me that the greatest thing I could do with my life was to die following Christ. My Christian school was full of required reading of missionary biographies exalting people who did just that. While other children were reading Judy Blume and Roald Dahl, I was reading John Foxe and his *Foxe's Book of Martyrs*. In the updated version of this book, the publisher's notes say it contains, "Stories of love of God and Christ. Stories of the amazing grace of God that enabled men, women, **and children** to endure persecutions **and often horrible deaths**." [29] (Emphasis mine.) That's what I wanted when I signed up to be a missionary. I wanted my life to be a sacrifice to God, like the blood sacrifices he craved in the Old Testament. The New Testament calls this kind of sacrifice reasonable.[30]

Lewis is pushing the Christian idea that people must be sacrificed to their gods: To Aslan or Yahweh or Jesus. That's all humanity is supposedly good for. In fact, when Jesus became human, Scripture says he became "obedient to death—even death on a cross," a terribly violent end.[31] What a lesson to emulate!

Gods out for blood encapsulate Bronze Age thinking. This is so much part of Aslan's character that the children understand implicitly that they must follow the signs to their death. They decide to be okay with that. Jill says, "Let's get it over. Goodbye, everyone!" Then they all chant, "In the name of Aslan," before cutting the madman's ropes. When he goes straight for his sword they tense to be slaughtered, but the madman instead swings it at the silver chair, ending his enchantment for good. (I know! Let's name an entire book after a chair that's in it for less than a minute!)

Our knight reveals that he is really Prince Rilian. "Duh," says my daughter. Our heroes rejoice and inform Rilian that he has been under

---

[29] ChristianBook.com. "New Foxe's Book of Martyrs, Publisher's Description." Available at: https://www.christianbook.com/new-foxes-book-of-martyrs-softcover/john-foxe/9780882708751/pd/08759#CBD-PD-Description
[30] Romans 12
[31] Philippians 2:8

an enchantment for ten years. He gets over the shock of that knowledge astonishingly fast so all is well.

Until Queen Green Dress Lady Woman enters the room that is.

The Silver Chair: Chapter 12

"Yay Puddleglum! Finally someone put out that fire!"
"I told you Puddleglum is the real hero of this story."
"Then why do you keep rooting for the witch?!"
"Do I? Oops."

***

Once a lady, then a queen, now clearly a witch, this nameless beauty enters the room with our heroes. She is angry that the prince is free but she remains chill AF. She immediately starts an enchantment on everyone in the room with the help of magic powder thrown into the fire. Then she calmly talks to them while playing an instrument. She's no longer rolling her Rs "delightfully" at all. Little Bit is r-r-relieved since I r-r-read those parts hor-r-r-r-ridly.

The enchantment causes all four of them to start to doubt that the overworld is real, the sun is real, or Aslan is real. Whenever they claim those things are real, the whip-smart witch talks them out of it. Puddleglum finally steps on the fire with his foot, which lifts the spell just enough to allow him a clear head. He uses this moment of clarity to give an impassioned sermon.

While Puddleglum preaches at her, the witch takes the opportunity to turn into a giant serpent. The Marsh-wiggle and the prince hack her neck off, and her death makes "a nasty mess." The villain's death is about as anti-climactic as Boba Fett getting accidentally knocked into a Sarlacc pit by a blinded Solo.

In Christianity, the serpent is a picture of evil and appears prominently in the very first story—that of feminine weakness, ignorance, and failure. The snake of Eden, often considered the devil, is sometimes depicted as a woman in historic art—perhaps a reference to Lilith who once controlled Inanna's Huluppa tree. The dragon in The Book of Revelation called "that serpent of old" is even mounted by a woman. The misogynistic idea that women are natural allies with the devil goes way back in Christian thought and works. The *Malleus Maleficarum*, a Christian treatise from 1487, warns, "All witchcraft comes from carnal lust, which in woman is insatiable."[32] The thinking in early Christendom was that since God was good and the devil was the opposite, then men were close to God and women, their opposite, were closer to the devil.[33] Women will either join the devil snake out of ignorance and naivety like Eve, or joyfully out of dark desires for power. Weak or wicked, good or bad, virtuous or impure: women were often one-dimensional characters when described by men from antiquity. Martin Luther, father of Protestant faith, proclaimed, "The word and works of God is quite clear, that women were made either to be wives or prostitutes."

Before Abrahamic subversion, the snake was a symbol of goodness and femininity. The Egyptian hieroglyph for goddess is a snake. During the time of the early Israelites, Asherah was the resident goddess in the so-called Promised Land.[34] She was also worshipped by the children of Israel and is most likely who the Bible calls the Queen of Heaven.[35] They also worshipped another god from the Canaanite

---

[32] Part I, Question VI

[33] This summary borrowed largely from Stuart Clark and Robin Briggs who researched the reasons why Christians loved burning witches.

[34] Karen Garst, 2016. *Women Beyond Belief: Discovering Life Without Religion*, (Durham, NC: Pitchstone Publishing), pp. 251-262.

[35] Jeremiah 7

pantheon we've already discussed named El.[36] Israel literally means "He who struggles with El." **El**ohim, the name for God in Genesis that is the plural form of El, likely refers to Asherah, his wife, as well as the other gods under his banner who had a hand in creation. When the pantheon was condensed into a single entity by early Jewish religious authorities around 4,000 years ago, El absorbed all the other deities' abilities, including Asherah's powers of creation. What was the symbol associated with Asherah, goddess of new life? The snake—a creature who could shed its skin and appear like new.

Now if I were a new male-dominated patriarchal religion on the scene, what story would I use to subjugate women? One where women brought on death itself and now must be under men's rule? Perfect. And what symbols would I use for evil? A goddess symbol from the current, local female deity? A bit on the nose, right?

***

The boys all fought the symbol of feminine power, I mean the giant snake, while Jill sat down, kept quiet, and hoped she wouldn't faint, blub, or "do anything idiotic." Sigh, girls sure are worthless. So are women. Just takes a bit of hacking and they're defeated.

Then they all celebrated while drinking wine because tipsy children are hilarious. That's where the chapter ends.

Puddleglum's speech that allowed the witch time to transform was an interesting one. I had to read it aloud to Little Bitsy twice because the first time I thought he was still in a trance, spouting nonsense, and I got the tone all wrong. When I got to the end, I realized he had been serious the whole time and was being used by Lewis the Theologian to attempt to give children a philosophical proof for God. Yikes!

---

[36] Available at: https://www.ancient.eu/Yahweh/

Suppose we *have* only dreamed, or made up, all those things—trees and grass and sun and moon and stars and Aslan himself. Suppose we have. Then all I can say is that, in that case, **the made-up things seem a good deal more important than the real ones.** Suppose this black pit of a kingdom of yours *is* the only world. Well, it strikes me as a pretty poor one. And that's a funny thing, when you come to think of it. We're just babies making up a game, if you're right. But four babies playing a game can make a play-world which licks your real world hollow. **That's why I'm going to stand by the play-world. I'm on Aslan's side even if there isn't any Aslan to lead it.** I'm going to live as like a Narnian as I can even if there isn't any Narnia.[37]

YES! Go Puddles! Play-world! Play-world! Play-world! He's going to stand by his imaginary world, why? Because make-believe is better than reality! And reality is hard! That's why! And that makes it more important than the real one, how? Because making up something in your head makes it more real, okay! Obvs!

Of this speech Lewis has said:

"I have simply put the 'Ontological Proof' in a form suitable for children. And even that is not so remarkable a feat as you might think. You can get into children's heads a good deal which is quite beyond the Bishop of Woolwich."[38]

I wouldn't brag about getting children, if I were Lewis. The man saw *Snow White and the Seven Dwarves* the year it came out and both he and his movie date, Tolkien, hated it. I think most children at the time would disagree. Lewis, never one to shy away from a vicious and prejudiced takedown of someone he didn't like (the Bishop of Woolwich being no exception), said of Walt Disney:

---

[37] Emphasis in bold is mine.
[38] Lewis wrote this in a letter to Nancy Warner in October 1963.

"What might not have come of it if this man had been educated—or even brought up in a decent society?"[39]

I think Walt did okay.

Lewis may have hated Disney for his depiction of Dwarves, something the gatekeeping Lewis felt ownership of, but he disliked the Bishop of Woolwich for his criticisms of old-fashioned Christian theology. The bishop wrote a book called *Honest to God* that introduced a picture of the Christian deity which deviated from an old man living in the sky, as the ancient people who wrote the Old Testament believed, to an entity that was the "ground of our being"—something grander, more spiritual, and more familiar to modern Christians. To Lewis, however, God was a male patriarch. Full stop. And probably White. Likely English.

As to Lewis' ontological proof, he uses a philosophical argument that states the possibility of God's existence entails his actuality. Or in other words, God must exist simply because we can imagine it. Just like how Candy Land must exist. As a kid I dreamed of roads made of cinnamon and sugar lined with chocolate rocks. Rivers were ice cream, and trees were the kind of licorice that actually tasted good. It was easy for me to imagine this world. Too easy. So easy it must exist! In fact, it was so intuitive that when I would talk to my friends about it, they could correctly guess which desserts went where. I don't know a child who couldn't easily imagine such a world. And there's a whole board game celebrating such an idea! Further proof it's real!

To make the ontological argument official we'll follow the formula: It's *possible* such a Candy Land world exists somewhere. Maybe not likely, but *possible*. There are countless worlds out there after all. If this world possibly exists then it exists in some possible worlds. And if it exists in some possible worlds, then it exists, possibly, in all possible

---

[39] Quoted from a letter to A.K. Hamilton, 1939.

worlds. Therefore, it must exist in all possible worlds! Now let's take it home! I claim that not only is Candy Land real, it's exactly like how I've written it down while inspired by it, and knowing it exists should inform how I live my life. Join my group or be forever candyless. As true Candylandians, we will lobby for laws that enforce Candy Land ideals and call it freedom of religion!

For Puddleglum and Lewis, the idea of Aslan or God is not imagined by accident, but the mere fact it *can be* imagined must mean it is possible to exist. Then, of course, *if* it can be thought up and therefore possibly exist then that is the foundational proof it actually exists.

(My head hurts now.)

When I was small, I was told that the fact I can clearly imagine Heaven and God means those things are real. Let's ignore that their exact attributes were poured into my head starting at birth and my spiritual leaders got angry if I imagined them differently than our holy text allowed. God has "put eternity into man's heart"[40] so that's why we know places like Heaven are real and souls can't be destroyed. It's rather circular reasoning at its worst. Is it any wonder humankind needed the scientific method to ground us to reality?

Little Bit cheered Puddleglum on, and rightly so. The overworld is real after all. Yet it is his logic, not his courage, that falls flat. Lewis is trying to prove God's existence to children using these words. This fallacy will fail children in every other logical pursuit.

Lewis is also introducing a reworking of Pascal's Wager. Blaise Pascal once had a personal wager found sewn into his coat lining and published after his death where he decided to bet his life on a belief in God. His arguments are long and varied, and really can't be summed up so simplistically as I'm about to do, but it's generally agreed upon that he thought the benefits of going to Heaven and avoiding Hell

---

[40] Ecclesiastes 3:11

were important enough to risk wasting a life devoted to these beliefs. He would bet on the play-world with the bigger pay off.

Pascal was a Christian, and so his only two options were the Christian god or no god at all—a binary that assumes there are no other gods to choose from, which is hilarious considering the Pentateuch specifically mentions the existence of other gods when telling believers to choose the Jewish one.[41] This wager is problematic in a lot of ways besides its lack of options. For one thing it assumes the choices are equally likely. It also promotes bludgeoning one's brain into belief by avoiding the need for "piling up proofs of God" since they are not to be found. Finally, he advocates "subduing your passions" in order to "naturally cause you to believe" and "blunt your cleverness."[42] Damn. Pascal was in it to win it.

Puddleglum makes the case for choosing to believe something for the benefits of having something better to believe in. If Candy Land world were part of a majority religion, I could see the Pascals of the world placing their wager for it and trying their best to believe in it. If they are wrong, sure, they wasted their whole lives to chocolate's service, but if they are right, oh what a world of cake awaits them! The obvious caution here is treating the made-up ones as "a good deal more important than the real ones." That can be downright antithetical to survival. When fantasy replaces reality, people get hurt. Plus, those who live in fantasy worlds are usually causing harm or being harmed.

Puddleglum's infamous speech is all the more endearing among Lewis fans for the simple reason that it equates belief in God with belief in the sun, stars, and world above the ground. One online Christian commentor thought Lewis was trying to communicate choosing faith over evidence for its intangible benefits.

---

[41] Exodus 20:3

[42] Blaise Pascal (trans. John Warrington), 1932. *Pensees*, (London: Dent, Everyman's Library No. 874).

[Even] if by some chance we are wrong about all this: about God and the existence of God and the whole purpose of life. Even if we're wrong, we're better off continuing to act like we're not. **Because at least we still have purpose, and love, and hope.** I'd rather live my life as a Christian even if there is no Christ. I'm on Heaven's side even if there is no Heaven.[43]

Oh, sweetie. I couldn't imagine life without Christ either. It was easy for me to project what I thought non-Christians would feel onto them. *What poor hopeless, loveless, purposeless losers they were.* I heard many pastors from the pulpit do the same. Now I sit here filled with purpose and love; I'm even downright hopeful. More than anything I have an inner peace Christianity always promised but never made good on. It helps when I don't think of myself as a dirty condemned sinner for simply being human. If atheists were miserable and hopeless as Lewis and my former church believed, then they would have higher levels of mental health issues such as depression or anxiety. In fact, they don't.[44] I know my depression evaporated the moment I gave up the thing causing me all the mental distress: Christianity! That's not prescriptive, and I'm not promising that will happen to others, but it for sure happened in my case. I was taking my play-world way too seriously.

Pascaline reasoning can also be applied to contradictory beliefs. Is it better to believe we're reincarnated because it makes us act more ethically? Is it better to believe all trees have spirits so we will appreciate nature? Is it better to believe my kids are perfect so I can feel like a confident parent? The lesson of the book for believers seems to be this:

---

[43] Emphasis mine; comment available at: http://worldsthewoodworlds.blog-spot.com/2011/12/puddleglums-speech.html

[44] J. T. Moore & M. M. Leach, 2016. "Dogmatism and mental health: A comparison of the religious and secular," *Psychology of Religion and Spirituality*, 8(1): 54-64.

Forget what's true. Stick with wishful thinking. Only then can we have purpose, however inflated or false.

In the end, there's only one life we know for sure we have. Wasting it then would be an immense and immeasurable loss. The deities we imagine seem to only be as powerful as our imaginations, and only as real as we allow them to be.

The Silver Chair: Chapters 13-16

"Dying is good if you do it for Aslan because then you can live in his land."
"I wonder why he makes you suffer and die to get there."
"Aslan isn't nice so you have to do what he says or he'll be mean to you."
"Is that someone you'd want to live with forever?"
"Once I got to his land, I'd run far away from him!"
"Way to work the system."

***

Where did we leave off last bedtime? Oh yeah. Ding dong! The witch is dead and the party is standing around her gory mess drinking. They bandaged up Puddleglum's burnt foot with butter (don't do that) and planned their escape from the underground castle while chaos erupted outside. The witch's death broke the spells that controlled this place. Suddenly a chasm appeared under the earth and the underground sea started rising to drown the city. The city itself, which was once silent, is now loud and panicked. Despite everything going on, people are making time to set off fireworks. Lewis wants to convey an air of celebration that doesn't really seem to fit with the expediency of the situation.

Hearing the blasts and assuming there is some sort of battle happening, Prince Rilian takes his shield for battle and notices that it has magically gained the image of the lion on it. He proclaims, "This signifies that Aslan will be our good lord, whether he means us to live or die." Sorry, you don't get to be known as a "good" lord if you are all-powerful yet make someone die in your name. That pretty much makes the word "good" meaningless.

They all sycophantically kiss the image on the shield and say goodbye to each other *once again* expecting to die for their lion. Jill and Eustace use each other's "Christian names" at this point even though "one didn't do it at school" to make the whole sacrifice thing more religious. They also probably weren't told to die for Jesus at school, either. What a terrible institution.

On the way out of the noisy city, Rilian orders the boys to catch one of the Earthmen to question him. Jill thinks stopping to snatch a person from a hostile group is a bad idea, and she's not wrong. She is, however, a powerless girl whose opinion holds no weight.

> "Then, Madam, you shall see us die fighting around you, and you must commend yourself to the Lion."

In other words, who cares if it's a bad plan and everyone dies. I'm in charge and there's nothing you can do about it. Bonus! Dying for our lion god is a great option!

I'm getting sick of how death is presented as this honorable thing if it's in a prince's or lion's service. Dying for others can be heroic but dying for a master is a much darker business. It comes down to a matter of choice and freedom and consent. I don't like stories where dying for a master's interests is not only acceptable, but also expected.

Puddleglum slips into the dark alley to catch a random Earthman. This completely random Earthman will only be around for a few minutes and is just a plot device so our heroes can learn some information. He is not important. He is not around long. He is just some guy. Some random guy!

SO OF COURSE HE GETS A NAME!

The Earthman's name (which no one cares about) is Golg (dumb). This name is so obviously half-assed. Why couldn't Lewis put half that effort into the main villain? It's not hard! Golg could have been the witch's name for all I care! WOMEN ARE PEOPLE. (*Must breathe. Breathing now.*)

Stupid Golg (sorry, Golg, it's not your fault) learns that Rilian killed the witch so just like that, in a *Wizard of Oz*-type twist, the witch's minions are now all on the side of our party. They had been enchanted this whole time and are now free. The fireworks going off is them celebrating that fact. Learning this makes Rilian finally stop pointing his sword at the poor Earthman's neck. Such a great guy, this Rilian. (He did have a father keen on battle axing people.)

The Earthmen are also all rushing towards the red glow of the chasm that opened up since it's an entrance to their home, a lower world called Bism. Golg (who gets a name because he's *not* a woman) jumped down there and was gone. (Bye forever Golg, we hardly knew you. *We knew your name though.*) Eventually the opening to Bism sealed itself shut. That is the entire story of Golg, who got a name for being a dude.

The party follows the green lamps that led to the part of the overworld the witch was going to conquer. (Spoiler: It's Narnia.) The flood waters followed them close behind, but they began to climb high above it. Jill briefly wonders about Father Time and the dragon-looking creatures sleeping in the caves until the end of the world and is assured they are probably fine. (So random.) Jill then screams when she notices the lamps going out because that's what girls do. This prompted Rilian to say, "Courage, friends. Whether we live or die Aslan will be our good lord." So that's a super comforting and completely helpful thing to say.

Thankfully they were very near the surface at this point. Coming to some soft earth above their heads, they lifted Jill up to the opening. Some Narnians having a party noticed her and helped her out. The same kind folks tried to dig out Eustace, but he responded by shoving a sword in their faces until they could explain who they were and what they were doing. Boys and their violence, right? Finally, Puddleglum and their prince emerged to everyone's excitement.

Rilian told them the story of the wicked witch who was "doubtless the same kind as that White Witch who had brought the Great Winter on Narnia long ago" and her plan to use him to rule his own kingdom.

> "And the lesson of it all is, your Highness, that those Northern Witches always mean the same thing, but in every age they have a different plan for getting it."

The moral of our story is that evil women always want power when they should instead be submissive. Witches take after the headstrong Lilith, but Daughters of Eve know it is better to leave the power to men.

Eve's first and only act of recorded agency had monstrous consequences. As part of her punishment, Elohim tells her that childbirth will now be painful and that her husband will "rule over" her.[45] This curse was, in essence, further loss of agency. She had no control over her body and the results of what Adam did with it would cause her excruciating pain nine months later.

Eve's rough treatment is why religious men throughout the centuries have felt justified in denying women's rights. Women must be subjugated; this command comes directly from their god,

---

[45] Genesis 3:16

conveniently written down, taught, and enforced by men. (It's not like women were allowed to teach.[46])

Christian theologian John Calvin had many thoughts on Eve and none of them included an acknowledgement that she was a person in her own right:

> "Thus the woman, who had **perversely exceeded her proper bounds**, is forced back to **her own position**… she is cast into **servitude**."[47]

There is no evidence that Eve was more than a story device, but for the believers who think she was a real person, her story has been used to malign the character of all women and validate their subjugation. John Wesley, founder of the Methodist movement, once said to his wife that she should be content to be an "insignificant person."[48] He believed that the role of a wife was to silently do all the work while the husband was given all the praise and power—things he specifically told her not to desire. Their marriage was unsurprisingly a painful and unpleasant one.

This is the context for why every witch in every age wants "the same thing." Notice how Narnia is always ruled by a king, never a queen. If Narnia has a queen, which it often does, the queen never rules and is instead subordinate to her husband or brother (even if he's younger). Even our Lady of the Green Snake Dress knew this; that's why she needed Rilian. In Lewis' world you always need a man to rule. The Eves will be good because they will give up their power. The Liliths will be bad because they will claim it.

---

[46] 1 Timothy 2:12

[47] Emphasis mine; Michael Parsons, 2005. *Reformation Marriage: The Husband and Wife Relationship in the Theology of Luther and Calvin*, (Eugene, OR: Wipf and Stock Publishers), p. 328.

[48] Henry Hupfeld, 1877. *Encyclopedia of Wit and Wisdom: A Collection of Over Nice Thousand Anecdotes, and Illustrations of Life, Character, Humor, and Pathos*, (Philadelphia, PA: David McKay Publisher).

After this discussion about witches, Rilian leaves to greet his father, King Werewolf Caspian, who had been tipped off by Aslan to return to Narnia and see his son. Caspian dies in his son's arms seconds after getting off his ship. Aslan couldn't be bothered to tell him to leave earlier.

While Rilian starts crying and grieving his father's loss, Aslan decides the adventure is over and takes Eustace and Jill back to the afterlife, compounding Rilian's loss. Not to worry, Caspian is there when the kids get back. I mean, he's lying there dead, but he *is* there. In order to wake him up, and this is weird, Aslan asks Eustace to stab him in his paw. Eustace doesn't want to, but Aslan makes him and the blood that comes out wakes Caspian up. I know this is an allusion to the cross and how Christians need to be figuratively covered in Jesus' blood, but ew?

Eustace and Jill haven't died yet and can't stay there so they are sent back to school with weapons! To beat children! The end!

And that is the story of *The Silver Chair*. What exactly is the chair? Where did it come from? Maybe Lewis should have named the book *The Stupid Signs* instead.

Bitsy was right. We should have just read the horsey book.

6
Racism and His Boy

The Horse and His Boy: Chapter 1

"His name is Sheesh? Really?"

"No, *Arsheesh.*"

"Sounds like 'ah sheesh.'"

"Maybe his father was Yikes and his aunt was Jeez Louise."

"I can tell you're joking because women don't usually get names."

"*Jeez Louise!*"

"Are you still laughing at your own joke, Mom?"

***

Welcome to Calormen, a country of *colored men,* and the evilest place on the whole flat planet! This is the setting of *A Horse and His Boy,* colloquially known as "the horsey book" by the local ten-year old. In this fictional land, Lewis will present a jaw-dropping stereotype-ridden downright offensive view of Middle Eastern people. Oh boy!

Calormen is located to the south of Narnia and is home to villages of men (possibly also women) with dark faces, dirty robes, long beards (maybe not the women), turbans, and shoes turned up at the toe— pretty much the entire cast of Disney's Aladdin, minus any redeeming qualities. Buckle up for explaining good old fashion orientalism to your children while our author from the West depicts the East in the most patronizing way possible. It's only a fictional country, as any

Narnia apologist will tell you, so we can claim total incapability! What fun!

Seriously, there's so much explicit racism in this little book that even my White middle-aged self, who is probably missing half of it, is horrified. We are clearly supposed to know these Calormene people are the enemy from their opening physical descriptions before they are even specifically described as greedy wicked liars.

There might be a Mark of Cain connection to the evil people of Calormen. Just as so many of Lewis' themes and plot points for this series come from Genesis, so also does the Mark of Cain myth. If only the Eden story had ended when a woman ruins the world, but no, Adam and Eve go on to have a couple children. One of which, Cain, murders the other one, Abel. Then God is like, "Whoa, what the... what's going on? Where's Abel? What happened?"[1] Which is how any deity would react this early in the ancient tales before he is retroactively given superpowers like omniscience. God figures out what happened to Abel when Abel's magic blood tells him. He responds by putting some sort of undescribed physical mark on Cain. Some say this mark was a Hebrew word, which makes sense considering Cain is the Son of Adam, a mud golem formed of the dust of the earth. In Hebrew mythology, golems have three letters written on their forehead: *aleph*, *mem*, and *tav*, that spell out the word "truth." If someone were to erase aleph, the letters would spell out the word for death, and the creature would die. Refusing to accept this lore, some believers instead embrace a belief that Cains' mark is Black skin—an idea particularly popularized during the American slave trade by White Christians.

The Church of Jesus Christ of Latter-Day Saints has a history of not allowing Black men into the priesthood. (Women, as yet, are not even up for consideration.) Its founders, Joseph Smith and Brigham

---

[1] Genesis 4:8-10 (paraphrased)

Young, held the belief that the Mark of Cain was Black skin, and ascribed many negative attributes to it. Black skin was a curse from God, like we see in The Book of Mormon where people who hardened their hearts against God had their "white, and exceedingly fair and delightsome" skin changed to a "skin of blackness"[2] which God didn't find so, er, delightsome. Even after the restrictions of Black men were lifted in 1978, the idea that Black skin was a curse was not officially contradicted until freaking 2013!

On the non-Christian side of Abrahamic faith, we have a Hadith of Islam[3] which states that those who reject faith after accepting it will be given black faces and go to torment in Hell while those who keep the faith go to Allah's Mercy and are given white faces. Now maybe I'm interpreting those verses wrong, and there are certainly enough motivated people to argue that point, but when I read about black faces going to Hell and white faces being delightsome, I thought *is that really not racist?* Really? And Occam's Razor is just a tool in the shaving kit of a guy named Occam.

Researchers Deborah L. Hall, David C. Matz, and Wendy Wood have done a meta-analysis of fifty-five major studies on racism and found a very strong and undeniable link between racism and religion.[4] Of the over twenty thousand participants of these studies, the majority were Christians. In the authors' conclusion they confirmed, "Only religious agnostics were racially tolerant."

Maybe young readers should hold an agnostic's hand before continuing this story.

The bulk of *A Horse and His Boy* may take place in Calormen, but over in Narnia it is the "Golden Age" when Peter is high king and the

---

[2] 2 Nephi 5:21

[3] Surah Ale-Imran, verses 106-107.

[4] Deborah L Hall, David C Matz, Wendy Wood, 2010. "Why Don't We Practice What We Preach?: A Meta-Analytic Review of Religious Racism," *Personality and Social Psychology Review*, 14(1): 126–139. doi: 10.1177/1088868309352179

other three Pevensie children are kings and queens in Cair Paravel. If we were reading in chronological order, this tale would follow *The Lion, The Witch and The Wardrobe*, but of course we are a publication order family **as the Good Lord intended**.

The story opens with its protagonist, a boy named Shasta, living with a cruel father named Arsheesh. *That sounds Middle Eastern-y enough*, thought Lewis. The name does not have any cultural origins or etymological meaning and seems to be chosen at random. Although, I did find a disturbing naming site online that listed "Tisroc" and "Tarkaan" among related baby names to Arsheesh. If ever I am judging my decisions as a mother, it will be helpful to know there might be a little Tarkaan, named after a Calormen lord in a racially problematic book, running around out there. My own parenting choices won't seem too far outside the bell curve by comparison.

I couldn't remember this book as well as the others and started to get excited that at least this setting would mean our main character would be a boy of color. Then I remembered what I was reading. The main character will be White and a kidnap victim from a civilized (read: White) kingdom to boot.

One day a Tarkaan demanded to stay the night with Shasta and his father while on a journey. Shasta overhears the Tarkaan offer his father money to make Shasta a slave. In trying to get a higher price for the boy, Arsheesh attempts to convince the Tarkaan that his only son is very valuable to him. The Tarkaan sees right through this (emphasis mine):

> "This boy is manifestly no son of yours, for your cheek is as black as mine but the boy is fair and white like the accursed **but beautiful** barbarians who inhabit the remote North."

We hate those gorgeous, super attractive White people! Gosh darn their accursed delightsome faces!

A White man wrote words into the mouth of a Black man about how White people are more attractive. Yikes. This kind of thing has some icky consequences, like we see in the Doll Test[5] where children were asked which of two dolls, one Black and one White, they thought was the pretty one. The majority of both Black and White children pointed to the White doll. When asked which doll was the good one, the same children pointed to the White doll again. When asked which one was the bad one, the majority of both Black and White children pointed to the Black doll. It was heartbreaking to watch Black mothers break down in tears knowing their words of beauty and worth over their own children were not penetrating through society's destructive messaging.

Shortly after signing up to be a foster parent of kids with disabilities, the foster system dropped off an eight-year-old at my door. I had tons of experience with her wheelchair, casts, splints, and braces, but none with her long afro. At the salon while learning to do twists, a man I didn't know pulled me aside to tell me how important it was to tell this girl how beautiful she was. "Nah, you gotta do it," he emphasized after hearing how I didn't like to focus on my girls' physical appearance, "She's different than y'all White kids. She might not feel it. You gotta tell her because she'll believe you."

Lewis wrote in his diary in the late 1920's that three groups he disliked, "Women, Indians, and Americans," were coming to Oxford and that "one feels a certain amateurishness in the talk and look of the people."[6]

Our author clearly has some issues.

Maybe the racism present in Lewis' work up until this point has been something those of us not affected by it didn't think was so bad.

---

[5] Get tissues ready: https://www.youtube.com/watch?v=tkpUyB2xgTM
[6] David C. Downing, 1992. *Planets in Peril: A Critical Study of C.S. Lewis's Ransom Trilogy*, (University of Massachusetts Press), p. 151.

Sure, characters with Black features like Nikabrik were evil, but that was just code for something "dark." See? Innocent enough. Entire races of creatures are bad simply for being born into that breed, but it's a magic world after all.

It's easy to be dismissive of racist things when it makes us uncomfortable. However, it shouldn't have to get to the point of the N-word or a book about an entire country of colored men with evil hearts to take it seriously.

Some of my friends say they come across many racist actions that White folks dismiss because these actions haven't crossed some impossible line, like being done while wearing KKK robes and setting a cross on fire. Broad, negative generalizations about people of color like telling someone they speak "well for a Black person," following someone around in a store, assumptions about someone's home life or number of children or welfare status, arguing *those* people should move out of *our* country, and jokes that spread stereotypes are all legitimate forms of racism. Brushing this stuff off as minor assumes incorrectly that these things don't have a cumulative effect. News stories abound of property damage being grieved more than the oppression and devaluation of Black lives; Black-sounding names are being rejected[7] at much higher rates than other names on job applications; communities are being destroyed by our ridiculous incarceration rate of Black people which is higher than at the height of apartheid in South Africa;[8] and Black girls are being punished by their schools more than White girls[9] for the same offenses, which I saw firsthand working at a school

---

[7] David R. Francis. "Employers Replies to Racial Names," *The National Bureau of Economic Research*, (Digest Cambridge, MA). Available at: https://www.nber.org/digest/sep03/w9873.html

[8] Keith O. Lawrence ed., 2011. *Race, Crime, and Punishment: Breaking the Connection in America*, (Washington D.C., The Aspen Institute).

[9] Data from The Office of Civil Rights at the US Department of Education reported by The New York Times in 2014: https://tinyurl.com/y5mtm7d3

in Texas and again when fostering. Glad all this discrimination is completely random and not at all due to racism because I don't see any guys in white sheets setting fires, do you?

We didn't grow up loving these stories because of the racism, but we sure as hell are not going to ignore those aspects now!

**

Shasta overhears his father admit he is not the boy's biological parent during this conversation with the Tarkaan. Lewis mentions that eavesdropping was wrong, but that Shasta "had never learned that" because he lived with evil people in an evil country. This sin of overhearing adults will come up repeatedly in this book and it reminds me of my childhood where grown-ups were granted the right to privacy whereas children were not.

Shasta is immediately relieved he has no biological connection to Arsheesh because he never loved the man. Granted, the father is a bad dude who comes from a land of bad dudes, but honestly the boy never loved him? The story may be attempting to give our main character the attribute of goodness by saying he would never love anything evil, similar to the biblical mandate to not love the things of this world,[10] but in actuality it means our hero has major attachment issues.

Eventually Shasta leaves the men to argue over his price while he visits the stables. As he pets the Tarkaan's horse, he wonders what his new master might be like. He talks aloud about how he wishes the horse could tell him. The horse, in turn, speaks back! It's a Narnian horse named Breehy-hinny-brinny-hoohy-hah. This name is meant for the readers to ridicule, so Shasta renames him Bree because screw his real name. (At least he has a name.) Turns out Bree was also

---

[10] 1 John 2:15

kidnapped by those evil Calormene jerks. He informs Shasta that the Tarkaan is (*fake shocked gasp*) *terrible* and the young man would be better off dead than a slave to such a person. Then the two agree to run away together—out of this evil country, away from these evil people, and onto righteous (White) Narnia.

The Horse and His Boy: Chapters 2-3

"If war means killing people, why would anyone *want* to do it?"
"Maybe to defend their land or lives."
"Okay, but why look forward to it?"
"Warriors get honor and glory out of killing in battle. It shows how strong they are."
"That shouldn't get you honor and glory."
"I know."
"Grownups are wrong about a lot of things."
"Probably."

***

Bree and Shasta decided stealing the Tarkaan's money as well as wine for young Shasta was fine since it was "booty" and "spoil." Bree even called it "raiding" instead of stealing to drive home this point. They established that Calormen was the enemy and anything done to the enemy by the good guys was okay. The Christian Scriptures often encourage stealing land, livestock, and even women and children[11] from other people whom their god deems wicked. I'm fine with Shasta stealing supplies in his escape, but it's funny to me how Lewis must twist

---

[11] Numbers 31:30, Deuteronomy 2:35, Psalm 135:12, Judges 6:9, Exodus 33:1, Deuteronomy 10:11, Joshua 1:6, Nehemiah 9:8, etc. etc. etc.

himself into knots to explain away what he would otherwise condemn as bad behavior.

War is an element of these stories I took for granted as a child, but now I see its veneration as disturbing. This is the "Golden Age" of Narnia where it will never get better, yet wars are everywhere. What does that say about the Christian view of peace? Even in the last book of the Bible when Jesus finally saves his followers and gives them peace, he comes with a sword for a tongue[12] and death and destruction in his wake.[13] This is the future I was taught to crave as a child. How awful it tastes to me now.

Bree was a warhorse, and fought in Calormene wars, but he longed to go to Narnia where there would be peace under Aslan. No, I'm kidding. He *longed* for Narnian wars! That's literally his entire motivation for leaving.

> "Give me the Narnian wars where I shall fight as a free Horse among my own people! Those will be wars worth talking about."

The pair traveled for "weeks and weeks" until one day they heard a snarling and "utterly savage" roar. They ran for their lives while the lion gave chase. Then a second lion appeared on their other side forcing them to a specific spot. Another horse and rider were also being herded by the lions until Shasta and Bree were galloping alongside the new horse and rider. When the two horses tried to put distance between each other "two more lions' roars" on either side of them drove them back together. This is, what? Three lions now? Four? A million? Just lions everywhere. It was lousy with lions. The horses dove into an inlet of water out of desperation and the "shaggy and terrible" lion (just one now) finally stopped following.

---

[12] Revelation 19:15
[13] Revelation 12:7-17

They were terrified they would die and be eaten, so that's our clue, after reading enough of these books, that all of this was due to one "terrible" and supernaturally fast lion named Aslan. He was just being a dick per usual. I'm sure there was no other conceivable way to get these two riders and horses together without scaring the shit out of them.

Shasta noticed the other rider was slender and "he had no beard," but when they got out of the water and he was afforded a better look at the rider, Shasta sees, "Why, it's only a girl!" Notice the immediate downplay of this new character. This girl, Aravis, was very rude, defensive, and indecent (read: out in public while female). She particularly dislikes Shasta and he responds by sulking. So naturally they'll get married later.

One thing I've realized while reading through this book for a second time is that there's no mention of Aravis having dark skin. We know she must since she's not only from Calormen, but from a long line of Calormene patriarchs. In fact, she's a true Calormene with all the greed, pride, lying by embellishment, looking down on others, talking too much while female, and other personal failings Calormene folks have. Her figure is remarked upon (slender), and her face (smooth), but not her skin color. I remember reading about her as a child and assuming she looked like me because it was not clear she didn't. Maybe Lewis avoided a description of her skin color to make her more appealing to his White audience? Maybe her skin color would have said something evil about her character, in keeping with the rest of the series, so he just left it out of her opening descriptions?

For those playing at home: This is called r-a-c-i-s-m. Despite the blatant tokenism, Aravis is regularly used as a counterexample when discussing Lewis' racism. Lewis can't possibly be saying the entire country is bad *because there is that one girl!* Let's not forget she must reject her entire country in an ethnocentric show of solidarity with a White country in order to qualify as good.

The horse Aravis is riding, Hwin, is also a Talking Horse from Narnia and had been kidnapped like Bree was. It's assumed she hid her talking abilities as well. Her journey is largely ignored and not given the same focus as Bree's. The important thing is she's a girl horse so our girl character won't be scandalously riding a boy horse.

Aravis is fleeing a forced marriage set up by her evil stepmother. This is doubly gross because she's not yet hit puberty.

> "You're not grown up. I don't believe you're any older than I am. I don't believe you're as old."

Since Shasta is currently fourteen it's assumed Aravis is thirteen or younger. This means she is still a child and she's being given in marriage, in a children's book, to a man in his sixties. So what does she do? Well this *is* a children's book after all so she naturally goes to kill herself after the engagement is announced. Thankfully Hwin saves her by agreeing to run away to Narnia with her.

Aravis had a plan to get away while going to make sacrifices that were customary of brides. Calormen is so backwards that they were all about killing animals for the god Tash. (Didn't they know they *should have* been doing sacrifices to the god Yahweh instead?[14]) During the sacrificing trip, Aravis drugged the maidservant who was with her and ran. It was a good plan and it worked, but girls are not afforded the same excuse as boys of getting away with things done to the enemy while fleeing for their lives. Shasta self-righteously and rather hypocritically points out Aravis' maidservant would surely be beaten for falling asleep on the job. He accuses her of being selfish even though her actions mirror his own: Aravis flees to avoid sexual slavery, leaving her maidservant to maybe be punished. She takes her own horse with

---

[14] Hebrews 13:11-13

160

her. Shasta flees to avoid slavery leaving his father to be punished or killed by a violent Tarkaan. He stole the Tarkaan's horse to do so.

Avaris is portrayed as having sinned and later severely punished for it by Aslan. He mauls her for it. Shasta avoids any consequence whatsoever and his behavior is considered completely understandable. Aslan rewards him for it.

Could the difference in response be, oh I don't know, because one is, to quote Shasta, "*only* a girl"?

To make this story triply gross (if that's possible), Aravis also had a letter written up pretending to be from her father's brother. In it, her biological uncle supposedly says he grabbed his niece in the woods and forced himself on her. Apparently, this kind of incestual kidnap marriage is normal for Calormen (and children's books). Aravis hopes anyone looking for her will go to her uncle's house that's in the opposite direction and it will buy her some more time to get out of the country. Kidnapping children! Raping girls and forcing them into marriage! What kind of book is this? The Bible?!

Anyway, the new party of four decide to flee to Narnia together. There is only one last Calormene city in their way: Tashbaan. After that is a stretch of desert leading to the country of Archenland in the mountains. Get it? Land of mountain arches! ARCHenland. Remember the last book where there was a land of giants? It was named Ettinmoor, which is literally Ettin's[15] moor. Lewis was just in the shower one day thinking, "This land has arches! This land has giants! This land has colored people!"

Archenland will be important later because it's a nation of civilized (read: White) people. When Bree was proving Shasta was *trustworthy* he said our hero was "certainly either a Narnian or an Archenlander"

---

[15] Ettin is another word for giant.

because of his skin color. White equated to trustworthy, and one's nationality was a legit defense of one's character.

Waiting for them in Tashbaan will be some very familiar characters from *The Lion, The Witch and the Wardrobe*.

The Horse and His Boy: Chapters 4-5

"What's a litter?"
"It's like a bench that people carry you around on."
"Can I have one instead of my wheelchair?"
"No."
"Please?"
"No."
"Please!"
"No."
"..."
"..."
"And you and Daddy could carry me around on it!"
"No!"

***

Tashbaan is the most beautiful city and its pure grandeur is described in such relish detail it feels almost real. Shasta can't stop looking at it. Before the reader can fall too deeply in love with the place, we enter its gates and are met with the strong smell of bodily odor and piles of dung. Christian Scripture talks of unbelieving people being seemingly wonderful on the outside but full of rotting death on the inside like a beautiful tomb over a corpse.[16] Similarly, Calormen can be lovely, but must contain filth within it.

Aravis has been told she must act like someone who has been "kicked and cuffed and called names" all her life instead of the Tarkeena she really is. It is to blend in among the crowds who would live in such a city. As they go, Shasta gets a stolen carrot thrown at him by soldiers and a punch in the face when he doesn't react in humility.

Lewis spends a bit of ink making sure readers who might have been enchanted with the opening description of Tashbaan learn how its heart is horrible and violent. I've been inside the British Museum and know how taken the West is with the wonders of the East. I've also read the museum's pamphlet regarding whether they should return all the stuff they stole as an imperialist superpower, to which their answer is basically "lol nope."[17] The ugly message behind the pamphlet's words is that the East is inferior. They may not care for their things properly like we will. They are barbaric.

Along the main street are huge statues of the gods and heroes of Calormen, which Lewis describes as "mostly impressive rather than agreeable to look at." If it were only the gods this statement referred to, and this was an isolated negative statement on Calormene looks, we could blame the comment on the gods' possible inhuman characteristics. But it was also about the people, and not just any people, but the best of Calormen. This is a repeat lesson to young readers that dark-skinned people are not pleasing to look at.

In the city streets, crowds had to part whenever an important person went by carried on a litter by slaves. A crier would yell "Way, way, way!" and everyone else knew to press up against the sides of the street.

---

[16] Matthew 23:27, and I wondered why so many believers didn't treat me like a good person after deconverting.
[17] British Museum, London, UK. The pamphlet in question was specifically about Greece's Parthenon, but the arguments could be applied more broadly to their other collections. Read on September 15, 2019.

Well, this happened for a group of important White people from Narnia. The crier himself points out the group's whiteness for extra emphasis of their importance. Lewis piles on descriptions of their fair skin and fair hair and how much better they were than the Calormene officials the crowds have previously made way for. Unlike the Tarkaans, these fair lords had a swing in their step and were talking, laughing, and one was even whistling. It's clear they are not only much better, but much friendlier than the locals. They were also decked out in fancy clothes and jewels. Jewels and fancy clothes are always implied to be the height of arrogant vanity when a Calormene does it. For this group, however, it's tasteful. Hmm, I wonder what the difference is?

Shasta "had never seen anything so lovely in his life." White people are just the prettiest, Lewis. Delightsome even. We get it. Calm down.

In another example of It's Fine When the White People Do It, one of these pretty pretty lords, the king in fact, suddenly grabs Shasta by the shoulder and hits him! Seriously! Shasta is just a punching bag today. But wait! Narnians don't just hit people like evil soldiers do! So to make it clear that this kind of hitting is done by good guys (so it's good) and the other kind of hitting was done by the bad guys (so it's bad) Lewis adds, "a smack—not a cruel one to make you cry but a sharp one to let you know you are in disgrace." See? All better now. Moving on.

The king and another lord held Shasta "very tightly by both hands" and forced him to go back with them to their rooms. This king berates Shasta the whole time they walk. He drills him with questions and when Shasta won't say anything the king denounces his behavior as that of a Calormene slave. Which begs the question, are slaves bad guys? Or just acting like one is wrong?

Shasta feels this whole experience is "very unpleasant" but only because, get this, he wished he could make a better impression on the king who he could tell was "the nicest kind of grown-up." *What?!* Okay the only impression this king has thus far left is one of a man who grabs, hits, yanks, and berates young teens. But he's the nicest?! How?! In what world? Well, besides a world where children deserve to be hit, have no bodily autonomy, and everything is permitted with the right skin tone. So, a world like the church I grew up in I suppose.

The king is King Edmund—yes, *that* Edmund—and it turns out Shasta bears a striking (heh) resemblance to Prince Corin of Archenland, who Edmund is supposed to be watching. Corin ran away last night to get into brawls while Queen Susan (yep, *that* Susan) has been up crying all night over his disappearance. Which, backing up a bit, is in direct contrast to how the king and lords were acting in their introduction mere moments ago, swinging their arms and laughing. The entire scene was meant as a comparison to how the important Calormenes would go through town "grave and mysterious" so we are meant to think the Narnians are better people. Knowing what we know now, that a prince had run away and the queen had been crying all night, means these guys walked around happily—"One was whistling"—and didn't give a flying fig for their missing child.

Once back in their royal rooms everyone starts grilling Shasta to figure out where he had been. It's only when Tumnus (yes, *that* Tumnus) points out that Shasta looks sunburnt and is probably dazed from dehydration that they stop questioning him and have him lie down and eat some sherbet to cool off. Here he listens in on the conversation between Edmund and Susan after, of course, mentally noting how the White people in the room "had nicer faces and voices than most Calormenes" because **we hadn't had enough of that yet.**

Edmund starts in on his sister who has been up crying all night.

"Have you yet settled in your mind whether you will marry this dark-faced lover of yours, this Prince Rabadash, or no?"

The Calormen prince literally has the word "bad" in his freaking name! Also, we are clearly pointing out his skin color and it's dark so that's clear foreshadowing that he's no good.

> Susan says no. Edmund is relieved and tips his hand of conditional love.
> "I should have loved you the less if you had taken him... it was a wonder to me that ever you could find it in your heart to show him so much favour."
> "That was my folly, Edmund, of which I cry you mercy."

Susan feels the need to apologize for her inferior love interest. Turns out she had fallen for Baddy, the nick name Bitsy and I have given Rabadash, when he had won some war games in Narnia. (When they're not in an actual war they are playing war games.) Now that they were on the prince's home turf, he showed his true colors: "a most proud, bloody, luxurious, cruel, and self-pleasing tyrant." So, you know, a regular Calormene then. However, everyone agreed Baddy was perfectly nice and kind at the time he visited Narnia which means Edmund's clear revulsion for the prince from the beginning had nothing to do with the prince's actual, not-yet-revealed character. Hmm, I WONDER WHAT IT WAS THEN.

It's likely that Lewis is doing his own version of the Black Peril—that baseless fear that Black men would be unnaturally attracted to White women and cause all kinds of problems. During the times of British colonialism of India and Africa, Black Peril fears were an excuse for White men to take violent or criminal actions against men of color.[18] Lewis could use this inherent bias to portray Rabadash as the worst of humanity, giving our heroes a villain to defeat and a damsel to save. It will also excuse our White saviors' actions which would

---

[18] Diana Jeater, 2002. "Review of Rhodesia Black Peril, White Virtue. Sexual Crime in Southern Rhodesia, 1902-1935 by Jock McCulloch," *Journal of South African Studies*, 28(2): 465. Available at: https://www.jstor.org/stable/823397

otherwise be considered sin—all the lying, stealing, and so forth—similar to Shasta's actions when fleeing the Tarkaan.

We later learn that Edmund's question for Susan was not sincere. It was a test. He asked if she was marrying this guy knowing full well he was going to imprison them all and rape Susan if she said no. Edmund didn't think to tell Susan this until after she'd told him her heart. Repeatedly in these books it's assumed that girls' empty little heads will just explode with worry if told actual information about their own circumstances. Like, *maybe* the whole Baddy-will-take-you-by-force-if-you-say-no thing was some pertinent information Susan should have known in order to make an informed decision! But *noooooo*. No one in her present company seems to think she needed to know this stuff. It was not just Edmund; they *all* knew. They all *knew*. Freaking Tumnus even got wind of this from the Grand Vizier. No one told her.

I was surprised at how gross our redeemed hero, Edmund, truly was. He was making "some light common jests" about women with the Calormen prince when the prince became "angry and dangerous" and "threatening." BUT THEY STILL DIDN'T TELL SUSAN THIS. Did I mention Susan is older than Edmund? She defers to him in everything because he's male even though not too long ago she was a mom to him as their own mother was dealing with WWII. This is just a plain ugly view of women as dependent, subordinate, and stupid.

The Narnians saw no other option but to flee Calormen. Goodness, every single character has this same goal now. The royal party hatches a plan to pretend to invite the prince to their ship for a grand meal. They'll go all out and buy food and hire dancing girls (do boys not dance?) and even pretend to accept Baddy's proposal. This is cover for them stockpiling their ship so they can sail away in the middle of the night before the prince arrives.

They also mention the fastest way through the desert when thinking of plans—information that will come in handy for Shasta later. Yay for eavesdropping! Even though this book repeatedly implies it's a sin!

Shasta must keep his mouth shut for fear they'll kill him now that he knows what they're up to. Yep, the "nicest kind of grown-up" is still probably all murder-y. After being served wine and being told he'll begin war training on his next birthday, Shasta falls asleep, dreaming, I'm sure, of drinking and killing.

A few hours later when Shasta is alone in the room, the real Prince Corin crashes in through the window. Where has he been? Oh, Corin has just been beating up (I assume Black) boys for Susan's honor. His behavior is not only given a pass; it's considered the only right course of action! He beat up the kid who said something about Queen Susan and even beat up that kid's brother who hadn't said anything. The young prince got caught by some guards who then beat *him* up. Then he got the guards drunk and snuck out. On his way back to his spoiled rich boy suite he stopped to beat up the original boy a second time just for the heck of it. Sweet kid, this Prince Corin, but he's the good guy. I mean, he doesn't even have the word "bad" in his name, and all his actions are excused as virtuous for defending a silly woman. The fact that these young people of color suffered violence simply for speaking is of no consequence to our main characters.

Shasta and Prince Corin look exactly alike. Spoiler: they're twins. Shasta informs Corin that he was brought up in Calormen but must really be from the north and was escaping to Narnia with a Talking Horse. Corin didn't for a minute ever think of getting an adult or trying to save a horse that was clearly Narnian by way of the ship everyone was leaving on. Oh no, that would be a boring, short story. Aslan wouldn't get the chance to torture anyone in the desert yet. Can't have that. Better help your look-alike escape out a window into the night instead.

Seriously, that's how it should have ended. Right there.

The Horse and His Boy: Chapters 6-8

"I know all about marriage."
"Oh really? Enlighten me."
"Well you hug and kiss a lot, and you fight over the thermostat and hide the video game controllers."
"That's actually pretty accurate."
"No one should be forced to do those things. That would be wrong."
"You're right. Someone should always have the right to choose to enter a relationship, especially one that requires bogarting video game controllers."

***

Shasta is alone. He makes it out of Tashbaan and to the tombs bordering the desert but no one is waiting for him there like they should be. He's forced to stay the night by himself in the spookiest place he can imagine and hope his friends make it out of the city to join him. His fear is heightened by the growing darkness and a belief in ghouls. In these books everyone seems to be seriously afraid of ghouls while Lewis continually maintains that out of all the fantastic things in his pretend world, ghouls are the one obviously *not real* thing. Nymphs and dryads are totes for real, so are giants, mermaids, and underground monsters, but ghosts are silly made-up nonsense. This is probably only funny to me because I was taught that people who believed in ghosts were ignorant. Demons, though, were for *sure* real. There are quite a few people who have irrational fears of devils, demons, and Hell, yet the people responsible for teaching them such things, if they are anything like the ones I know, may strongly maintain that it's ghost stories that harm children.

Fear has real consequences on the brain and body. My son, Bitsy's bitty brother, has a history of trauma. In the first five years after joining our family through adoption he still had nightmares that rocked his world. The most random things have triggered him, putting him mentally into the dark world he came from, and this affects him physically. During the times my son is afraid, it's my job to minimize his fear and bring down his cortisol levels. This is not the time to test him or teach him a lesson. That's why when Aslan, established as our Jesus deity, pulls the next few stunts to an isolated and terrified child, it makes my blood boil.

At the height of his fear, Shasta feels something touch his leg. He is so terrified he freezes, but it just turns out to be a cat. It would only be a horribly bad cat if the cat had any awareness of scaring the poor lonely child. Spoiler: It's Aslan. And he knows.

Shasta asks if the cat is a Talking Cat to which Aslan flat out refuses to talk to him. Shasta goes to sleep by lying down next to the cat, but the cat abandons him when he is woken up by jackals coming to eat him. To get some idea how terrifying the ghouls were to Shasta, he chooses to face wild predators rather than hide anywhere near the tombs. The jackals get closer and closer until a lion appears and roars so loudly the sound shakes the sand. This would scare Shasta as well, who had just run for his life from lions earlier. Then the lion shrinks back down into the cat which gaslights Shasta into thinking he's crazy.

Not only is Shasta being terrified when there were at least a thousand ways Aslan could have avoided this—talking to Shasta, letting Shasta know he was approaching, staying with Shasta the whole effing time, making sure Shasta could see him during danger, not leaving in the first place, reassuring Shasta he was sane—Aslan will later take credit for comforting Shasta in the tombs! Ha! That's rich considering Aslan was the scariest part of the experience! Bad kitty!

Shasta then says he'll never be mean to a cat ever again and Aslan responds by scratching him! Ouch. Little Bit didn't get why Aslan did this when Shasta's promising to be nicer to cats. Well, we're not supposed to question when Aslan hurts children. Shasta spends the whole next day by himself wondering if his friends left him or were caught. Finally, he decides to make the trek across the desert by himself, but thankfully before he sets out, he sees Hwin and Bree coming towards him with a groom! No Aravis though.

Aravis had made the mistake back in town of looking up at a passing litter that had a friend inside who recognized her. Lasaraleen, the friend, has an awesome name, not the usual word-play mess Lewis usually pulls out his ear. I half expected her to be named Darkfriend or Girlface. Good work, Lewis! (Someone give him a cookie.) After being recognized, Aravis had no choice but to join her friend in the litter and tell her what she was doing dressed as a slave. Lasaraleen is assumed to also be thirteen or younger, but she has a husband who is much older and out of town. She offers Aravis her place to hide since it turns out Aravis' father is in the city looking for her!

Lasaraleen is the worst kind of girl in Lewis' mind. She cares a great deal about her new dress. She also laughs at nothing, enjoys nicer things, revels in the latest news, and loves being close to the palace as well as to the princes and princesses inside it. We'll see in the last book that Lewis absolutely hates this kind of socialite and assumes his god does as well. Lasaraleen can't understand why Aravis doesn't want to be married to an old man in his 60's who has a hunchback when he also has three houses and nice clothes! I really don't think our author had a clue what thirteen-year-old girls would actually think of old men raping them. There is really no number of pretty dresses to make up for that, Lewis!

This book cannot stand womanly foolishness, so it says a lot about the Tarkeena that she was a "terrible giggler" for one thing, and she says "darling" a lot. By contrast, Aravis loves archery, dogs, and swimming. Spending time with Lasaraleen makes Aravis feel better about leaving this life behind as her friend's interests are implied to be universally despised. Now, I may be on Team Aravis in terms of taste, but no one ever has my permission to put down another woman. There's nothing wrong or inferior with being high femme. Period. If someone tries to compliment one person by putting down others, it's not a compliment.

Lasaraleen can giggle her head off and buy nice dresses and enjoy the company of royalty. That's a great thing for middle-schoolers to do. Sadly, her view of those in different socioeconomic brackets than herself is troubling, but she's not a grown-up yet and still learning. *Go paint your nails, honey! You do you.*

The two friends plan to go to the palace the next day since Lasaraleen has visiting privileges. That way Aravis can sneak out through the gardens there. The horses are sent with Lasaraleen's groom through the gate to meet Shasta. Why couldn't Aravis go with them? No real reason except to set up the next scene where the girls run into the Tisroc, the ruler of all Calormen. (But not the best baby name, in my opinion.)

Once in the palace, the girls see the Tisroc coming and dive into a room to hide from him. Unfortunately, he goes into that exact room to discuss some secrets with his son, Prince Baddy, and the elderly Grand Vizzier whom Aravis is engaged to. The girls listen in from their hiding place in the room and overhear the conversation this whole contrived subplot has set them up to overhear.

Also, eavesdropping is a sin, kids.

Prince Baddy noticed the Narnian ship was gone and wants to give chase and kidnap Queen Susan, whom he calls all sorts of names.

Baddy's daddy won't go to war with Narnia because he fears the strong magic there. Baddy responds with a suggestion that he take 200 men and conquer Archenland, Narnia's White neighbors, then ride north to Narnia to do a quick kidnapping. Once they have Archenland they will build it up slowly under Narnia's nose and finally take Narnia as well. Since the Tisroc can't sign off on this officially, as Narnia would retaliate, they all agree to pretend Baddy conquered their peaceful neighbors on his own. If caught or killed, the Tisroc can just say his impetuous son did all this without consulting him first. Plus, there have been five Tisrocs who were killed by their impatient eldest sons, so if Baddy meets a bad end, it will give the Tisroc a little breathing room. It's a win-win.

It's hard to read this section because it's so falsely poetic, and over-the-top wordy. Why use two words when twenty will do? It reads like, "O, my [adjective] son, light of my [noun], may you ever [verb], by the blessing of [name of god] ([parenthetical statement about god]) that the Tisroc ([parenthetical statement honoring Tisroc]) who wise men once said was [long-winded maxim]." If you want your readers to hate these guys, definitely write them this way.

At one point, rather obviously, the Vizier even directly says that Narnians are inferior because, "their poetry is not, like ours, full of choice apophthegms."[19] We're breaking some forth wall here, or at the very least that's some super self-awareness about one's own culture that would be most beneficial to a third-party observer and not, of course, to other people in the room.

The accusation that the Calormenes add obnoxious quotes into their speech and the Narnians don't is not totally correct. Queen Susan and King Edmund's informal discussion three chapters ago was

---

[19] Meaning: A short, witty instructive saying. I thought this was a misspelling of apothegm, and so did my word processor, but nope; it's just how they spell it in the UK.

lousy with aphorisms, like, "It is an old saying: see the bear in his own den before you judge of his conditions," Or, "Come, live with me and you'll know me," Or, "Just as the beggar's only difficulty about riding is that he has no horse." How's that much different? Perhaps the author assumes his audience will get the difference between insufferable sayings and wise ones. (A helpful shortcut to figuring that out is to note a character's nationality and skin color.)

The sexism and violence against women evident in this conversation is downright inappropriate. As Arsheesh's aunt would say, "Jeez Louise!" (Bitsy is rolling her eyes somewhere.) Their evil plot relies on the sexist idea that women are so flighty and impossible to understand that no king would ever send an army to take Susan back if she's kidnapped and raped because, who knows, maybe she is magically fine with it now. I mean, "women are changeable as weathercocks" and don't really know what they want until a man tells them. Plus, she'd be damaged goods.

The men think it's completely reasonable to teach Susan a "sharp lesson" for rejecting the prince's proposal. While all this talk of forced marriage and painful lessons don't use the word rape directly, it's still pretty terrible to have this in a children's book! I mean, some older children are putting two and two together and realizing they're not just talking about taking away Susan's access to the video game controllers!

Lastly, this mission only works because King Peter, who is the high king and ruler of Narnia, is off committing violent acts against folks in a different war. Ah, the "Golden Age." It can't just be me who wonders if the Pevensie children should be tried for war crimes. Yet Narnia is at war in the name of their god, Aslan, so it's a *righteous* war. They are the good guys, after all. The reason for Calormen to go to war is almost the same reason—they consider themselves blessed and directed by their god—but we are supposed to know one god is

174

ridiculous and his wars unjust, and the other, more familiar god is reasonable and those wars just.

It will shock no one to learn this story is leading up to its own war so the victorious survivors can retroactively declare their god the right one.

The Horse and His Boy: Chapters 9-10

"Lions are really bad!"

"Just this one."

"I was talking about the ones in Calormen, too."

"They are all the same one."

"Wait…it's Aslan? Really?"

"Yeah it will all be revealed in a chapter or so."

"But these lions were all shaggy and bitey."

"It was still Aslan."

"He's really awful."

"Agreed."

***

Once the Tisroc, Baddy, and the Vizier leave the room, our girls start to breathe normally again. Lasaraleen is trembling so much it shakes her whole body, but Aravis has no real empathy for her friend. When Lasaraleen begs Aravis to go back to safety, our hero responds by shaking her and threatening to give away their location if they didn't stick to the plan. "But we shall both be k-k-killed!" the poor Tarkeena cries. Aravis ignores her and forces her to the garden gate. Lasaraleen is shaking so badly at this point that she cannot open it so Aravis does it. You'd think our frightened child would say a quick farewell and run back home, but our author had things go another direction.

Lasaraleen, who is supposed to be practically wetting herself at this point, decides it's the *perfect* time to strike up a conversation about marrying the Grand Vizier we just overheard helping to plot murder and rape! It's a gendered stereotype on steroids; preteen girls just cannot help themselves from chatting about weddings! This part of the book is just *lazy*. It is completely contrived and hangs on some pretty misogynistic ideas about what young girls would be concerned about under these circumstances. Aravis scoffs that she would rather marry "my father's scullion" than someone like the Vizier. A bit classist, but at least she recognized his lack of moral character. This gives Lasaraleen an opening to say that the evil plot they just overheard "must be right if he's going to do it!" Oh, sweet heavens! I love that she's appealing to Divine Command Theory in the same way Christians have all my life. Lewis is inadvertently holding up a mirror to his own arguments' holes.

Aravis shoves off her friend's "affectionate" embraces and leaves Tashbaan for good. She "hated every minute of her time in Tashbaan" so eff you very much, Lasaraleen, and your baths and meals. Aravis has finally broken free of the kind of femininity that's social, talkative, fashionable, overly affectionate, and emotional—the exact kind Lewis despises. Poor Lasaraleen did not deserve a friend who used her. Baby girl needed someone who loved to watch her twirl in her pretty dresses.

It's not that Lasaraleen is my favorite character, far from it, but that's the point: she's no one's favorite character. And the reason is kinda sexist. In reality, she was a freaking hero who gave refuge to a friend in need, protected this friend from her father even though she didn't agree with her decision, and put herself in danger to help someone she cared about. I just feel like she needs more credit.

Aravis gets to the tombs and "her heart quailed" due to thoughts of the ghouls. She sees the horses and dismisses their groom who runs away since he also feared the ghouls. Everyone fears these things!

Shasta comes out from hiding and shares what he overheard from Edmund and Susan on how to get through the desert. Aravis relays her info about what Baddy is planning. Now they have a mission to get to Archenland first and warn King Lune, Corin's dad, what's coming. The band was back together and off on a mission from god!

**

This quest took our heroes down an endless path through sand. At one point the sand was so hot it burned Shasta's feet, forcing him to ride Bree after that. He must have felt guilty about riding while Aravis walked because he made it a point to remark upon her wearing shoes. Lewis notes that upon hearing this: Aravis said nothing and looked prim. Let's hope she didn't mean to, but she did.

Aravis is doing the hard work of walking through the endless desert while Shasta rides and saves his energy, but a look she may or may not have given him, one of looking too "prim," is bad? What kind of face policing is this? Can you guess how many times Shasta gave looks, mostly sulky ones, and Lewis opined that it would be best if he didn't mean them? I'll give you a clue: NEVER. Boys are allowed to wear negative feelings on their faces. Girls? It's unladylike. Feeling impressed by men is proper. Feeling superior to men in any given situation is not.

Proper female characters are also not allowed to be opinionated or in command. After a day's march through unforgiving sand, they found a river and slept. The next morning Bree wouldn't set out until he'd eaten. Everyone thought this was wrong since it was late and lives were on the line. Hwin tried to communicate how important it was to continue the journey, but she had to do this in the most round-about, careful way to avoid being demanding. Once Bree put her in her place, Hwin "made no answer, being, like most highly bred mares, a very nervous and gentle person who was easily put down." When she speaks, she's shy, and when they travel, she silently sets the pace even though she's weaker. This quiet grace is what Lewis thinks femininity is all about. Hwin will continue to be gracefully mute as Bree does what he wants. In my church it was the best kind of woman who quietly submitted to the will of the men in her life, even when the consequences were costly. So, you know, *that's bullshit.*

A black swarm appeared in the distance. It's Baddy's Band of Bad guys! Now our group had to gallop! Remember they've been riding hard for a while already. They are going very quickly, but Aslan demands more.

> And certainly both Horses were doing, if not all they could, all they thought they could; which is not quite the same thing.

You know what would make them go faster? Fear for their lives! Enter His Dickness. Aslan chases them while roaring, terrifying the horses into greater speed. It's assumed their pre-adrenaline efforts were not good enough, and somehow this is a personal failing on their parts.

Bree obviously is faster than Hwin, who the lion targets. Why Hwin? Because screw females, that's why. Aslan wants to claw up Aravis' back as a punishment for getting away from her arranged marriage by leaving her handmaid behind. Does he also want to claw up Shasta for leaving Arsheesh to his fate? Nope. Anway, Hwin, who was a sinless character from Lewis's point of view, screams "one of the most terrible noises in the world" as the lion snaps at her hind legs. Seriously, what in the world did Hwin do to this jerk?! Then Aslan rips Aravis' shoulders to shreds on Hwin's back. Shasta jumps off Bree and "half mad with horror" yells at the lion. The lion was done playing cat-and-mouse with our heroes and leaves.

They make it to a strange, green gate conveniently just ahead and are greeted by a prophet-like dude called The Hermit of the Southern

March. Hermit guy knows all about Baddy thanks to magic and tells Shasta to run to the king. (Hermit didn't go himself even though he had been sitting on this knowledge because he didn't feel like it, *okay?*) Shasta is close to passing out but obeys. *Take a freaking horse!* we all shout at the book.

Aravis is severely injured and placed on the best bedding "she had never seen or heard of" before. As if Calormen didn't trade with Archenland that was literally a day's travel north and a high-bred Tarkeena in the land of sin and pleasure wouldn't know of good bedding! Okay, *whatever* Lewis.

Her body was so gruesome that Hwin asks if she will live. The hermit tends to her wounds and says they don't look infected and will heal. Aravis makes the mistake of saying she has good luck and is quickly told that there's no such thing as luck. Why? Because Aslan is so sovereign that coincidences don't exist. This reminds me of the time I made the mistake of telling my friend's new husband at her wedding that he was a lucky man. He was a devout Christian and looked taken aback at the thought. I got immediately corrected, "Not lucky, *blessed!*" They were married in a church. They did it right. God would now reward them with blessings, not mindless luck. Didn't I know? Didn't I believe in God and his blessings?

They're divorced now.[20]

Luck means that some outcomes are random. A member of my former church thought of luck as witchcraft. It went against his view in an all-powerful and sovereign deity and was therefore a completely pagan idea to him. It wasn't until I was a 30-year-old brand-new atheist that I learned coincidences were clearly real and meaningless[21] as they continued to happen after I stopped believing in a god who

---

[20] Is this the pettiest thing I've ever written? Hmm, maybe?
[21] Why Coincidences are Meaningless:
https://www.youtube.com/watch?v=H1TxH0zf07w

winked at us through life's little blessings. I was honestly surprised by this as if good things only happened to believers. Indoctrination is truly a head trip.

***

Aravis can't be left alone to sleep off her pain because there's more emotional labor demanded of our ladyfolk! Bree is sulking. And how! He says he's going to go back to Calormen and be a slave. *Sure* he is. This has nothing to do with getting the girls, one of whom is recovering from bodily trauma, to cheer him up. Bree beats himself up for running to safety while the lion—his own god, unbeknownst to him—had hurt the others. The hermit says it's a good thing Bree is completely miserable because it means the horse has lost his self-conceit. Humility is something all decent believers must have. Enter the worst sentence in the chapter:

> As long as you know you're nobody special, you'll be a very decent sort of Horse.

There it is: Christianity's most mixed message.

It seems our lion deity got what he was after, to hurt Aravis, scare Hwin, and decimate the self-esteem of Bree. What did he do to Shasta? Well, he's off doing it right now! The next chapter is called "The Unwelcome Fellow Traveller." As Shasta travels in Archenland, our favorite furry asshole will be stalking him.

The Horse and His Boy: Chapter 11

"If Aslan is powerful, why didn't he save Shasta as a baby by sending him back to his family instead of giving him to someone who would abuse him all his life?"

"Good point, I…"

"Why can't Aslan just blow them to where they need to be like he did in the last book instead of scaring them into running there faster?"

"Um…"

"If Shasta is dying of hunger why can't Aslan magically feed him like he magically gave him water?"

"Er…"

"If Aslan knows everything, why can't he just clearly tell them what he wants so they don't make him mad?"

"Well…"

"Why can't Aslan…"

"ASLAN WORKS IN MYSTERIOUS WAYS, OKAY!"

***

I think Lewis *might* just be a sadist. Maybe possibly.[22] Shasta is running so hard he's shaking, his side aches, and the sweat is stinging his eyes and blinding him as he stumbles forward. He's also starving. Oh, and his face is covered in flies, too, randomly. What else? He hasn't slept or showered in a freaking long time either. He's sore, thoroughly exhausted, sun scorched, cat-scratched, oh yeah and his feet are still burnt from the sand earlier. That would not feel good considering he's running barefoot. Did I miss something? Let's just say he's in a lot of pain right now.

How many main characters will we see frozen or tortured or hurting or bloody or near death in this series? I'm not necessarily opposed to characters experiencing the harsher side of life in children's adventure stories, but my problem is that these books are presenting torture as rightful service to Jesus and necessary for proper sanctification.[23] If

---

[22] It's well established that Lewis had an obsession with sexual sadism.

[23] 1 Corinthians 3:15; 1 Peter 1:7; Zechariah 13:9; Malachi 3

the goal is to show young readers who the Christian god is then be prepared for a version of God who plans, causes, and voyeuristically oversees human tragedy and suffering. Additionally, a child who does not respond the *proper way* to brutal testing by their deity is deserving of *additional* pain or punishments. This may not be the lesson all Christian parents want to teach their children, especially all the denominations who don't gulp their doctrines of violence and righteous tyranny straight from the holy source.

Speaking of sadists, the biblical god fits the description perfectly. In the *good book*, he often hurts people. A lot of people. He perpetrated seven genocides in the space of thirteen verses, personally threatened to lift women's skirts so they could be raped,[24] and terrorized people for the express purpose of showing off.

I know I'm harping on a collection of books written in the Iron Age, but people to this day are telling their kids to worship this character and what one worships is what one starts to emulate! Sometimes, as we see in 2 Samuel and 1 Chronicles, even the Bible can't tell the difference between its own god and the devil. The same exact story is repeated in both books with one version having Satan in the place of God.

Imagine telling someone to pay respect to a god who is pro-slavery and anti-women; who performs genocides and infanticides and slaughters animals for pleasure; who hates certain people like Esau before they are even born; who is xenophobic, misogynistic, homophobic; and who commands unbelievers to be killed in the Old Testament and tortured eternally in the New! Even Lewis himself once called God the

---

[24] Jeremiah 13:15–26, the KJV says "heels made bare" instead of "skirts lifted up" to obscure the fact this is sexual assault. Isaiah 3:17 says "the Lord will discover their secret parts," literally "expose their vaginas" [Hebrew: *poth* meaning vagina]. These examples taken from Dan Barker on the FFRF blog about the ten worst verses in the Old Testament.

"Cosmic Sadist."[25] But to quote Lasaraleen, "Must be right if he's going to do it!"

***

Shasta finally runs into King Lune on a hunting party and explains that Baddy is coming! The king initially mistakes him for Prince Corin and is shocked to discover it's not the son he raised. Oh, and for a titch of racism, King Lune is fat just like the Tisroc is fat, but Lune is described as jolly and the Tisroc was described as disgusting. I wonder what the difference is!

They all race back to defend their kingdom. The horse they gave Shasta won't gallop so he gets left behind. Why wouldn't they check on him? Why wouldn't the horse keep up? Oh, it's so we can do more eavesdropping for the fourth major and super convenient time in the same book! (Sinful!)

Prince Baddy stops at a fork in the road while Shasta pulls around the other side. Not one of the two hundred men happens to notice him or his giant horse just standing there within listening distance. Baddy explains that once inside King Lune's palace at Anvard they are to kill everyone who is male, including babies, and keep everyone who is female to be divided up among themselves. It's because, young reader, the womenfolk are good for raping. This reminds me of another similar story I read as a child. To quote it:

> Now kill all the boys. And kill every woman who has slept with a man, but save for yourselves every girl who has never slept with a man.[26]

[25] C. S. Lewis, 1963. *A Grief Observed*, (New York, NY: Harper & Row).
[26] Numbers 31:17-18

Who said that? Moses.[27] Lewis' bad guy may be less evil by comparison because at least Rabadash would let all the women live to be sex slaves. Moses on the other hand only wanted the pre-pubescent girls. *Remember kids, it's only bad when the bad guys do it, but kidnapping little girls for sex is fine when Mr. Ten Commandments orders it!*

Shasta decides to keep following the road Baddy didn't take. His horse straight up refuses to do more than walk so that's the speed they are going when a "sudden fright" gets him back into the panicked state Aslan so loves in his followers. There was a large creature he couldn't see walking besides the horse. "It was a horrible shock," but Shasta decides to try talking to it with a fear-stricken faint voice. Aslan does speak back this time but stays freaking invisible, so Shasta immediately thinks he's a ghoul and freaks out. In an out-of-character exception, Aslan reassures the boy that he's not a ghoul. I've come to expect next to nothing from Aslan, so I am surprised any time he's halfway decent.

Aslan confirms that all the nasty lions terrifying them have all been himself. He also informs Shasta that he gave the boy to the fisherman who beat him and enslaved him for years when he was a baby. When Shasta asks who he is, the lion just answers, "Myself" and the Earth shakes and all that. This is a reference to Scripture when Moses asks God who he is and gets the answer "I AM WHO I AM" which is the same as saying "Myself." *I'm me! ME! Enough said! Go get me some sex slaves already!*

This show of power fills Shasta with a "new and different sort of trembling." Oh here we go. Aslan shone with a bright "whiteness" (heh, a bit on the nose) and "no one ever saw anything more terrible or beautiful."

---

[27] I realize there is no archeological or historical evidence for a real-life person named Moses, and the biblical books (Pentateuch) he supposedly penned include his own death and what happened after it, but sufficient to say, God's Chosen People were the ones either committing or condoning this particular atrocity.

184

My eye roll was so exaggerated it hurt.

The Bible repeatedly says to fear God. Enter the millions of Christian apologetics trying to make that into something reverential, even when the Bible is very upfront about the whole "scary god" thing. Take verses like Amos 3:6: "Shall there be evil in a city, and the Lord hath not done it?" Or Jeremiah 45:5 when God warns his prophet, "Behold, I am bringing evil upon all flesh." Often the biblical god is just actively threatening pestilence,[28] death,[29] and suffering[30] so that people will fear him, but we're still supposed to think this is a loving request for respect? *Please.* The characters in the Bible don't present fear of God as anything more than fear of his cruelty.

> Sanctify the Lord of hosts himself; and let him be your fear, and let him be your dread.[31]
> Therefore I am terrified at his presence; when I consider, I am in dread of him. God has made my heart faint, the Almighty has terrified me.[32]

Even Jesus presents God as scary.

> "But I will show you whom you should fear: Fear him who, after your body has been killed, has authority to throw you into hell. Yes, I tell you, fear him."[33]

Am I respecting the Hell-chucking guy? No, I'm damn well fearing him! This is why Aslan is always so terrifying. Terror is built into the love/worship/fear relationship biblical writers from violently tribal cultures had with their god.

---

[28] 2 Chronicles 7:13
[29] 1 Samuel 2:6
[30] Isaiah 53:10
[31] Isaiah 8:13
[32] Job 23:15-16
[33] Luke 12:5

Shasta falls off his horse before the lion's feet in worship. I assume Lewis meant to write paws instead of feet here, but he probably just mixed up his Jesus with his lion. Aslan is then transfigured and lifted up to Heaven, yet another nod to Christ. Shasta discovers he is on the path to Narnia and proclaims, "What luck that I hit it!—at least it wasn't luck at all really, it was *Him*." Again, luck is bad theology so none of that now. All praise to Aslan for getting us to the place safely! Never mind when he didn't do it safely and don't blame him for all torture! He's only responsible when we like what's happening!

Here's where the chapter ends, with Shasta in awe of Aslan, even though Aslan just admitted to attacking them multiple times, terrifying them, clawing up his close friend, and giving him to an abuser as a helpless baby. Shasta is on the ground in worship, even drinking water from the lion's footprint! Little Bit and I are just sitting here in unbelieving bafflement.

The Horse and His Boy: Chapters 12-15

"And he didn't get to do war anymore so that was the worst punishment of all."

"Awww, poor guy. Aslan is so mean!"

"No war for you! And war is great so you're missing out!"

"No killing for you!"

"Too bad!"

***

Shasta made it to Narnia and runs into a Talking Hedgehog. "It won't be a woman hedgehog," predicts Bitsy who has adapted to these androcentric worlds. A bunch more Talking Animals show up who are also all male to hear the news that King Lune will soon be under attack. The stag among them runs the news to Cair Paravel so they can mount a response lickity split. A few Dwarves, who are all men, see that Shasta is starving and serve him breakfast.

Shasta's breakfast was "all new and wonderful to Shasta for Calormene food is quite different." It says he didn't know what toast was, and then it says he didn't know what butter was. Apparently, a couple days' ride is much too far away to ever trade such basic things. Also, why would a boy raised in a different country his whole life not like the food there and prefer foreign food? That's unusual. This negative comparison with Calormen seems stretched. Even their food is subpar? Really?

Shasta got to finally sleep and woke up to the sound of the Narnian army coming. Among them was Edmund and Corin who had arrived back from Calormen already. King Edmund finally learns who Shasta is and gives him his first ever lesson that eavesdropping is morally wrong. Finally! If this plot device got used a *fifth time* I was done.

A fan favorite, Queen Lucy, is there as well! She is decked out in armor to Bitsy's delight. What happened between this and the first book when Lucy is told it's bad when women fight? Whatever, we'll take it. Lewis makes it clear she'll be with the archers away from battle and protected so it's not like she's an equal party or anything. Queen Susan is the better archer but she's also a proper lady so knows her place is not in a battle. When talking about Lucy we hear she is not as good as a man, but "at any rate as good as a boy." Yes, because boys, not even men, are above women, so elevating Lucy to a male child is some sort of backwards complement. I'm choking on the sexism.

Almost immediately Corin gets into a violent fight with the Dwarf who was ordered to keep him out of the battle. Corin breaks the Dwarf's ankle, takes the Dwarf's armor and horse, and gives them to

Shasta. When Shasta looks confused, Corin asks incredulously, "Don't you want to?" Corin can't understand why anyone wouldn't want to join in the killing fun. The boys sneak into the army after being ordered not to so they can be violent. Yay! This is supposed to show how valiant and brave they are! It's clear Edmund knows what Corin is up to. When Lucy asks where he is, Edmund tells her to "leave well alone."

Corin has a huge war boner and starts chatting about how the birds circling overhead will get fed some dead people soon. He really is a psycho. When the Narnians finally arrive and see the Calormen army using a battering ram on King Lune's gate, they charge. Everyone starts praying for their lives and Shasta thinks to himself, "If you funk this, you'll funk every battle all your life." Note: I accidentally might have misread that first "funk." Bits didn't seem to notice.

Shasta is confused and scared and does nothing much in the battle. We will get the details of the battle from our sports-announcer-like hermit back in the Southern March looking through a magic pool, which is only considered evil witchcraft when a woman does it.

Aravis and the two horses get the play-by-play as the hermit describes a lot of glorified violence like a giant taking a weapon through the eye and dying horribly or the five Calormene soldiers dying as arrows pierce their bodies. Tiny teen terror Corin slaughters a man and is practically gleeful about it. A bunch of Talking Leopards and other cats kill the horses by ripping them up. (Little Bit is downright salty about me reading this.) King Edmund takes someone's head off. It's bloody chaos.

Not to beat a dead Calormene horse, but the men who are killed or captured in this battle are given names. We just met them and will never hear from them again, but they get names. We *still* have no idea what Aravis' maidservant's name was despite her being so important Aravis gets tortured over slipping her a Mickey. We also don't know

Aravis' mother's name or the name of Aravis' stepmother who arranged her marriage. Guess whose names we do have: Aravis' father, Kidrash, grandfather, Rishti, great-grandfather, Kidrash again, great-great grandfather, Ilsombreh, and great-great-great grandfather, Ardeeb. How useful is having Aravis' great-great-great grandfather's name when two characters who are part of the plot go nameless? Sexism: Not very helpful.

At the end of the battle the Calormenes are all dead, dying, or captured. Rabadash is hanging on the gate by a hole in the back of his hauberk. He did this by jumping down from the gate and getting stuck. Everyone starts laughing at him so he starts crying. It's a whole scene.

King Lune reaches out to give Shasta a bear hug and kisses him. Shasta is really confused until the king asks the court to witness the twin brothers standing together. Shasta is royalty! (Surprise!) Prince Corin gets lectured about sneaking into battle by his dad but "everyone, including Corin, could see that the King was very proud of him." Boys will be boys. One just killed a guy and loved it so, like, maybe have him see a therapist?

Back at the hermit's place, Bree doesn't want to leave until his tail has grown out enough that they could cut it off to disguise him in Tashbaan. He is worried because he's entering "the best society" (read: White) and wants to make a good impression. Aravis says he's as "vain as that Tarkheena" referring to Lasaraleen because they cannot leave my girl alone!

Bree keeps saying "the Lion's Mane" which is like a Narnian solemn swear, making Aravis ask what that's about. I mean, doesn't this horse hate lions? Bree starts proselytizing about Aslan, but he doesn't say every theological point exactly right. For one thing, he thinks Aslan is a god instead of a lion, whereas technically Aslan is both at the same time. This may be important because Lewis believed Jesus could only be the stand-in sacrifice for humanity if he was fully human, but Christianity had already developed the character into a deity on par with Yahweh. (Even though it honestly doesn't sound as good to say Jesus was an immortal god who had a *bad weekend* for your sins.) Now Jesus had to be both unlimited god and limited human at the same time in a logic-bending way. Why this means Aslan has to be fully lion is beyond me, but any excuse to have Aslan attack folks as punishment for dumb things is good enough. Aslan jumps the wall, scares the girls into silence, and terrifies Bree who "shot away like an arrow to the other side of the enclosure." Why? Because Bree got his theology slightly wrong since he was kidnapped as a child and didn't go to the right church.

I'll point out that when Bree focused on Aslan's deity, he was threatened, but when Shasta focused on Aslan's lion-ness on the road to Anvard, Aslan gets all deity-afied on him and shakes the earth until he gets worshipped. Whichever one they pick to focus on is always wrong.

Hwin and Aravis are temporarily frozen, but Hwin gathers her courage to fight off the lion and save her friends. Ha! *Nope!* Hwin, our role model, goes and submits herself to Aslan *to be eaten!* Yes **eaten**.

> "Please, you're so beautiful. You may eat me if you like. I'd sooner be eaten by you than fed by anyone else."

My eyes are bleeding from reading this crap. Do we really want to teach children that their deity can eat them for his pleasure? Or that this kind of submission is a good thing and should be rewarded? Sure enough, Hwin is rewarded with a feeling of joy. Aslan says he knew she would "not be long in coming to me," and is all proud of Hwin for being what the Bible calls "a living sacrifice." No. *No no no.*

Aslan makes Bree call himself a fool and then says, "Happy the Horse who knows that while he is still young. Or the Human either."

That's a direct message to our young reader: You are a fool! Know it well! Foolishness in this context doesn't just mean innocent silliness or ignorance, but the charge can be serious enough to get fundamentalist kids a harsh beating growing up. The Bible says the heart of a child is where foolishness is found and can be beaten out with a blunt instrument.[34] These godly words from the inspired Scripture have consequences.

In 2010, fundamentalist Christian parents Kevin and Elizabeth Schatz beat their children thinking it was what God wanted based on biblical passages. Seven-year-old Lydia Charity Schatz sustained massive tissue damage that led to her death. Her last beating was simply for mispronouncing a word. In 2013, Larry and Carri Williams beat their daughter, Hana, to death. They were following the same biblical instructions. In 2015, Deborah and Bruce Leonard beat their son Lucas to death for trying to leave their church and severely injured their other son. In 2017, a Christian mother named Rhonda Shoffner beat and strangled her daughter for not knowing Bible verses well enough when reciting them from memory.

I don't think I'm being too critical when I say these religious ideas are dangerous and wrong. I was also beaten quite a lot growing up and was taught to submit to my own abuse. Learning to accept abuse from deities, or more likely those claiming to be in the deity's service, creates even more victims. It's no shock to me the church has a sexual assault problem (#churchtoo). Aravis is told the reason Aslan ripped out chunks of her skin and she responds, "Yes, sir." That's supposed to show character growth. It's vomit-inducing!

Aslan disappears when Shasta, now called Prince Cor, arrives. No one is supposed to call him Shasta anymore, because that's a dirty Calormene name. He invites Aravis to stay with him at Anvard and

---

34 Proverbs 22:15

she accepts. Shasta more than once moans that he will get an education now that he's royalty.

Once at Anvard, they had to get Queen Lucy to come make the rooms pretty for Aravis because King Lune's wife had died and royal women do that sort of work. (Guess what King Lune's wife's name is. It may shock the reader to learn she does not have one. Wuuuuuuuuuuuut?) All Lewis says of Aravis and Lucy's interaction is that they talked "about Aravis's bedroom and Aravis's boudoir and about getting clothes for her, and all the sort of things girls do talk about." Here's a salute to… GENDER STEROTYPES!

Our entire war party then gathers at the grand banquet to talk about what to do with Prince Baddy. Head chopping is suggested, but instead they decide to give him their list of conditions he must meet in order to be freed. He just curses at them instead of listening. Corin asks if he can hit him while he is chained to a wall in keeping with the boy's lovely character. All the valent menfolk jump to their feet ready for a fight with their tied-up prisoner. Easy fight to win. Before anyone hits Baddy, Aslan enters the room and gives Baddy a chance to be humbled and lose his self-worth like all his other followers have, but Baddy won't do it. (Don't make me cheer for Baddy!) In response, Aslan turns him into a donkey. Everybody laughs at him. Again. (Everybody is always laughing even though they just finished a battle they probably lost friends in.) Baddy will get turned back to normal on the condition he never leaves the city to commit war. Since war is just the greatest, this really was some punishment!

Shasta goes on to have quarrels, "even fights," with Aravis until they became so used to this arrangement that they get married "to go on doing it more conveniently." Corin became a great fighter who is known for beating up a bear. Figures. Everybody gets married. Aravis has a son, so *whew*, no icky girl as high queen. As if there's such thing as high queen. I guess this is about as happily as these things end.

7
Long Live the Queen

The Magician's Nephew: Chapter 1

"Buckle up, little girl! This is my favorite book in the series."

"Are people treated better?"

"I admit there are still problematic elements, **but you must love this one.**"

"Why?"

"Because it's my favorite!"

"Does it at least have women with names?"

"Yes! My favorite character, and the witch from the very first story, is named Jadis."

"Okay."

***

Finally! My daughter and I made it to the best story: *The Magician's Nephew*! This is the second to last volume in publication order, although chronologically it takes place before the others. HarperCollins order would place it first, making it many readers' introduction to the series.

> "You can't go back and change the beginning, but you can start where you are and change the ending." —C. S. Lewis

Unless you're writing Narnia books.

Bitsy and I have had some rough times with this series, yet we're cleansing our palates for a new adventure and fresh story. It felt right to start over and feel the enthusiasm that I once felt. Breathe it in.

The Magician's Nephew is the backstory of backstories. Like any good prequel, it adds depth and meaning to the main story while also taking us to new territory. Publication order families like mine get to experience "so *that's* where that came from!" moments while chronological order readers merely get slight spoilers of the next book. This is why I believe it's best to read the books in the order they were penned. Like anything of quality, it's worth the wait.

Lewis' concept of a world between worlds in this book was so influential that it inspired Lev Grossman to recreate it in *The Magicians*. Many have said the concept of interworld travel is the best metaphor for a library—each book can be entered just like each pool in Lewis' in-between place led to a different world. Many of my church leaders were convinced that acknowledging our universe was big enough to have other life-sustaining planets, ones where maybe Jesus didn't die, was the height of blasphemy. So having this element in my Christian literature was especially thrilling to me.

The Magician's Nephew breaks out of Narnia even as it informs its beginning. The imagination is completely untethered for the first time in this series, opening the story to include potentially endless adventures. The flat planet containing Narnia always felt so small after *The Voyage of the Dawn Treader*. The only unexplored country left was Calormen and it was sufficiently covered in the last book. Maybe Lewis felt that same claustrophobia I did. The magic of finding a wardrobe and something *new* behind it was fading. The surrounding areas had been thoroughly mined. What was left? Alexander the Great was said to weep when he realized there were no more lands to conquer, yet Lewis simply created more. Just when we thought there was nothing new to explore, he picked up his pen and took us to Charn.

Our story begins in the days of Sherlock Holmes. *It says that.* Will there be racism and sexism and prejudice and ableism and weird religious weirdly weirdness? Okay fine *yes.* However, I want the stories I'm reading to Bitsy to come alive rather than be dissected. Up until now I have allowed all sorts of interruptions to discuss moral elements of the story and I watched as the imagination train at bedtime turned into a lecture hall. I began reading this one with a new mindset. I was highly enthusiastic about this plan. *Pure magic and enjoyment ahead.*

Then we started reading.

***

[Content note: Child endangerment and creepy guy acting creepy with kids.]

In the days when schools were nastier (Lewis' words, of course), there was a boy named Digory and a girl named Polly who lived in adjoining row houses in London. Upon meeting, they immediately began making fun of each other's names like little sinners. One day Digory was crying, and since he's a boy, there's some fuss made to spare his feelings. Yay toxic masculinity! Turns out Digory's dad is in India, his mom is dying, and he lives with his uncle and aunt, an unhappy brother and sister. The uncle is, well, kinda, *fine...* he's a pedophile.

> "How would you like to lie awake listening for Uncle Andrew's step to come creeping along the passage to your room? And he has such awful eyes."

To explain why this strange uncle is always up in the attic, the totally acceptable guess the characters give is that he's keeping a wife with mental illness locked up there. Because that's totally a normal and humane thing to do to women.

One thing I loved about this book was that Polly had discovered a small space in the attics of the homes that connected them all. I remember finding a tiny room hidden in my aunt's old house when I was a kid, which was a bit of a thrill! Polly and Digory learned of an empty house in the row of homes and planned to go through this little tunnel and come out into it. Just a bit of B&E. No big deal. Digory was all about this and "was a good deal more excited than you'd have thought from the way he spoke." Probably since it would be a safe place from his uncle.

Well they made their way across rafters and into the empty home, only instead of being empty it was filled with science equipment and literature. Turns out they hadn't made it from Polly's house to the empty one but had instead come up into Digory's uncle's house. Unfortunately, Uncle Andrew had been sitting in a high-backed chair and rose "like a pantomime demon coming up out of a trapdoor."

First thing creepy uncle does is walk across the room to lock the door and trap the children behind him so his sister couldn't get in and rescue them. The children try to back away to the attic door they came out of, but Andrew is quick and runs around blocking it. Polly begs to be let out, and he refuses. He wants to experiment on them first.

It's clearly a dreadful situation and the children silently make a pack to humor the guy so he won't hurt them. They first try to appeal to the law or his sake of goodness—saying that he *must* let them go. They get the response, "Must?" He has all the power here similar to a certain lion we've dealt with before.

Then Uncle Andrew starts talking to Polly about how attractive she is and offers her a pretty ring. She's the age that if she had been, according to Lewis, "a very little younger she would have wanted to put one in her mouth." Yikes. The greying uncle going on about how lonely he is and how attractive she is, you know, (*clears throat*) classic literature! Nothing to worry about!

Uncle Creepy gives Polly a ring "with my love" and has "an eager, almost a greedy, look on his face." Digory shouts for her to get away, but it's too late. She touches the ring and disappears entirely.

The chapter ends ominously: "Digory and his Uncle were alone in the room."

The Magician's Nephew: Chapter 2

"Polly shouldn't have touched the ring bracelet."

"Why not?"

"Because it was magic!"

"She didn't know that."

"She should have known that!"

"How?"

"I don't know."

"What if a guy named Tom handed you a book, would you take it?"

"Books are normal things, so yes?"

"Well, did I mention his name was actually Tom RIDDLE?!"

"No! Voldemort!!! I'm cursed now!"

"And who would be at fault?"

"The Dark Lord!"

"Exactly, it's the fault of the person causing harm, not the victim who didn't know."

***

Womenfolk just can't resist jewelry and any sense we supposedly have goes right out our pretty little heads when we see even one sparkly piece of the stuff. This is a universal truth. Why, right now I have on twelve cursed rings, six necklaces, and effing St. Edward's Crown.

(Don't ask where I got it.) It's a lesson to gals everywhere that it's their own fault when our beloved trinkets transport us to other dimensions.

The parts of the Bible my childhood church focused on could be fairly anti-jewelry.[1] Even though eye-catching bling was a no-no, women were still summed up as objects to be looked at for pleasure or, conversely, for punishment according to Jesus and his cultural disdain for women in public.[2] (Jesus was fine with men in public so there's no corresponding warning.) A former pastor of mine once called makeup and earrings false advertising, like a pretty paint job on a junk car. The message I received was that it was my responsibility to be pretty, but I couldn't cheat.

I was taught that Esther, in the biblical book named after her, was the model of godly modesty for refusing to don too much jewelry. In one of the most celebrated and messed up stories of the entire Bible about rape, Esther is brought before King Xerxes to sleep with him without any thought to her consent. The king ends up choosing her to be queen out of all the other women of his harem. To prepare to have sex with the king, all the women were given year-long beauty treatments with oils and perfumes, and each could wear jewelry from the royal treasury. Part of the reason why Esther is chosen, I was told, was because even though she was able to take as much jewelry as she wanted for this "encounter," she didn't go jewelry crazy:

> "She asked for nothing other than what Hegai, the king's eunuch who was in charge of the harem, suggested."[3]

I was taught this was a lesson against womanly excess. If you type in "Christian women wear jewelry" into Google you will get some "Should they?" posts mostly written by men.

---

[1] 1 Timothy 2:9
[2] Matthew 5:28
[3] Esther 2:15

However much my church pushed the idea, making the story about jewelry a stretch. A reading of the original story doesn't seem to emphasize a modesty theme at all, but instead strongly implies Esther was chosen as queen, a position that saved her people, for her performance in that one-night stand. I was never informed that it was her particular sexual talents and not her pure heart or lack of jewelry that caused her promotion in life. I didn't even get this not-at-all-subtle message until I was long since grown and reading the story without evangelical blinders. Want to save your people? Get good at the whoring, children!

You know what my Christian school taught me about Esther? Was it that rape was bad? Nope. Was it that women are people? Hell no. It was that Esther was a good girl who SUBMITTED.[4] (*screaming internally my entire childhood*)

Growing up in church, little boys could play David slaying giants or Moses parting seas, but little girls had a limited selection of biblical role models to emulate, the majority of which had a story that included rape, birth, or sex work. There are only two books of the Bible named after women, and the other is Ruth. Ruth offered her body up to Boaz out of desperation and poverty by sneaking into his bed at night. This prompted the horny man to propose. That's how you 'get your Boaz,' girlfriend.

The New Testament Bible, found in many hotel rooms, talks about how women shouldn't wear jewelry, but should instead shut up like proper slaves, er, I mean *practice quietness and submit obediently to their husbands.*[5] (There that sounds *much* better.) This anti-jewelry piece of Scripture is followed up three verses later with the ageless marital advice to call your husband "lord" and know your place in the

---

[4] Link to an image from my Christian textbook showing children writing sentences about God using Esther because she submitted: https://tinyurl.com/y36afpuc
[5] 1 Peter 3

master/slave relationship. (Kinky.) Ah the universal and timeless Word of God!

Lewis' religion is, or can be, somewhat jewelry-phobic and dangerously misogynistic. When the Bible tells women that their prayers aren't good enough without covering their hair[6] or that they should wear specific things when worshiping[7] it's due to a belief that women's bodies are inherently dangerous and sinful. They must be controlled.

***

Polly valuing the pretty ring had a dark consequence, as many believers think it should have. Digory was left trapped alone with his uncle who immediately pounced the boy, covered his mouth, and, even worse, forced him to endure endless exposition. (Sick bastard.)

These books should be renamed: *The Chronicles of Men Explaining Things to Us.*

Uncle Andrew's backstory involves a witchcraft-loving godmother who went to prison for being "bad." It's not really explained what illegal things she did, if anything, but what else happens to bad women? Before she died, she gave him a magical box and ordered him to destroy it with some spells. He promised to destroy it. He didn't.

Digory points out it was rotten of his uncle not to keep a promise, and his uncle responds that rules like that are for "little boys—and servants—and women" but not for real people. This wisdom sounded to Digory as "something rather fine" (*of course it did*) especially since he said it with a face "so grave and noble and mysterious." It was only after remembering the uncle's earlier actions, specifically when his face was twisted with evil, that Digory realized this meant his uncle could

---

[6] 1 Corinthians 11
[7] 1 Timothy 2:9-10

just do whatever he wanted. Welcome to my former religious world, Digs.

Uncle Andrew is on top of the hierarchy; he's human, male, rich, able-bodied, White, and older. By hierarchy standards, he should rightfully have power over almost everyone else. That means that if he is truly awful, the only ones who can stop him must also be on his level. When I was young my church taught that God put men over women, husbands over wives, and fathers over families. The only time I ever saw anyone balk at this set up was when the man in charge was clearly a monster. Even in these cases, many pastors still tell children and women to obey the men anyway, even submit to abuse![8] While that may be biblical advice, it certainly differs from modern Christian morality that has outpaced Iron Age Scripture.

Give godly men or lions an advantage over others, where even the rules of common decency and good behavior don't apply, and there's not much pushback. Aslan has killed or maimed many children many times by this point in the series and he's still considered (by the book's worldview) the highest kind of good. This is the essence of Divine Command Theory: It's fine if our righteous god commands it even if it's morally reprehensible otherwise. Give this same power to a man like Andrew, and only then is it a problem.

As I was repeatedly told growing up, the patriarch/headship system is godly and perfect, so all the misery it seems to be creating is really the fault of the personal sin of the people under that godly leadership.

---

[8] Julia Baird and Hayley Gleeson, (updated) 2018. "'Submit to Your Husbands': Women Told to Endure Domestic Violence in the Name of God" Australian Broadcasting Corporation News. Available at: https://www.abc.net.au/news/2017-07-18/domestic-violence-church-submit-to-husbands/8652028

If a marriage is failing, for example, it must be because the wife is not submitting *hard enough*.[9]

***

Armed with a broken promise and a magic box from Atlantis (because why not Atlantis), Andrew learned how to manipulate the sand in the box to do magic, eventually making rings from it. He had to meet some "devilish queer people" and do some "very disagreeable" things which robbed him of his health in order to learn this knowledge. Young Christian readers will recognize "forbidden" knowledge as the very thing Genesis warns folks not to pursue!

Digory's uncle was driven by curiosity—the desire to *know*. The whole time he talks of magic, he is in fact describing what would take place in a science lab. "Can't you understand that the thing is a great experiment?" he says. It drives home the point that science and education require religious gatekeepers.

In the Bible we see education rejected as *foreign* and wisdom labeled "Greek." Aversion to these things then is born out of xenophobia. One biblical passage can be me summed up as, "Those foreigners are elitist when they use logic. Those smarty pants just don't get spiritual matters!"[10] This might be the worst passage in Scripture since it kicks anti-intellectualism into high gear. Verses on genocide, rape, and Hell are inexcusable, but a passage that advocates rejection of reason in favor of obedience to authority is how all these other evils get their foundation. Biblical literalists are already hobbled enough by commands not to lean on their own understanding[11] and to cling to their

---

[9] My former pastor once implied that if wives would just submit to marital rape more often then they wouldn't get raped so much.
[10] 1 Corinthians 1:22-24 (paraphrased)
[11] Proverbs 3

own ignorance of the world.[12] Even Jesus is said to want his followers to be like ignorant children,[13] not grown-ups with pesky fully developed brains and higher reasoning skills. Evangelical Christianity like the kind I was raised with bases its advice for followers on anti-intellectualism[14] for this reason. Don't listen to reason! It's elitist! It's *Greek*!

Uncle Andrew's hair turned grey from all this book learning and experimenting, showing the root of his very head is now poisoned with forbidden knowledge. Digory calls out his uncle's honor after hearing his tale, but Andrew waves it off as something stupid that would come from one who was "brought up among women." During all this exposition, Polly remains a lost damsel in distress off-camera. Girlfolk may lead to the downfall of society, but gosh darn it we can't forget to keep rescuing them!

Taking some rings from the box, Digory decides to use them to follow Polly wherever she went. I mean, it took a bit of convincing by his uncle, but any other action would have reflected badly on his manhood which was already dinged from crying over his dying mother earlier. (Nothing toxic about any of this!) He touches the ring and off he goes! It might be an evil ring, but it's fine when a good guy uses it. Best not to think about it too hard.

Digory is entering a truly magical place fueled by pure imagination—the Wood Between the Worlds.

The Magician's Nephew: Chapters 3-4

"What's wrong?"
"Nothing."

---

[12] Romans 16:19
[13] Matthew 18:3
[14] John Piper, 2016. "Five Strategies for Avoiding Intellectualism." Desiring God, (September 19). Available at: https://www.desiringgod.org/interviews/five-strategies-for-avoiding-intellectualism

"Is this part getting scary for you?"

"Pssh. No Mom, I'm fine."

"Okay, but something is wrong. You look slightly upset."

"Just keep reading!"

"Okay…"

"I NEED TO KNOW IF THE GUINEA PIG IS OKAY."

***

In Western society we have fairy tales and scary stories set in the woods. It's a mysterious place, full of unknown dangers. Even the Garden of Eden is beautiful and peaceful likely because it is a haven from the surrounding wilderness. Adam and Eve are banished from it into dangers unknown. Like any good story, ours is going into the woods.

Digory was sucked up into a void upon touching the evil ring. He finds himself floating in water yet completely dry. He comes out of a pool into a thick, empty forest dotted with even more pools. The trees there, thick and surrounded in green light, were living off the magical waters. Digory could almost feel them drinking and growing. He lost all thought of Polly or his uncle or his dying mother. He lost all sense entirely.

He was high as a kite.

Polly is lying down nearby with a similar stoner expression. She spoke in a "dreamy, contented sort of voice" and asked Digory if she knew him. He thought maybe they knew each other but he couldn't be sure. It felt as if they'd been in this place forever with no memory of what came before, but Polly informed him she had just watched him come out of the pool, so it couldn't have been that long. This whole scene needs a Pink Floyd soundtrack and a cameo from Harold and Kumar.

The reefer children notice a guinea pig with a magic ring taped to it. Andrew had tested out the magic on the guinea pig before he did on the children. Bitsy is relieved to know the guinea pig was happily rooting around in the grass. Seeing the ring made them notice their own rings. They had to will themselves into sobriety to remember who they were and why they were there.

Digory realized going back home meant going back into the arms of his uncle. Why do that when they now have access to pools that can take them to entirely different worlds? Curiosity, that vile thing that got his uncle into trouble, was driving him. Would it lead to new wonder and understanding? Or would it unleash a terrible evil and cause destruction? Well, that depends, I suppose, on the book's view of knowledge and what the moral consequences should be. (Spoiler: Lots of destruction.)

Digory figured out that this Wood Between the Worlds, as Polly coined it, connected many different places similar to their crawl space between row houses; it was not really a part of any one house but led to all of them. Suddenly, endless possibilities existed, endless worlds. Any young reader would get a thrill from this revelation.

Polly, as the female protagonist, had to be the brakes, the sense of reason, the *mom*. She wants to make sure they can make it safely back before exploring. At her discretion, the children jump back into their own pool to make sure they can get home, but with a plan to switch rings before they return completely. As they leap, they see lights all around them that turn out to be stars! Digory even thought he saw Jupiter quite close.

THEY WERE IN A FREAKING STARGATE! (Nerdgasm.)

After it was clear they were indeed heading back to London, they switched their rings and returned to the Wood. Digory immediately heads out to find a new pool to explore and once again Polly must be the responsible one and remind him they need to mark the correct pool or risk never finding their way home.

Our author lost his mom at a very young age, and then moved in with a friend's mom who sources say became his lover as well as mothered him. I wonder if this is why all the girls he writes about have to be the mom in these stories. I wonder what Freud would say about this.

When Digory and Polly finally enter a new pool, they come out to find a world dark and destroyed. No living thing can be seen or heard in the rubble. The children slowly walked through the ruins until they came upon a standing building with golden doors. Inside they were astonished to discover people—not alive, but almost like waxworks dressed in fancy clothes with jewelry and crowns. Polly sees fancy outfits on them and goes right on in! Oh for heaven's sake! Girls and their trinkets! Lewis states, "If you were interested in clothes at all, you could hardly help going in to see them closer." Polly and her girl brain can't help it.

While Polly swooned over the pretties, Digory was more interested in the faces. These people were taller than regular humans and were sitting in stone chairs. Their clothes had not rotted away like everything around them because of a strong, palpable magic. The people in the chairs had pretty faces in the first chairs, then cruel but happy faces in the next chairs, and finally cruel and unhappy faces near the end. It reads like a timeline of events they must have experienced. The last row of faces was downright despairing as if they had "done dreadful things and also suffered dreadful things."

At the very end in the last chair was a lone figure of a giant woman who was extremely beautiful. In fact, she was the most beautiful woman Digory had ever seen. Petty Polly claims to not have seen anything specifically beautiful about her. Girls and their jealousy.

In the middle of the room was a pillar holding a golden bell and hammer. Written underneath was a warning:

Make your choice, adventurous Stranger;
Strike the bell and bide the danger,
Or wonder, till it drives you mad,
What would have followed if you had.

Once again we see curiosity being presented as a lure of the devil. We must remain safe in our bubbles and never risk learning or doing something new. It would be wrong just like Eve's quest for knowledge in the Garden was wrong and led to death entering the world.

In ancient times mapmakers would fill in unknown territories on a map, usually at sea, with the warning, "Here be dragons!" The unknown, unexplored areas of life are the most dangerous. Straying from Christ is a similar danger, and its consequence is death and eternal damnation. I stayed a Christian out of fear for years. Freedom from it was scary. Thankfully all the warnings of releasing giant witches, terrible curses, eternal fires, or even the wrath of God didn't come true.

Digory ignores Polly's motherly protest and claims he is overtaken by magic to ring the bell. Polly sees right through this baloney and calls him out on his lie. Digory argues that girls are too dumb to know these things.

"It's because you're a girl. Girls never want to know anything but gossip and rot about people getting engaged."

Polly has had enough and reaches for her ring to return her to the Wood. Digory yells "None of that!" at her in a nasty voice and grabs her wrist, hurting it "quite badly." Then he elbows her other hand out of the way and quickly grabs the golden hammer to ring the bell.

I'd love to say the book shows Polly as the clear victim of this violence, but it actually portrays her as bickering with Digory the whole time as if she had it coming. This is to excuse him hurting her "quite badly."

> Within two seconds, however, they had something to think about that drove their own quarrels quite out of their minds.

Our narrator presents Digory's actions as if they were both simply quarreling, and everyone was equally to blame, and no one was particularly at fault for Polly getting hurt.

The golden bell gave out a note that didn't die away but grew louder until they couldn't have heard their own screams over it. A huge earthquake followed and the whole room, weak with age, starts caving in with great blocks of masonry falling all over the place. The note eventually dies, and the dust clears, but their horror is just beginning. For at that moment the terrible giant woman at the end of the room rises from her chair.

The Magician's Nephew: Chapters 5-6

"How scary! I wouldn't want to be grabbed by Queen Jadis!"
"Um... yeah... *clears throat* that would be... awful... No grown adult would love that."

***

The most terrible and beautiful queen rises from her chair. She is cool, collected, vicious, flawless, fearless, and powerful. Also *evil*, naturally. This is the Empress Jadis.

In a big deviation from the norm, Jadis gets called by name[15] and I had to wonder why Lewis would start using a woman's name instead

---

[15] Jadis' name appears only once in *The Lion, The Witch and The Wardrobe* in a notice nailed to the floor of Tumnus' ransacked home.

of merely her title (witch, queen, female in dress) after all this time. It is obviously more practical to name a main character, but he has been fine with leaving female characters, even primary ones with large speaking roles, nameless in past books. On a hunch, I looked up when Lewis' relationship with his wife, Joy, started since she was quite the intellectual and likely helped humanize women for our author. The timing is close enough: The *Magician's Nephew* was published in 1955 and Lewis married Joy in early 1956.[16] Yet even with the timing, this conclusion is a stretch. While Lewis' marriage story is fascinating, it gets nowhere near explaining Jadis.

Under all that theocratic bunkum, C. S. Lewis had a well-docu-mented S&M side. He once asked people at a party whether he could spank them. He also became drunk at another party and started beg-ging people to allow him to whip them. According to one of his biog-raphies,[17] Lewis referred to himself as "lover of the whip" in letters to his friend, Arthur Greeves. I experienced Lewis from his Christian apologetics, and never got to know the true spank-happy party animal with the drinking problem.

Lewis loved to dole out violence on his characters in relish detail, which arguably could be related to his kinks, though I credit it more to his view of the Christian life being an excruciating experience. Lewis thought "God's best" for us included pain.[18] Of course someone who

---

[16] In case I get pushback, I realize this is the date of their civil marriage in order for her to stay in the country and they weren't *Christian married* until 1957, but she was most definitely in his life around the time he was writing this book.

[17] Alister, McGrath, 2013. *C. S. Lewis—A Life: Eccentric Genius, Reluctant Prophet*, (Tyndale House Publishers. Carol Stream, IL).

[18] "We are not necessarily doubting that God will do the best for us; we are wondering how painful the best will turn out to be." *Letters of C. S. Lewis*, (29 April 1959), para. 1, p. 285—as reported in *The Quotable Lewis* (1989), p. 469.

loves a bit of pain might be drawn to the Cosmic Sadist[19] all the more for it.

Knowing these things about Lewis does color some of the scenes I'm blushingly reading aloud *to my child*. Upon meeting Uncle Andrew, Jadis wishes out loud that she'd brought a whip to lash him with. A whip! I get it now! Of course Jadis is a dominatrix! Think about it! (Because you know I have.) She doesn't need high heels because she's already tall from her giant blood and she's so powerful that when she grabs the children upon first meeting them Polly mentally notes she easily could have broken their arms. Even Digory notices her "white, beautiful" hand was "strong as steel pincers." She even wears revealing clothing that Andrew's sister will try to kick her out of the house over.

She demands silence, punishes those who break her rules, has fond memories of her castle's dungeon, commands people to do her bidding—she's everything a dom should be and magically more!

Jadis was obviously born from the mind of Mr. Lover of the Whip rather than Mr. Pious Theologian and **I am here for it**. I was talking about this stuff with a friend of mine from my missionary days who has an English degree. She ran across Lewis' fantasy life while doing research for her Master's thesis. She recalled one sexual fantasy Lewis wrote about was imagining taking a woman home who had passed him on the street, whipping her, spanking her until she begged him to stop, and then having sex with her.

I can't help but laugh at how my slut-shaming, sex negative, purity culture church practically made Lewis a patron saint! I love this so much! It's like Christmas. *Okay, where was I? I think I was reading a children's book?*

---

[19] Lewis called the Christian god a "Cosmic Sadist" and "Eternal Vivisector" in his book *A Grief Observed* (1961) which he published under the pseudonym N. W. Clerk.

Jadis calmly AF tells the children they are in danger. Then she grace-fully grabs them and yanks them effortlessly out of the palace that is collapsing around them. She shows zero signs of fear and Digory thinks, "She's wonderfully brave. And strong. She's what I call a Queen!" *Me too, buddy.*

While Jadis is being a total badass, Polly is trying to reach her ring to return home, but she can't quite do it. As they run through the palace, Jadis coolly comments on where the torture chambers were, or the banquet hall where seven hundred people were slaughtered, or where the dungeon door used to be. All her favorite memories and places are drenched in blood. She comes to the exit—this enormous metal gate—and with a bit of magic and very little effort she crumbles it to dust. Then she warns this is what happens to anyone who stands in her way. (I love her.)

Beyond the dusted gate is a dead world. The sun is huge and red and near its end; it gives off very little heat. The cities below are in ruin. Nothing lives here. Jadis reminisces about when she could hear people being whipped in the street. (More whipping! It's the fetish that keeps on giving!) Then she tells the children how all the people of this world died. (Women are suddenly allowed to give exposition?) Turns out there was a war between her and her sister, a nameless war-rior queen who was on the front lines in battle, and Jadis won by kill-ing everyone on the whole planet with a single magic word.

Upon hearing about all the genocide, Digory is now also reaching for his ring to return home. Jadis hears of the children's world and its young sun and all the people she could rule there and decides to go with them.

The children make to escape by putting on their rings to return to the Wood Between the Worlds. Unfortunately for them, Jadis gets pulled along simply for being in contact with them. The cannabis-like effect of the Wood works differently on our queen and ends up draining her power and strength. Being powerless is not something Jadis does well *at all*. Seeing her in a sympathetic state makes Digory hesitate before going back to London, and Jadis uses that moment to grab his ear. Now Jadis is on Earth, in London, and of all places, in Uncle Andrew's study!

> In Charn she had been alarming enough: in London, she was terrifying.

Charn is one letter from the word charm and is full of magic. Lewis' affinity for lazy naming works rather well here.

Jadis' powerful presence has something to do with her height, but also "her height was nothing compared with her beauty, her fierceness, and her wildness." When she speaks softly the whole room quivers. She demands to know who the magician is who summoned her and quickly makes Andrew her slave. She then demands either a flying carpet or a dragon (he gets her a taxi) and starts making plans for conquest of the world. This lady does not mess around. There's more talk about whipping at this point as well. (Glee!)

Lewis is now calling Jadis a witch and not a queen; this is a noticeable shift that communicates how everyone sees her at this point. (Not me though. #JadisMyQueen4EVA).

When the children are finally left alone, Polly starts to get the heck home. Digory wants her to return as soon as possible and demands, "You can't leave me alone in a scrape like this."

I stop reading at this point to yell at him, "Polly darn well can, idiot. She owes you nothing! You're the one who violently grabbed her to release the best character ever (thank you) and it's all your fault if she conquers England! Not Polly's!"

Polly says he should at least apologize for what he did.

"Sorry? Well now, if that isn't just like a girl! What have *I* done?"

These blanket statements about girls never receive proper pushback. The boys do terrible things, the girls get blamed for being a member of their gender, and everyone is presented as quarreling equally as far as the narrator is concerned. Hearing Digory say this made Little Bit growl and I about dropped the book in exasperation. We both lowkey hate Digory right now. Polly mentions a laundry list of wrongs he damn well did, but she includes how Jadis wouldn't have gotten to London if he hadn't turned back for her in the Wood and allowed her to get his ear. This is much too *Lot's wife* for me, as if Digory's sympathetic hesitation and backwards glance was in any way wrong. Digory did some very real, violent things; let's not add imaginary, biblically-fueled nonsense to the list! Digory sort of apologizes weakly, "There: I've said I'm sorry." Then orders her to "be decent and come back." Controlling jerk. Boo.

One floor down Uncle Andrew is getting rather drunk, putting on his finest clothes, and repeating about Jadis, "A dem fine woman, sir, a dem fine woman." (I'm sure "dem" is not supposed to count as "damn" in a children's book.) Andrew thinks this goddess might have sex with him.

> The foolish old man was actually beginning to imagine the Witch would fall in love with him.

The book makes clear this thinking is partially inspired by booze just in case the young readers want to know the particulars of getting wasted. His vanity is condemned and tied to the reason Andrew wanted to become a magician in the first place. Seeking out knowledge is just another vanity. (There is a bit of delicious hypocrisy at play when our author gets on Andrew for fantasies about a woman he just met.)

It won't go well for Andrew, because Jadis does NOT need a man. That's part of why we love her, and, sadly, also why this book condemns her squarely to the evil category. Bitsy and I are ready to see Jadis loosed on London.

The Magician's Nephew: Chapter 7

"Will Digory save his mom?"

"I don't want to spoil the ending."

"I would rather know!"

"Okay fine, yes, he saves her."

"Good, I just didn't want you to get sad if the mom died."

"Me?"

"Wouldn't that make you sad since your mom died?"

"Sometimes I get sad that my mom never met you. Sometimes I even wish I had a magic fruit to go back and save her."

"Okay now THAT was a spoiler."

"Oops."

***

Chapter seven has a bit of everything. There's the delightful chaos of Jadis meeting London police. There's also the suffocating sexism when, well, Jadis meets London police, or any other man in the street for that matter. And tucked almost indifferently between action scenes is a nugget of breathtaking pain as a little boy grieves for his dying mother whom he is helpless to save.

Lewis really truly thinks that no matter the circumstances, women will be catty. Despite being in the presence of a violent and powerful queen, all our female protagonists are petty, compare their beauty, and put each other down. It makes a bit of sense in cultures where women are powerless objects that they would preserve their own economic and social standing by talking down a competitor. Yet it speaks to Lewis' view of women's inherent nature that these beauty and purity put-downs would be kept up in fantastical and extraordinary circumstances. Women are assumed to have a gendered sin issue with words. This may be why the Bible repeatedly urges the silencing of women.[20] Or to further quote the *good book*:

"I found one upright man among a thousand, but not one upright woman among them all."[21]

Now that Jadis is in the presence of Aunt Letty, Uncle Andrew's sister, more cattiness ensues:

"Now, slave, how long am I to wait for my chariot?" thundered the Witch.
[…]
"And who is this young person, Andrew, may I ask?" said Aunt Letty in icy tones.
"Distinguished foreigner—v-very important p-person," he stammered.
"Rubbish!" said Aunt Letty, and then, turning to the Witch, "get out of my house this moment, you shameless hussy, or I'll send for the police."
[…]
[Aunt Letty] did not approve of bare arms.

Letty is older and there is a hierarchy of age at play, which may be why she pointedly refers to Jadis as a "young person" to show who should hold the power here and who should not. Letty, as a woman in Lewis' world, will be vain enough to hate Jadis for her looks—her bare arms a sign of both youth and sexuality—but the true judgement will

---

[20] 1 Timothy 2:11-14; 1 Corinthians 14:34; 1 Peter 3:1-6; Ephesians 5:22-24; Colossians 3:18; 1 Corinthians 11:3-12
[21] Ecclesiastes 7:28

be a righteous one since Jadis is breaking the rules of purity culture, which is particularly strict when it comes to women. Who did Aunt Letty think Jadis was? Every adult reading this series might easily assume she was Andrew's prostitute. But Lewis, in the role of narrator, adds unconvincingly that Letty assumed Jadis was from the circus. (Circus folks are "shameless hussies"?)

It's time for Jadis to punish Letty. She makes the same motion she did on the gates in Charn that rendered them to dust, but London does not have enough magic to channel, even for the best magician, so Letty is unaffected. The realization that her magic was gone should have been a devastating blow to our queen's world domination plans, but this is Jadis, mind you, and she does not show disappointment or worry, not even shame or self-doubt. She's a professional dominatrix, er, dominating conqueror, so she leaps to action picking up Letty by the neck and flinging her clear across the room. The housemaid is downright thrilled by this, by the way.

Digory comes down the stairs just as Jadis and Andrew leave. Letty is still crumpled in the corner, but only bruised. The giddy maid tells "Master Digory" (eww, social class does not sound right on children) about what happened before calling the police.

Digory hatches a plan to wait for the witch to return and somehow slip the ring to the Wood Between the Worlds on her. It's a good idea since we know what happens to her in that place. In the meantime, the boy stands guard at the front of the house. At his post he overhears that his sick mother is near the end of her life. There's no real time to process this as Jadis returns.

Pure chaos erupts. A cab pulled by a horse was coming around the bend. I can't do the description of her justice, so I'll let Lewis do it:

> There was no one in the driver's seat. On the roof—not sitting, but standing on the roof—swaying with superb balance as it came at full speed round the corner with one wheel in the air—was Jadis the

Queen of Queens and the Terror of Charn. Her teeth were bared, her eyes shone like fire, and her long hair streamed out behind her like a comet's tail.

I love that Lewis seems to enjoy this character as much as I do. Bitsy did not like that Jadis was flogging the horse, or that she whispered some magical thing to it that made it scream and rear up. This is the point in the story where Little Bit and I go our separate ways as far as enjoying the witch.

Following behind Jadis were the police, and then, for no reason, twenty boys whose only purpose was to cat-call the queen. Jadis is actively destroying property, including the cab she rode in on, and leaving a bunch of destruction in her wake. Turns out Jadis has robbed a jewelry store, leaving the proprietor with a black eye. Women and their jewelry. (Evil evil evil.) But who gets the blame for the robbed store? The man with her. The "most important of the policemen" ignores Jadis and questions Andrew about the chaos:

"Are you in charge of that there young woman?"

Lewis believed men to be so much better than women that they naturally would hold dominion over them. One of his theology books contains this gem:

[Only] one wearing the masculine uniform can [...] represent the Lord to the Church: for we are all, corporately and individually, feminine to Him.[22]

Feminine here meaning subordinate and inferior. He goes on to defend masculine imagery of God as "inspired."[23] This kind of sexism

[22] C. S. Lewis, 1948. "Priestesses in the Church?" Originally published under the title "Notes on the Way." *Time and Tide*, Vol. XXIX (August 14). Available at: http://www.episcopalnet.org/TRACTS/priestesses.html
[23] Lewis, "Priestesses," p. 237.

definitely makes me want to start beating up people, but I'll leave that to Jadis.

At this point Jadis tries to kill the policeman with her horse. The horse's owner, a cabby whose lines are hard to read as he speaks with an accent, tries to talk to Jadis to get the horse back. He's a nice guy[24] who is portrayed as very kind.

This cabby pretty much calls Jadis hysterical and treats her like a small child, even calling her "Missie." He suggests that she needs to be a lady, get a nice cup of tea, and go lie down until she's not all murder-y. I'm surprised he didn't tell her to smile. Her response made me cheer:

"Dog, unhand our royal charger. We are the Empress Jadis."

Here is where the chapter ends, with Jadis about to throw down. This is the story having fun, but back at the previous scene where Digory learns his mother is not going to get better, that is where the story gets its heart. Letty had found time to gossip with a friend not long after being thrown across a room because the feminine tongue is so sinful that Letty can't even recover from trauma before following her base instincts. A friend had brought grapes and Letty mentions that it would take the "fruit from the land of youth" to save Digory's mom. It occurs to Digory that he has a magic ring with access to countless worlds, one of which could literally contain this magic fruit.

I knew Lewis' mother, Flora, had died, but I hadn't realized it was when he was nine years old, only a few years younger than Digory. This book will ultimately be a fantasy about saving her. After this loss, Lewis was sent away to a miserable boarding school where his mother was no longer there to protect him. The schoolmaster was horrible and eventually even declared insane! This explains Lewis' apparent hatred towards children's education and the incredibly violent ending in *The*

---

[24] Super sexist.

Silver Chair. In that story the head of the school is delightfully terrorized by Aslan, just as Lewis' schoolmaster should have been. Classic revenge fantasy!

Here's where Lewis becomes a completely understandable and sympathetic character. He is not actually in the books, but he has been here all along as the phantom narrator—not someone we're watching, but nevertheless a voice that directs the story. We have seen evidence he has already used his fantasy stories as a reaction at least once when it came to his abusive schoolmaster. One biographer compared his school years to his time in the trenches of WWI, so it's no surprise that in the Narnia series the schoolmaster is punished by Aslan, the school bullies are beaten, and the entire institution becomes better.

While I had picked apart the wrongheadedness of what Lewis assumed would improve a school, and been disappointed by his assertion that violence is a path to childhood moral development, I had missed this theme of redemption. *The Silver Chair* didn't end with an institution burned to the ground; after his cathartic revenge was doled out and he had unclenched his emotional fist, Lewis' fantasy became a school *made right*. That's important. He saw a bad world, and in his own imperfect way attempted to make it better.

Digory has a dying mother. Lewis had a dying mother. Digory goes on an adventure to save his mother. Lewis, around Digory's age, lost his. While my own mother was alive while I read the Narnia books the first time through, she died a few years later. I know what it's like wondering if I had done something differently. I know what it's like to dream I had.

In one of my favorite television series of all time, there's a particular scene where one of the characters talks to another who had died (and came back to life). He tells her what I would have told my mom given the chance:

But I want you to know I did save you. Not when it counted, of course, but, after that. Every night after that. I'd see it all again... I do something different. Faster or more clever, you know? Dozens of times, lots of different ways... Every night I save you.[25]

C. S. Lewis, the powerhouse of evangelicals, the crammer of Christendom, here becomes the child in the story. This time around, he'll save her. Every night he'll save her. Tonight, it will be magic fruit from a magic world. Tomorrow, maybe a whole new story.

It resonated deeply within me when Digory started to hope.

It was no good trying to throttle this hope. It might—really, really, it just might be true. [...] Mother well again. Everything right again.

In the following chapters we'll see what happens when hope runs the story.

The Magician's Nephew: Chapters 8-9

"What if the leopard didn't like the other leopard?"
"Well, too bad they have to populate Narnia."
"Oh, Mom! There are only two people! Human people!"
"Well, they're already married at least."
"But what about *their kids*? Who do they marry?"
"I think you just stumbled upon the biggest ick factor in the creation story."

***

Using her Kryptonian strength, Jadis reaches up and easily takes an iron cross bar off the lamppost she recently plowed her cab into. She

---

[25] "After Life." *Buffy the Vampire Slayer*, written by Jane Espenson, directed by David Solomon, United Paramount Network, 2001.

got sick of the cat-callers and is about to bludgeon them all with it. Honestly, I'm not hating this. (Violence is bad though. *cough*)

First, she takes out the chief of police who falls like a ninepin. Then she starts down the line of men. While the crowd is distracted, Polly of all people rushes the scene with magic rings in her pockets. It seems she had the same idea as Digory about getting the witch back to the Wood. Digory then takes charge for no reason other than he is a boy. He tells Polly to put on her ring when he gives the signal.

Jadis is having a blast. She just took out another officer who crumpled to the ground and she's on the kind of murder rampage I imagine would make her happy. She starts triumphantly shouting that she's going to destroy London when Digory grabs her ankle. Well, he tries, but she kicks him and splits his lip, filling his mouth with blood. For someone with superhuman strength, why didn't this kill him? This not-killing-him inconsistency means Diggyboy has two more opportunities to grab at her until finally he gets ahold and signals to Polly. Now they are flying through the Stargate back to the Wood Between the Worlds.

And so is the cabby. And Uncle Andrew. And the freaking horse, too!

At once the witch becomes ill and her powers start to drain. A bunch of plot-driven stuff must happen so the narcotized aspect of the Wood is completely forgotten this time around and everyone is in their normal state of mind. The horse goes to get a drink from a nearby pool and upon seeing this Polly yells to put on the rings. Why? It makes no sense. Maybe she saw the horse and decided that another world was best? Another world where the witch could regain her strength? Anyway, it's not super clear why she would have done this and why Digory was quick to oblige, except how else are they getting to Narnia? So the entire party went into the world that is connected to the pool the horse was standing in.

Except, it didn't exist yet.

I was so excited about this next part while reading to Bitsy. It felt like when I was a kid and I had an experience sharing a TV show I loved with a neighbor who had never seen it before. As the theme song started playing, I had this euphoric feeling. I looked over at my friend to share this moment with her, but she was just politely sitting there enduring both the show and my hard stares. Bits' response was not much different.

This world was a fetus world; it was not dead, just unformed:

And really it was uncommonly like Nothing.

Then, surrounded by complete darkness, a musical note begins. It is joined by others—stars coming to life. The sun is born, both younger and brighter than Earth's sun; it erupts in joy revealing with its light a barren world—not barren as in used up and old, but a blank, tabula rasa waiting for the wonders to come. What is driving the creation of things? Music! Aslan is singing, despite having a lion larynx, and at this point all the Christian children are going "OH HEY I KNOW WHAT IS GOING ON!" It's creation, people! Breathed and spoken into existence by the Jesus beast! Unlike the original tale from antiquity, Lewis has Aslan make the sun *before* the plants that relied on it. Almost like he knew more about how these things worked.

Again, as in the first book, Aslan's presence has a different effect on different people. The witch is all clenched fists, Uncle Andrew wants to hide, and the children and cabby are having some woo-woo spiritual experience. Before all this, the cabby had been leading the children in a hymn so it's clear that he's a good religious type. Yet the cabby started singing the hymn because he was scared, and I just realized that instead of reassuring him that they could totally get home whenever they wanted since they had teleport rings, the kids joined in singing to show off their holiness cred. It's like when someone is in need and religious folks make a show of praying instead of actually helping.

Jadis overhears Andrew talk about the rings being the way to escape from this place with the scary lion so she plans to take them. Digory and Polly threaten to leave them all behind in an instant if the queen tries to grab at the rings. They even tell the cabby that they are about to leave him behind, too. He doesn't care because Aslan has made him brainlessly worshipful. He has a wife at home but screw her, right? He'll die listening to lion music because he's on a spiritual high right now.

As the lion roamed the world back and forth[26] while singing it into existence, he came nearer and nearer to Jadis. She responds by chucking that iron lamppost bar as hard as she can right at Aslan's head! The bar hit the lion between the eyes! Then Jadis runs off leaving the rest of the party standing there paralyzed as the lion, still singing, comes straight at them! Another familiar scene is played out where everyone was terrified of the lion as he approached and hoped it wouldn't look at them, but at the same time "in some queer way they wished it would." The faithful want the lion to maul or eat them, to be "living sacrifices." Their holy book tells them human sacrifice is fine if done for the right deity.[27]

As the lion sang, the trees grew up all around like a time lapse video. A lamppost also started to grow from this magic earth where the rod fell to the ground and stuck there. It was a living thing, and even had a flame come on inside. This would be the same lamppost Lucy would discover in *The Lion, The Witch and The Wardrobe*! Uncle Andrew immediately began making plans to plant bits of metal and make battleships or whatnot grow from them. He even starts wondering if he

---

[26] Fun fact: The Bible talks of one like a lion roaming back and forth on earth, but it's the devil: 1 Peter 5:8.
[27] Genesis 22

could make a health resort out of this place since the air is making him feel younger. At the mention of health and youth, Digory remembers his plan to save his mother. He mentions it to Andrew, but the older man doesn't care. (People who don't care about your mom are bad. Now ignore when Aslan does it.) Digory then runs to ask the lion for help.

Aslan is making new music now which influences the humans, making them want to "rush at other people and either hug them or fight them." It made Uncle Andrew super horny. Turns out this kind of song is for making babies! Where do babies come from? Well, first you feel like *hugging* or *fighting, wrestling* really. This music creates animals who come out of the earth like mole hills exploding. Even elephants pop out because no one cares about proper habitats. Aslan goes around arranging their marriages by pairing one male and one female from some of the animal groups, but not all of them; they have to leave something to eat.

He anthropomorphized the pairs: beavers and rabbits become bigger and smarter and elephants became smaller. Then Aslan stared at them "as if he was going to burn them up" because the guy can't do anything without it being scary or violent. He starts to chant magic:

"Narnia, Narnia, Narnia, awake. Love. Think. Speak. Be walking trees. Be talking beasts. Be divine waters."

OH MY GOSH, IT'S FREAKING NARNIA!!!

The Magician's Nephew: Chapter 10

We interrupt the usual dialog between mother and daughter to bring you: Bitsy decides to communicate only in barks tonight.

"So what did you think of…?"

"Ruff ruff ruff!!!"

"How did you like…?"

pants and cocks head "Rrrrrrrruff!"
Bulldogs were mentioned and she's ten. Just keeping it real.

***

In the last chapters we saw aspects of two biblical stories from the book of Genesis: Creation of the World and Noah's Flood. These allusions provide mile markers for the young Christian reader to let them know where we are in the story. I must admit, creating whole worlds from pure imagination is a great fantasy. Having two of each kind of animal populating the world is curious though. Like, how would this work exactly? Incestuous couplings over generations without genetic breakdown forming eventual societies of those animals who retain their original parents' looks and intelligence? Sure! Don't sweat it. It's just a children's story. It's not like anyone takes this kind of thing seriously.[28]

All the animal people, including bulldogs who were just created, join in one voice to say their very first independent thought:

"Hail, Aslan. We hear and obey."

Okay, so they say their first *extremely dependent* thought. It reminds me of how my church presented God as a master to be obeyed. Slavery is a-okay in both the Old and New Testaments. How did God become everyone's master? By default, for creating us. In response to this gift of life, the Scriptures tell us our response should be to "only fear the LORD and serve him faithfully."[29] I always thought the word "only" in this verse made it seem as if it's the simplest little thing to be a deity's scared (according to the verse) slave for life. There are, of

---

[28] Hahahahaha *sobs*
[29] 1 Samuel 12:24

225

course, torturous consequences for disobedience so it's not a true choice, but it's *so darn reasonable* that why wouldn't we just fall in line?

To sum up the Old Testament god's plan: Here's life! Now use it to obey me by killing a bunch of strangers. I gave them life so they could die hated by me! Some of you can become rich and prosperous by following my bizarre instructions and some of you can die violently by not following my bizarre instructions well enough. Also, there is no eternal reward; it's all about this life. Obey or suffer!

The New Testament contains a similar idea that because a person received life, even if they didn't want it or ask for it, they must now be a slave as a thank you for that life. Since people "have been set free from sin" they must now "become slaves of God."[30] God is so thoughtful he even molds people into his servants with tasks he prepared for them ahead of time, as if that was the very purpose of them even being alive.[31] One task could be to worship God while dying of starvation. That is literally something I was told growing up to excuse God's whole not-feeding-starving-children game plan. Another task could be never losing faith on the way to the gas chamber. Another valid part of God's loving plan! Just like in the Old Testament there's still torturous consequences for disobedience, only this time the torture is eternal!

The New Testament god in a nutshell: Don't be like the other people around you with their crazy blood cults. Join mine! Our death cult is a Jewish apocalypse religion and comes with my son dying a bloody death, his followers dying horrible deaths, and in the end times everybody dying horrible deaths! Don't worry about this life, though. Like seriously, don't worry: don't store up food, don't save up money, don't care about your clothing.[32] Why? Because this is the end times RIGHT

---

[30] Romans 6:22
[31] Ephesians 2
[32] Matthew 6:25-34

NOW. None of you standing around will die of natural causes before the world ends.[33] Just to be clear, 2,000 years <u>definitely</u> won't go by since the world is ending right this minute.[34] It's fine, though, because all this extreme misery on earth followed by the world ending in a few years will be rewarded eternally in the afterlife. Don't expect a lick of evidence for this afterlife, just take our word for it. And obey!

I shouldn't have to say this, but demanding slavery in exchange for life is wrong. Two people literally did create me (there was *definitely* either hugging or fighting involved) and even still I am not their slave. No good parent would demand this. Aslan is *not* a good parent and happily accepts obedience and servitude from the animals as if its rightfully his to take from them. He also creates a hierarchy, giving the animals control over the other animals whom they came from. He lets everyone know they were a chosen people, and if they go back to the ways of their unintelligent family members they will be cursed and lose the ability to talk, advocate, and think. If he then sent them into a land already occupied by people and ordered them to commit genocide, it would be an even closer facsimile to several biblical accounts.

The idea of "God's Chosen People" has led to tribalistic wars, blind hatred, justification for rape, and a host of victims in world history. The lesson is that God's people are better, smarter, and special-er; they can do whatever they want to anyone else. Our newly-made animal people can do whatever they want with the lesser animals, their version of the Caananites. They can eat them, use them, control them; they just can't become like them.

Aslan makes all the animals swear to him. One crow is a bit loud about it so his promises to Aslan come a beat after everyone else has quieted down. In response to this, Aslan encourages the other animals, who were presently trying to be polite, to laugh at him. The crow perks

[33] Matthew 24:34
[34] Matthew 16:28

up and asks, "Aslan! Aslan! Have I made the first joke?" Aslan responds, "You have not *made* the first joke, you have only *been* the first joke." At this, all the other animals continue to laugh "more than ever." At someone's expense. Aslan is... what's the word? Oh yeah. A **dick**.

What this new world needs is EVEN MORE HIERARCHY! Some animals had previously been ranked over other animals, but now they'll be ranked by gender and certain attributes, creating an in-group. This group consisted of the chief (male) Dwarf, the River-god (not goddess), the Oak tree (male), the He-Owl (not she-owl), and the Bull Elephant. (Not, um, ballerina elephant? What's a female elephant called? *A cow. We looked it up.*) It's clear who should be in charge: MEN! Aslan draws the predominately male leaders to his council to discuss what must be done about *that woman*. That right there is a good summary of Abrahamic religion.

The cabby and children approach the animal-people left behind. The cabby's old horse does not immediately recognize him, but eventually memories of hard labor on the streets of London come back to him. It was a horrible life from what the horse remembered. The humans have little sympathy to Little Bit's frustration and press gang the horse into service once more—having him take Digory to Aslan. In *The Horse and His Boy*, we learned that being ridden by humans outside of a war setting is offensive and demeaning to talking horses, yet humans seem to be able to force this kind of servitude upon others if they are a step higher up on the hierarchy. It's no different than Aslan forcing his will on everyone below him.

***

Uncle Andrew has been off experiencing things very differently up to this point. We're about to read yet another example of stupid unbelievers who must work tirelessly at their lack of belief. When Aslan first started singing the world into existence, Uncle Andrew, who really believed in Aslan *deep down* as all unbelievers do, "tried his hardest to make believe that it wasn't singing and never had been singing." That's totally how it works, by the way, we just disbelieve *really* hard.

Anytime the lion is obviously talking or singing, our stupid atheist only hears roaring. Soon, "he couldn't have heard anything else even if he had wanted to." Even the other talking animals seemed to make growling, baying, or snarling sounds instead of speech.

I have heard quite often since leaving Christianity that I am foolish. Only special believers can discern super special spiritual things and the rest of us just experience reality like normal.[35] (I'm told this despite my thirty years being one of those super special believers.) Coming to the wrong conclusion after weighing the evidence is hardly a vile deed, if that's what I'm being accused of, but the Bible claims unbelievers like me are evil[36] because of our unbelief. Even when doubt was unwanted in my case, it is still categorized as deliberate and spiteful, *just like all unbelievers' thoughts and actions are.*[37] Andrew only cared that the children have run up to the wild beasts because he's worried the magic rings will be eaten, not the children. It's said he didn't like animals after years of doing "cruel experiments" on them. He is evil in every way, just like all atheists supposedly are.

The Magician's Nephew: Chapter 11

"I was told I had to forgive the boy who hit me."
"That's up to you. You don't have to."

---

[35] 1 Corinthians 2:14
[36] Hebrews 3:12
[37] Psalm 14:1

"Then we'd both be wrong."

"He committed the wrong. Only him."

"Still, I'd have been the mean one if I hadn't forgiven him when they made him say he was sorry."

"You don't have to say 'It's okay' when it's not. I don't say, 'I forgive you,' in those cases where I feel the action is not forgivable. Instead I try simply to acknowledge the apology when appropriate and move forward."

"I just forgave him and said it was okay because that was easier."

"It's sometimes okay to choose the path of least resistance in an unfair system. Maybe someday when you're in a position of power you can help a victim of abuse rather than forcing them to absolve the criminal."

"Yeah, I would just protect her and not pressure her to make him feel better."

"My hero."

***

Uncle Andrew overheard some animals talking, but because he doesn't believe in animal speech, he interpreted the sounds as barking and snarling instead. When these snarling animals approached him, he freaked out! Of course, they were speaking English, the queen's English no less. The bulldog started asking him what kind of creature he was, but it came out as growls.

Shouldn't this bulldog be a wolf? Or are all wolves bad from the first book so we can't use one here? Bulldogs are adorable, but they came from wolves and were bred into respiratory problems. We're supposed to think that an all-powerful, all-knowing creator just made doggies with sinus issues? I realize this is a very minor quibble, but still, Aslan has created beings wholesale out of imagination, and he imagined them wheezing?

Andrew tried saying "Good Doggie" and backed away. Lewis says dogs like being called "Good Doggie" as much as "[the reader] would like being called 'My Little Man.'" I have two problems with this. First, Lewis is dumb and all doggos are good doggos. Tell them often. Second, Lewis assumes the reader is a boy. Parts of these books were hard to read as a girl, and impossible as a woman, but once the intended audience of "Little Man" is blatantly known, it makes so much more sense. Boys are people, after all. They drive the story. Girls are only the readership secondarily.

Andrew faints and the animals think the fallen man is a fallen tree even though they would have never seen a tree fall before. The bear thinks he might have honey bees in him, being a tree and all. It's hard to keep track of what these animals—brought into existence mere moments ago and repeatedly described as ignorant—know and don't know about the world. They already seem to have perfect English and a lot of 1950s idioms at their disposal, as well as a ton of knowledge about trees, bees, and minerals, but they don't know a creature from a tree when they see one. This seems to be written for laughs more than internal consistency as Lewis sets up a scene to make the unbeliever look ridiculous.

The animals decide that Uncle Andrew needs to be planted, so they bury him up to his knees in the dirt. He is slumped over so they think he's wilted and begin to water him. That will humiliate him even more! We are reminded that the important "husband" elephant is off doing leadership work which leaves the she-elephant (cow) the task of watering the Andrew tree with her trunk. The bulldog is offended when the elephant mentions she has a proper nose for the job. It's literally because his is smooshed, Aslan!

231

About this same time, Digory shows up to Aslan's council on the back of the cabby's horse. Digory is granted an audience with the lion who is described in the usual way: beautiful, big, terrible. (Gots to be scary!) Digory timidly asks for fruit to save his dying mother and Aslan the Dick completely ignores him, turns to his council, and announces, "This is the Boy who did it." Then turning to Digory:

> "Son of Adam. There is an evil Witch abroad in my new land of Narnia. Tell these good Beasts how she came here."

Ooh! Ooh! I know! POLLY said to put on the rings! Then she put on hers and Digory followed suit. Gold star for me!

How did Digory respond? With "the exact truth" saith the book. What was that?

> "I brought her, Aslan."

What? No. Nope. He may have woken her up in Charn, but he didn't bring her to Narnia. Polly did. He helped, sure, but my point is "the exact truth" would be more like: "Polly, taking the lead, helped me accidentally warp her here under really harrowing circumstances. Also, **we're children**."

This admission is not a case of him protecting Polly. No, he's taking the responsibility *from* her. Remember when she rushed Jadis with the rings and because Digory showed up he immediately was in charge? It's on him that he "allowed" a girl to lead that situation in the first place! We see this disregard for women's autonomy in the Bible when Eve gets the credit for ruining everything, yet Adam is held responsible for her as if she is a child. Eve is punished to the extreme, yet Adam gets spoken to by God just like Andrew got spoken to by the London chief of police. Women are not treated as full adults and girls are not treated as equals to boys. Aslan, as we will see, will hardly look at or talk to Polly. She's not important.

Additionally, Aslan does not say one word about how wrong it was to physically hurt Polly while he's making Digory confess his sins. Nope, just complete emphasis on how wrong it was for Diggy to follow his curiosity. The small boy is feeling truly hopeless at this point since he's sure he's blown his chance to save his mom. That's what the lion wants him to feel. Worthless. *Less than.* Humbled. Undeserving. That's how all good Christians are supposed to feel: "We are an unclean thing."[38]

"What is man that you should be mindful of him?"[39]

"We all have sinned and deserve death."[40]

As Lewis once penned:

"Every story of conversion is a story of blessed defeat."[41]

The cabby and Polly finally arrive on foot. Aslan focuses on the cabby and asks if the man recognizes him. It's implied that the cabby was a Christian and should recognize Jesus. We established at the end of *Voyage of The Dawn Treader* that that's who Aslan really is. The cabby is already a servant of his, a believer in Jesus, so Aslan asks if he wants to live in Narnia forever. Of course he does! He speaks on behalf of his wife, too! Yes, I'm sure she didn't need to have any say on whether she wanted to live without any other humans for the rest of her life. What? Are women people?

Aslan pops the silent wife into Narnia and announces they are the new king and queen. The cabby accepts and adds, "my Missus does the same," without checking with her. The man is not concerned with how his wife truly feels since if she truly is a good and submissive

---

[38] Isaiah 64:6

[39] Psalm 8:4

[40] Romans 3:23; 6:23

[41] Said in the foreword of Joy Davidman's book, *Smoke on the Mountain: An Interpretation of the Ten Commandments* (1954). Joy became Lewis' wife in 1956.

Christian wife, she'll feel exactly what he wants her to feel. His only concern at the moment is that he has no education or experience for the job of king. As we learned in *Prince Caspian*, Aslan likes his rulers male, stupid, violent, and humble, so the only thing Aslan really cares about is making sure the cabby will do his bidding. He gives the new king a list of three conditions in order to rule.

First: Future generations of people must follow in his footsteps. Aslan makes sure the cabby will raise his children and grandchildren to be rulers. Here is where Little Bit starts asking some uncomfortable questions about incest. I assure her Aslan is going to bring other humans over from London later, which is a lie I made up to get out of that conversation. Sue me.

Aslan tells the cabby his children will be "Kings of Narnia, and others will be Kings of Archenland." No women are allowed to rule. No Black people either since we've established that both those kingdoms are White folks only.

Second: Know your animals. Aslan makes sure the cabby knows which animals are special and which are not. The talking beasts are to be "free subjects" since they are "not slaves like the dumb beasts." Slavery is the process of dehumanizing people in order to justify their treatment. Here it's a bit on the nose with animals being animals and all.

The Bible does this same dehumanization process with human beings, especially the nations surrounding God's chosen people. The holy text even outlines how they should beat,[42] rape,[43] and trade[44] their slaves who are repeatedly referred to as "property."[45]

Third: Be violent. Aslan makes sure the cabby is violent enough to fight in upcoming wars. He literally just promised peace and all that

---

[42] Exodus 21:20-21
[43] Exodus 21:7-11
[44] Exodus 21:2-6; Deuteronomy 15:12-17
[45] Exodus 21:21; Leviticus 25:44-46

for hundreds of years, but already war is part of that peace. Apparently while he was creating everything, he also created evil things, just like the biblical god did,[46] to ruin the world for no reason. The cabby admits he has done some fighting with fists as part of his normal male experience and hopes that would translate to killing folks. (Good enough.)

Once done with the cabby, Aslan finally turns to Polly. What words of wisdom or rebuke will follow? Will she be awarded some royal status? Will she be blamed for picking the wrong pool to throw the party into? The only thing—the ONLY thing—Aslan asks Polly is if she's forgiven Digory for physically abusing her in Charn. It is her duty to forgive! It would be a sin not to! He won't make Digory ask for her forgiveness; she must just give it. He won't punish or confront Digory for this violence, which he has yet to even acknowledge, only the victim of it!

Compulsory forgiveness is bullshit. (I will repeat this until I die.) It puts blame on victims for not excusing their abusers. Forgiveness is more than just letting go of bitterness or moving on. No, we have other language for clearing the air, making amends, communicating hurt, accepting an apology, and acknowledging wrong. Forgiveness can include these things, but its implications are too broad. It can also mean not being angry at someone who has caused harm, implying anger is an inappropriate response to harm. In fundamentalism, the definition I got for forgiveness was to take the consequences from those who deserved them and put it on oneself. Christ did this on the cross, for example. In the Bible, Jesus commands everyone to always forgive bad people who caused them harm.[47] The Son of God goes as far as to say that failure to do so will result in God withholding forgiveness for victims of their own sins. Since sin leads to eternal torture if not

---

[46] Isaiah 45:7
[47] Matthew 6:14-15

235

forgiven, this is a real ultimatum for believers! The Lord and Savior warns, "Fear Him who is able to destroy both body and soul in hell."[48] This is forgiveness under threat of harm and is absolutely morally repugnant.

I have heard rape victims encouraged to forgive rapists as a way through their grief, only for them to find their grief complicated by added shame for doing so or added guilt for failing to do so. Pressuring people to forgive their abusers is an act of abuse.

Rabbi Danya Ruttenberg, told her Twitter followers that in Judaism forgiveness is not required.[49] It can be given if proper work has been done in the areas of repentance and repair, including having the one at fault accept the consequences of their actions legally, socially, professionally, and interpersonally. A public confession, as is often performed in Christian churches as the totality of repentance work, is woefully insufficient. Even after appropriate repair work is done, she says, forgiveness remains "complicated at best." If the harm caused was irreparable, no forgiveness is ever required, even if the perpetrator repents. I never thought after leaving one Abrahamic religion that I would have such high praise for the teachings from another.

It's not our fault forgiveness is a loaded word and we honestly don't have a better one. I've heard forgiveness pushed on people as the only way they will feel better. You know what feels empowering and great? *Not forgiving.* That does not imply holding onto the hurt forever or some such nonsense; it just means the blame stays where it stays. Where it belongs. Forgiveness is not something anyone ever *owes* an abuser. If it helps someone heal, then great! Forgive away! However, if it is compulsory then it's effectively meaningless. Plus, as in the case

---

[48] Matthew 10:28
[49] Danya Ruttenberg (@TheRaDR), November 7, 2020. Thread starts at 5:07 pm. Available at: https://tinyurl.com/y2kkx2cx

here, forgiving is often, *too often*, pushed on girls and women to excuse the behavior of men.

After one sentence (ONE SENTENCE) said to Polly, demanding the girl forgive her abuser, Aslan turns back to Digory without another glance.

"And now for the Boy himself."

Good thing we got all that wasted time talking to a girl out of the way. Onto the real hero of the story.

The Magician's Nephew: Chapter 12

"What about Polly?"

"Aslan doesn't seem interested in her."

"Well, that's probably a good thing."

"Not if she's going to live in his world for very long, it's not."

"If I were her, I'd pretend to be a boy."

"That right there is everything wrong with Narnia."

"And, Mom? Digory's mom will be okay, right? You said that earlier, but did you forget?"

"She'll live. He saves her."

"Aslan makes it sound like he won't save her."

"I think he's teaching the boy a lesson about his attachment with his mom and how he should prioritize his attachment with Aslan instead."

"I guess being a boy isn't so good in Narnia, either."

***

Now for the boy himself. Lewis is the boy, Aslan is Jesus Christ, and Bitsy and I are the incredulous audience with eyebrows permanently raised.

Unlike the only girl in the story, Digory gets tasked with a huge adventure. He gets to be seen and treated as fully human, fully capable, and fully in the driver's seat of his own story. The only thing outside his control is what the magical lion will do. He intuitively knows he must beg king kitty for his mom's life in *just the right way*.

What would I do if I were a god? Would I let a little boy live in fear of his mother's death when I could prevent it? Heck, would I end hunger, poverty, wage inequality, sexism, and racism? Maybe provide a cure for cancer, include knowledge of germs in my holy book, save dying children, design better human bodies, open up minds, stop rape before it happens, eliminate fear of eternal torture, make heaven attainable to all those I claim to love, and stop genocides? Even in childhood my limited intellect and incomplete knowledge of the world did not keep me from inventing any number of things I would do with love and power. Reasonable things. Helpful things. Things my own god was unable or unwilling to do.

To get around the problem of god's inaction, the Christians in my life stuck to horrible aphorisms: God has a plan for that rape. God works in mysterious ways when that child dies. His ways are above our ways. God loves us, but that love is wrapped up in a package that looks nothing like how any humane person in our life should love us. A parent may keep you from harm, but God? Not so much. Definitely not consistently. Hey, but if things *do* work out, we'd better praise him for it!

I feel for the excuse-makers. I do. I remember how difficult it was when I had to reconcile that loving god with an absentee. So how did

I do it? By inventing a god who *grieves*[50] then feeling so sorry for Sad God that I excused his absenteeism. Telling folks that God will mourn with them through hard times can be extremely comforting. I heard this at my mom's memorial when I was a teen. I was told that I may be hurting, but God was hurting *worse*. I may be crying, but God's grief was on a super-human scale.

There was a downside to this, however. I began to feel guilty about making God so sad. I was also made to feel wrong about grief over my mom's death by the "we don't grieve like those who have no hope" crowd. I should have known that the Bible promises her tragic end would work out for good[51] and that the death of a saint is precious to God.[52] I was even asked more than once if I had forgiven the teen boy who killed her. My story of holding him on the courthouse steps after his sentencing became a huge part of my Christian testimony. Crying through the night in deep depression almost two years later, that I left out.

The words on my mom's gravestone quote a verse about how dying is better than living.[53] Considering this idea heartless garbage was as close to accusing the Bible of falsehood that I could dare get. I just could not accept that the violence that destroyed her body was in any way a good or valuable thing. Why was I so sad since I'd obviously see her again in Heaven? Why did I get upset since God was in control? I was left with a belief system that feared death so much it was incapable of fully embracing the truth of it.

***

---

50 Isaiah 53:3; John 11:35
51 Romans 8:28
52 Psalm 116:15
53 Philippians 1:21

Aslan never once gives Digory hope or comfort, even though it is clear saving his mom was in the cards from the beginning. Isn't leaving your children in hopeless despair what God, if he exists, does every day? It's only when reading a story about a god character who can act and talk that we question it. It makes more sense for an imaginary god who cannot be seen, heard, or proven.

What did Aslan do in response to Digory's pleading for his mother's life? Aslan wept. Just so we could get another allusion to Jesus.[54] That's it. No action, no words, no promises, no hope. Aslan *boo-hooed*. And the book tells us those tears were better than Digory's, as if Aslan could feel more than a boy would for his own mother.

If some deity claimed, to my face, that he felt more grief than me at my own mother's parting, I would view it as the height of arrogance and egotism. If this deity were all-powerful, I would see it as malicious—a thief of my grief who is crying about the very pain he's causing. If this deity were all-knowing and even planning to raise her soon, I would see it as ingenuine. If this deity were also quoted as being downright gleeful at other people dying,[55] I'd see it as a complete farce. Yet somehow I know Lewis saw it as the height of comfort as he wrote it. Maybe to the child Lewis used to be, *it was*.

Aslan ignores Digory's request for his mom and focuses on a plan to keep Jadis away with a witch-repelling tree. Digory's task is to travel to a special garden and get an apple to grow this tree. Since the garden is much too far away for the little boy to travel on foot, Aslan makes the cabby's horse take him. The chapter is called "Strawberry's Adventure," yet Aslan immediately changes the horse's name to Fledge, after his new wings, in the custom of biblical characters getting name changes to show they work for God now. The talking horse is not

---

[54] John 11:35
[55] Psalm 137:9

given a choice in his mission, the changes made to his body, nor his re-naming, but seems more than willing to please his new master.

"Make me a servant, humble and meek," are words I sang in front of my church when I was little. I wanted to be a good servant. When I got older and learned that the Greek word for servant in the Bible literally meant slave[56] and was only translated as "servant" to soften it, I simply adjusted my desire and wanted to be a good slave instead. Anyone who *wants* to be a slave *maybe just possibly* has been brain-washed.

Strawberry, "or Fledge, as we must now call him" was given wings for the task since we're almost through the book and we just don't have time to *not* fly straight there. (I know of two children and a Marsh-wiggle who could have used this.) The wings grew out rather uncomfortably from the horse's back and it felt like flies biting all over. This description created a perfect visual in my mind for the sensation of wings spontaneously and uncomfortably breaking through skin, though it's another example of God's best for us being painful, as Lewis believed.

Aslan overhears the cabby's wife and Polly talking quietly in the corner as women who are not invited to the conversation tend to do.

"What are the two daughters of Eve whispering about?"

The female voices are clearly an unwelcome interruption. The cabby's wife timidly answers that Polly would also like to go on the adventure. *Please, pretty please? Can the girl character do something, too? Anything? Just for a laugh?*

Now both children are helped onto the horse's back by the cabby; Digory is given "a rough heave" and Polly is set there "gently and

---

[56] Doulos (transliterated), G1401 in Strong's Lexicon. In my Antient Greek class in seminary the mnemonic for remembering what doulos meant was "a slave should **do lots**."

daintily" as if "she were made of china and might break." This is supposed to show how boys and girls are supposed to be treated differently. Polly is put behind Digory and gets ordered around by him, but this is nothing out of the ordinary.

The next paragraphs of flying on a winged horse are excellent. What a beautiful, newly created world they get to see from high above! I loved these scenes the most. Eventually the horse grew tired so they settled down for the night to eat and sleep. The children had brought no food and there was nothing around.

"Well, I do think someone might have arranged about our meals."
"I'm sure Aslan would have, if you'd asked him."
"Wouldn't he know without being asked?"
"I've a sort of idea he likes to be asked."

There's prayer logic for you.

After eating some toffee in the bottom of a jacket pocket, the kids settled in to sleep. Too bad they weren't alone. A tall, dark (and gorgeous) figure was seen gliding around in the trees.

The Magician's Nephew: Chapter 13

"Digory will do the right thing."
"Yep."
"He'll go home and save his mom."
"Oh, wait, what? I thought you were going to say he'd finish the mission."

***

The children wake up to a newly-grown toffee tree that popped up overnight from a piece of toffee in their pocket. This world is still growing! They bathe in a clear river with brightly colored stones and flowers all around. Snow is mentioned, but no one is cold. Sunshine is mentioned, but no one has a burn. Even the spider webs are bright and silver and delightful. Bonus: No mention of actual spiders!

Soon the children come to the magical garden they were seeking. It was oriented towards the east which the books have repeatedly mentioned is the direction of Aslan's land. (The Garden of Eden is considered in the east so that's the religious connection.) When they come upon high walls and a gate Polly knew instinctively that she would not be allowed inside. I swear, "No Girls Allowed" is on a large sign over Aslan's childhood fort somewhere. Digory went alone.

This garden has rules because of course it does. The rules. The laws. The signs. It all comes down to random orders to show how obedient believers are. Here in the Narnian garden, the rules are not to climb the walls and to only take the fruit for others. See the test clearly now? Aslan ignores our boy's tears and pleas for his mother and sets up this tempting scenario where Digory will be given the choice to either take the fruit to save his dying mom or give it to Aslan as instructed.

When Digory picked one of the silver apples in the center of the garden that was clearly the one he was sent to retrieve, it smelled not only delicious, but it caused him a great hunger and thirst that only a juicy apple would satisfy. Aslan didn't just send the children on a quest without seeing to their meals as an oversight; he sent them hungry so the apple would be even more tempting!

Nearby was Jadis, just finishing her apple. I could just imagine Jadis wiping her mouth with the back of her wrist as silver juice dripped down her chin. (I would wear that image on a t-shirt.) She had clearly climbed the wall and was there to break all the rules like a total badass.

Digory ran from Jadis but she assured him she was not going to attack. She just wanted to give him "some knowledge" that would greatly benefit him. Knowledge?! Noooo! That's the worst! Does she even read the Bible?[57] Like the good godly boy he is, Digory answered that he would not hear any of it! Jadis kept talking anyway. She informed him that the apple gives life and eternal youth to those who consume it. Digory counters that he'd rather die and go to Heaven by following the rules. *Oh boy.* The witch continues to give him pretty darn good advice if this were any other character and circumstance. She lets him know that just one small bite of the apple will heal his mother. Then she goes into detail:

> "Five minutes later you will see the colour coming back to her face. She will tell you the pain is gone. Soon she will tell you she feels stronger. Then she will fall asleep–think of that; hours of sweet natural sleep, without pain, without drugs."

Holy crap! Jadis paints a pretty bleak picture of the torturous state Digory's mom is in. This is not even an exaggeration; the mom is in pure agony. Digory finally realizes "the most terrible choice lay before him." This is where Bitsy got a knowing look in her eye and confidently informed me, "Digory will do the right thing." I agreed, but she continued: "He'll go home and save his mom."

I stopped in my tracks.

I had assumed Bitsy would know that the *right* choice was to choose Aslan *over* his mother. How I love the pure motivation and wonderful morality of the unindoctrinated! I had to stop reading and hug my confused daughter. She really is the best.

There's a scene in the television show *Firefly*[58] where Mal and his crew take on a job to steal some cargo. It's presented as a Robin Hood situation, but it turns out they have unknowingly stolen medicine that poor people desperately need. Our heroes return it and are caught.

---

[57] Obviously the forbidden fruit tree in the Garden of Eden that led to the downfall of humanity was called The Tree of Knowledge.

[58] "The Train Job." *Firefly*, written by Joss Whedon and Tim Minear, directed by Joss Whedon, FOX network. 2002.

After seeing nothing is missing and acknowledging the good deed, the deputy says to Mal:

> "A man can get a job, he might not look too close at what that job is. But a man learns all the details of a situation like ours, well then he has a choice."

Mal's response is beautiful in its simplicity:

> "I don't believe he does."

Saving Digory's mother from unimaginable pain and early death is the right decision. A truly loving lion god would even reward this! The garden rules did say an apple could be taken to help others even though we're supposed to think taking it for his mom is selfish. There would still be plenty left over to plant the magic tree as well. It's not like his mom will eat the seeds! The only way saving his mom is not the right choice is in a world where this is all a sadistic test of blind obedience!

> "What has the Lion ever done for you that you should be his slave?"

Good question, Jadis. Digory will not engage in this discussion. He will defend Aslan with the incredible come back of, "He is—I don't know—" and choose to let his mom suffer and die like a good follower should.

One lesson I received in my small Baptist church was that Abraham was ordered to kill his son and went to mindlessly obey. God accounted it as righteousness. Warriors in Israel were told to kill people and obeyed. They were blessed. Jephthah sacrificed his beloved daughter in the Old Testament and the New Testament called him righteous. Likewise, I obeyed. I wore modest clothing, followed church rules, tithed my money, told people they were sinners, and threatened small children with Hell. Good slaves live for the words: "Well done, my good and faithful servant."[59] Good slaves know that human

---

[59] Matthew 25

feelings, health, life, happiness, and relationships are all secondary to following orders.

***

Jadis messes up and suggests Digory leave Polly and go save his mom. Digory capitalizes on that bit of bad advice to justify ignoring the rest of her arguments. Leave Polly behind? That would be *wrong*! Polly cheers him on and says, "Quick! Get away *now*." They would be happy to know that Scripture also commands people to flee knowledge, temptation, and conversation.[60]

I have to wonder at this point, what motivated the witch? Why on Earth did she care? Why did she say those things? Women just naturally like to temp boys, eh?

On the ride back to Aslan, Digory gets super depressed **as he should**. To assuage his guilty conscience, he simply thought of Aslan's face over and over. This made it feel like he was doing the right thing. Something may seem wrong, kids, but when you train your brain to align those thoughts with God's rules then you deaden that part of your conscience! (Three cheers for religious lobotomies!)

Digory finally arrives back to Aslan and hands over the apple, supposedly dooming his mother. Aslan responds like the biblical master: "Well done."

The Magician's Nephew: Chapters 14-15

"This was your *favorite* of all the Narnia books, Mom?"
"Yep."
"But we talked so much about everything wrong with it."

---

[60] 1 Corinthians 10:13

"True. You should never ignore the problematic things in something you enjoy."

"But you practically told me to at the beginning of this book!"

"Oh, right."

***

As we finished up *The Magician's Nephew* I realized how utterly and predictably I failed to avoid discussing the harmful aspects of my favorite book with my inquisitive kid. So much for simply sitting back and enjoying the story. I mean, it is fantastical storytelling! It has everything: flying horses, rapidly growing trees, dead planets, a giant dominatrix—even a stargate! Then in the middle of all the fun some cringeworthy line pops up like a smack in the face and steals all our focus. Part of me wants my daughter to lose herself in the make-believe world while the author's biases and beliefs become background noise. Maybe that's not the healthiest way to consume literature though.

When I ask Bits to summarize a Narnia book she talks about the adventure and magic, never the Christian allegories. Maybe that's what makes those religious parts insidious, but it also shows which elements are *lasting*. It's the pure magical goodness we remember and not the ham-fisted dogma. Not only children, but even adults like J. K. Rowling, who based aspects of the Harry Potter series on the Narnia books, admitted she somehow missed[61] how utterly "preachy" Lewis' books were.[62]

Laura Miller authored *The Magician's Book* that I wish I had discovered much sooner in our Narnia adventure as it takes a critical look

---

[61] The same way she missed her own horrible transphobia probably.

[62] Jennie Renton, 2001. "The story behind the Potter legend: JK Rowling talks about how she created the Harry Potter books and the magic of Harry Potter's world," *Sydney Morning Herald*, October 28. Available at: http://www.accio-quote.org/articles/2001/1001-sydney-renton.htm

into Lewis' themes. She had also missed the Christian messaging forced onto every page until re-reading the series as an adult.

> A critic has to write as well as read, and while the process of writing about a book can reveal things you'd never get from simply reading it, it can also make reading a less immediate and visceral experience. [...] Although I miss the childhood experience of being engulfed by a story, I would not willingly surrender my adult ability to recognize when a writer is taking me someplace I don't want to go."[63]

I wanted to enjoy my favorite book[64] but could not give up my critical eye to do it. Miller goes on to talk about how awful it was discovering Christianity had been threaded into the fabric of these stories, not only informing them, but being the very reason for their existence in the first place. This was a hard realization for her after having already fallen in love with Narnia, and by extension, with reading itself after initially consuming this series. She felt tricked.

While I had a different experience with Narnia as I was only allowed to read this series *because* of its Christian elements, I do identify with that feeling of being tricked. The Christianity of Narnia is very much the fundamentalist kind I grew up in where powerful men ran the show. Turns out that's not the heathiest nor kindest version. I find myself echoing Miller's words:

> Once you realize that a good story has the power to deceive you, it's impossible to wholeheartedly embrace the ignorance that is always a

---

[63] Laura Miller, 2008. *The Magician's Book: A Skeptic's Adventures in Narnia*, (New York, NY; Back Bay Books).

[64] *The Magician's Nephew* is my favorite *Narnia* book, but my absolute favorite book of all C. S. Lewis titles is hands down *A Grief Observed*. I read it right after my mom was killed and it landed like a heavy gut punch. When it felt like no one in the world understood what I was going through, Lewis did. It was so brutally honest, even admitting how cruel the Christian god could be, that the theologian wrote it under a pen name. He supposedly only admitted to being the author after so many of his friends recommended his own book to him to help him process his grief.

part of innocence. I was sorry, very sorry, to lose Narnia, but I always would have chosen to know the truth.

***

Digory realizes that the story of his adventure would be "handed down from father to son" for hundreds of years. Forget about Polly. Mothers handing stories down to daughters is of no importance.

Digory is granted kumbaya feelings by Aslan for ~~sacrificing his mom~~ obeying the lion without question. How could I, as an evangelical, feel good about myself after treating gay people, women, or unbelievers so badly? This is how. When I felt like I had pleased God, it didn't matter who I had hurt in the process. I would pray to God about it, thank him for his wisdom, and ride the spiritual high above the cognitive dissonance.

Digory throws the apple into the soil to let it *super grow* while the cabby and his wife are crowned. Lewis mentions that the queen, Helen, let her hair down and "it made a great improvement in her appearance." How pretty is the cabby with his hair down? Who knows and who cares. It's almost like the king is a person and worth more than his looks or something. Weird.

The crowns were made from silver and gold coins that fell from Uncle Andrew's pockets when he was being "planted" earlier. They had grown into silver and gold trees. The animals had been keeping Andrew in a cage of trees as a pet and torturing him in hilarious ways like throwing bees in his face, giving him thistles to eat that he sat in, and dropping worms on him. They name him Brandy because the drunk keeps repeating that word. It's Polly who takes pity on Andrew and asks Aslan to "unfrighten" him. She's also hoping Aslan can magically keep him away from Narnia so he doesn't ruin it with greed after he saw what a planted gold coin could become. Aslan asks her if

Andrew would want to come back after all this bad treatment, and since it's a question, Polly starts to respond when Aslan interrupts her to keep talking. Polly only gets to speak once and she's done. Aslan continues his gripe about how Adam's sons are too clever for their own good. Smart leads to evil, simple is good, and girls are trash, just so we're clear.

During the royal crowning, the apple tree has sprung up. The animals guard it so no one else could eat from the tempting fruit and get kicked out of Narnia. A guard around the tree? If only God had thought of that in the Genesis story!

The logic behind this magical tree is confusing. It seems, despite this being contradicted by events in *The Lion, The Witch and the Wardrobe*, that anyone who eats the fruit will be repelled from Narnia by the smell. The children do not know this only applies to those who have already eaten it, though, since Aslan only said that the smell of it is "death and horror and despair" which didn't match their image of the witch eating one without consequences earlier. Polly attempts to bring her concerns about this apple plan to Aslan's attention since there's a real worry the witch will come back and kill them all. Digory also noticed the supposed flaw in the plan but he stopped short of bringing it up for fear of "looking a fool." This leaves our girl the fool so she can get corrected by Aslan and we can all judge her for not trusting his wisdom.

While addressing the children, Aslan strings Digory along for a while before finally revealing that he can take an apple with permission and go save his mom. FINALLY. Aslan takes his sweet time explaining what would have happened to Digory's mom if the boy had taken the apple to her instead of to Aslan.

> "The day would have come when both you and she would have looked back and said it would have been better to die in that illness."

This makes Digory cry. After breaking him, Aslan then gives him permission to save his mom with another apple.

***

Lewis has a habit of putting a ton of information in the final pages of each book like a nail gun rapidly fired off to tie down loose ends. In like fashion, here's the last chapter wrap up: Aslan tells the children that their world better shape up or it will end up like ruined Charn. He predicts WWII and implies it's a judgement from God. He magically "entered into them" so they are spiritually woo'd about. (Don't do that with children. Good grief.) All humans are magically sent home. Uncle Andrew gets his brandy. Digory's mom recovers, plays with the children, and Lewis' fantasy is complete.

The children bury the rings and the magic apple core in the backyard. A tree grows from this pile and later a wardrobe gets made from the tree's wood. A little girl named Lucy will discover this wardrobe in Digory's home, only she will know Digory as the Old Professor. She will even be guided to Narnia by the light of a lamppost accidentally planted by Jadis. For those reading in HarperCollins order, this will mean nothing to them.

The sons of the cabby marry nymphs. My lie about Aslan bringing more humans from Earth is exposed, but at least it's not all incestual like we thought!

Uncle Andrew becomes nicer. He has learned his lesson due to all the abuse following the One Good Beating trope. The last line of the book is Andrew speaking of Jadis, "But she was a dem fine woman, sir, a dem fine woman." (Too true. Too true.)

***

Whereas this book was a book of beginnings, the next and last in the series will be a book of apocalyptic endings. We'll move from Genesis right into The Book of Revelation.

We saw Narnia born. Next, we'll watch her die.

8
It's the End of the World and We Feel Fine

"What are we going to read next?"
"We have one more Narnia book."
"Does anyone die?"
"Um, yes."
"Which one dies?"
"Er, more than one."
"Wait, what?!"
"Almost all the characters die."
"Wuuuuuuuuuuuuut."
"I have utterly failed to hype this book correctly."

***

This final installment of the Narnia series will lead us through discussions on loyalty, wisdom, justice, sexism (yes, we'll get to Susan) and our human aversion to endings. Let's begin by acknowledging the theology that informs so much of the ethos of this book: Christian eschatology. (Oh joy.)

In a cultural anthropology class I took (*mumbles large number* of years ago) with my sister and our friend from church, the professor asked everyone to write down what we thought would happen after we died. My evangelical heart lived for this kind of thing, and I immediately started preaching furiously on my 3x5 card. I had Bible verses quoted in full with steps on how to be "Christian saved" and everything. The professor then rattled off the contents of our cards unceremoniously one after another: "Nothing." "Heaven if we are good." "I don't know." "Our bodies rot or are donated to science." "Reincarnation." "Heaven or Hell." "Worm food."

Of all the cards, I will never forget the most amusing and ludicrous one our professor read aloud; he even lost his composure about halfway through. It was long, longer than mine even, and had all sorts of specific elements to it. This afterlife included a giant tree of life with fruit on it. Food was mentioned on a long table. There was slavery of some kind—people serving the food for example—but everyone working there was happy. The sea was gone because God got rid of it and the sun too. There was a city with walls made of jasper and twelve gates each made of a single gigantic pearl. The buildings inside were made of gold and had exact measurements written out on the card. A throne was set up in a prominent place because this city had a ruler to tell the slaves what to do. Over in the distance was a fiery lake of burning sulfur where cowards, witches, and those who broke the sexual rules were all thrown into it by order of the ruler.

This card was worse than mine, but slightly less pretentious *if that's possible*. At some point I leaned across my sister over to my friend from church and whispered while giggling, "Sounds like a crazy cult!" I still remember the look of hurt and confusion on her face when she responded, "That's my card."

My memory beyond the expression of her face is fuzzy, but I think she was trying to be a good witness for Christ by describing the biblical afterlife in perfect detail. Everything there was all taken straight from our Christian Scripture, not even from the apocryphal bits. She was more accurate and thorough than the Revelation Bible study we had just done, and unlike that happy-go-apocalypse study, she didn't gloss through the weird parts.

The other thing I remember vividly was my own shock at how I had not recognized the place I was supposedly going when I died. I recognized elements of it, sure, but I had assumed this card was written by someone in a cult, not someone from my own mainstream, non-denominational church! There was just something about all those details being rattled off by a secular professor that didn't make it feel real. Why hadn't the specifics really stuck with me when reading them from the Bible? Did I not really believe this stuff?

Reading through Lewis' descriptions of Aslan's afterlife was fun, delightful, and even thoughtful, but there's something about laying it all out there that betrays how ridiculous it truly sounds. *The Last Battle* reminded me of that niggling doubt I had after hearing the biblical description of New Jerusalem read with a smirk in that large classroom. It's so weird, and specific, and dated, and culturally limited, and *human*.

Even when a person is not completely convinced by their holy book's claim of the existence of specific necro-destinations for themselves and others, these doctrines can still inform their view of humanity. Want to really get to know if a religious person values people or not, get to know their eschatology. Who is going to the good place like them? Who is not worthy? (Why are women so often less worthy?) Who is a second-class citizen? Black folks have a real hard time getting into Lewis' version of Heaven. When we do see one, it shocks our main characters.

The concept of Hell with its burning sulfur once motivated my missionary work, far more than the rewards of Heaven ever did, but I wonder how I was ever capable of shrugging at the knowledge of people going there. Even at my most fundamentalist, I soft-peddled the crap out of the concept of eternal torture when questioned directly about it. I went from "obviously all unbelievers go there" to "only God knows for sure" in the blink of one uncomfortable conversation involving direct eye contact.

Lewis has said of Hell:

> "There is no doctrine which I would more willingly remove from Christianity than this, if it lay in my power. But it has the full support of Scripture and, specially, of our Lord's own words; it has always been held by Christendom; and it has the support of reason."[1]

Undoubtably, the "support of reason" does not mean Hell is reasonable. No moral society would torture the worst offender daily for a thousand years, let alone for *eternity*. I believe "reason" here merely means the concept can be *reasonably* supported by the New Testament.[2] It's true that I could not stop believing in the idea of Hell until I had been fully convinced the Bible was bologna.

While Lewis did dip a toe into interpreting Scripture generously at times, our dear theologian dared not lose it as a source of authority completely. His position of power, above women for one thing, depended on the divine right afforded to him over them. His life's work is absolutely predicated on people believing the Bible.

Our author's main goal is not to write something simply for the enjoyment of children; he must use this story to warn them, scare them, save them. This book will be propaganda. It will be old timey Christianity on steroids. For this reason, it is not commonly a fan favorite.

---

[1] http://www.cslewisinstitute.org/CS_Lewis_on_Heaven_and_Hell_FullArticle
[2] Hell was invented during the writing of the New Testament and does not exist in the Old Testament.

The Last Battle: Chapter 1

"Ugh, I want to save the donkey from the bad ape."

"Me too, but he doesn't know he needs to be saved."

"He's too dumb."

"It's not morally wrong to have gaps in our knowledge. It's only wrong to *choose* ignorance over education, especially when people tell us we are causing harm."

"Yep. '*When we know better, we do better.*'"

***

This last book of the Narnia series starts out with two brand new characters: Shift the smart ape and Puzzle the dumb donkey. The two discover a lion's skin in a pool while taking a walk one day. Shift sews it to fit over Puzzle and reveals a plan to trick people into thinking the donkey is Aslan so they will mindlessly obey him. It's a how-to guide for starting any new money-making religion. Why was Shift so selfish? Why were they walking? Where to? How did the skin end up in the pool? It really doesn't matter. The point is they have a convenient lion's skin! Let's get to the plot already!

Maybe Aslan set the skin in the water in the first place? He does love his evil tests and Shift certainly thinks he is behind this.

"Probably he sent us the lionskin on purpose, so that we could set things to right."

The ape wants to make a power grab, and sees the path to do so, therefore, the local god must be behind this plan. Although we get the impression this ape is too clever to believe his own self-serving argument. I know when I tried to pull this as a child my sincerely devout parents instantly became born-again skeptics! It would take me a few years to learn how to expertly use my "I feel this is God's will" card.

257

While the text does not state that Aslan directed the lion skin to fall into the hands of the greedy ape, keep in mind that Lewis worships a sovereign deity whom Aslan is directly based on, who "works out everything to its proper end—even the wicked for a day of disaster."[3] It wouldn't go against his nature to do an evil act to justify hurting people; just like when Pharaoh got tortured and his firstborn slaughtered by God for actions that were later revealed to be God's own doing?[4]

The source material for this story, The Book of Revelation, is not a happy book of bedtime stories; it's a violent nightmare of death and terror doled out by Jesus "the Lamb" Christ, who sets up horrors for the loosely defined "wicked" to fall into so he can justify brutalizing them. Anyone with a lick of morality will shudder at the gratuitous amount of collateral damage this master plan entails. It is unfortunate *The Last Battle* draws from such a blood-filled well.

Despite the dearth of action in this opening chapter, the conversational interplay between the ape and donkey communicates a lot of information without relying on those long stretches of exposition Lewis constantly falls back on. He even includes little details that add depth to these interactions. I especially loved when the ape scratched himself the "wrong way up" like apes do and the description of the cowed donkey falling into mental traps left and right. Little Bit was immediately engaged with these two animals and easily saw through Shift's manipulation of Puzzle. We didn't have to sit through a paragraph about how Shift is shifty (yes, once again Lewis' cheap naming choices on display) since hearing him twist the puzzled Puzzle's words around made this obvious.

I do have quite a few issues with some of the themes already at play in these first pages. I'm uncomfortable with how we've stumbled *once*

---

[3] Proverbs 16:4
[4] Exodus 4:21

again down the easy path of painting the intelligent character as the evil one. It reinforces the biblical narrative that philosophy is out to trick people into leaving Christian faith.[5] Puzzle's true sin was listening to the wrong source: a friend who was smarter than he was. When wisdom relies on obeying a godly authority, and not on using critical thinking skills to judge what is best, then the wisest choice is to avoid educated arguments.

As a believer it was all so simple. It was not my experience, but my fear of a tyrant god that defined how wise I was.[6] I had an ever-shifting litmus test of what constituted wisdom, but at least I didn't have to do any icky thinking for myself. I just had to follow the checklist: Realize I do *not* want to make God angry. *Check.* Figure out what exactly made God angry by consulting a Bible or pastor. *Check and check.* Thoroughly consider the ramifications of following God and compare this approach with other systems of morality. Just kidding! *Left forever unchecked.*

In my home we follow the harm principle; what is right is determined by that which avoids or reduces harm. Too often sincere believers do what their holy book or pastor says to do even if it causes harm to others. Examples from my personal experience include denying women's rights, fighting marriage equality, voting against civil rights, denying adoptions to various groups, resisting advances in medicine, and rejecting sex education.

A counter lesson Bitsy has received multiple times in this series is that good morality is more than obeying the biggest deity. In the following chapters, the citizens of Narnia won't be evaluating if their deeds are right or not but will instead be evaluating if they followed the orders of Aslan well enough or not. If their deity had been legitimate, their loyal obedience would have been considered right. Too

---

[5] Colossians 2:8
[6] Proverbs 9:10

bad when fake Aslan orders the deaths of nymphs. Or for an equiva-lent, when the biblical god orders the death of women and girls on multiple occasions.[7] Mindless obedience is never okay in such situa-tions.

Physical descriptions being used to tell if a character is good or not is also back in this first chapter. The ape's physical description includes "ugliest, most wrinkled Ape you can imagine." Also, what color is an ape, hmm? The color that's rarely placed on Lewis' hero list, that's for sure. What does it teach children? *He has to be evil, just look at him!*

Lewis has an Orwellian "some animals are more equal than others" mindset informed by a clear hierarchy that cannot be questioned. For example, Reepicheap was a noble character, but lacked humanity, height, and was temporarily disabled. This is what allowed other char-acters who were human, tall, and able-bodied to treat him inferiorly while the author treated it as normal. Recall when High King Peter called him a "little ass" for fighting in the same battle as everyone else or when Aslan bullied him about the loss of his tail. Taking this hier-archy into consideration, the ape does something Lewis would find unforgiveable. He cuts in line. He rises above his station. And what happens? The world literally ends.

One last point I'd like to make is that the ape's plan relies on *a god who isn't there*. Aslan, as the book says, "never does turn up." At one point there is an earthquake after Shift reveals his tricky plan, and Puz-zle interprets it as Aslan being angry with the plan, but our clever ape interprets it as the opposite. There's no real authority to say one way or the other who is correct.

Aslan is the Wizard of Oz and the ape is playing the man behind the curtain. Lewis is writing about a common problem of a religious world longing for a god to speak. My pastors and Sunday School

---

[7] Judges 11:30-39; Exodus 22:18; Deuteronomy 22:20-21; Leviticus 21:9

teachers saw this silence and contorted all sorts of meaning around it the best they could. How many sermons did I sit through on how it *didn't seem like it*, but God was *right here* with us! Pareidolia is the tendency to interpret vague stimulus as something known to the observer, such as seeing Jesus in toast and interpreting it as a blessing or reading a verse in the Bible that is tangentially related to a personal trial and thinking it's God trying to communicate. Miracles like that happen all the time to those trying hard enough to see God in daily life.

I still remember exactly how it felt to learn that studies and scientific discoveries did not back up my church's claims. Christians were not blessed more than unbelievers or healed more than those without faith. In the largest, most expensive study ever done with thousands of participants, researchers found that intercessory prayer simply didn't work.[8] While some people may respond sarcastically, "*Wait, magic thoughts are worthless? Who knew!*" I was, sadly, one of those people devastated by the news. Prayer didn't change anything beyond the praying person's own brain chemicals. It was a cheap trick. What did make a difference, however, was medical advancements, wealth, access to care, and human hands.

If Jehovah was a god like Aphrodite, Thor, or Zeus, with their human-like personalities and faults, it wouldn't be as much of a problem when he decided not to show up and help humanity. The Hebrew god is not much superior in this regard early on in Scripture, but our American Christian version had evolved over time to become all-benevolent **and** all-knowing **and** all-powerful **and** omnipresent **and** all-sovereign. This is illogical, of course, as many of these attributes are mutually

---

[8] H. Benson, J. A. Dusek, J. B. Sherwood, et al., 2006. "Study of the Therapeutic Effects of Intercessory Prayer (STEP) in cardiac bypass patients: a multicenter randomized trial of uncertainty and certainty of receiving intercessory prayer," *American Heart Journal*, 151(4): 934–42.

exclusive in the face of tragedy. God can't know an innocent person will be violently murdered **and** be powerful enough to stop it **and** cause it in the first place through sovereignty **and** still be considered benevolently good.

Before I was convinced this kind of god was blessedly imaginary, I used to have pat answers to the Problem of Evil that make me laugh now. Tracie Harris once sliced through the problem neatly while taking callers on *The Atheist Experience*:

> "You either have a God who sends child rapists to rape children or you have a god who simply watches it and says, 'When you're done, I'm going to punish you.' […] If I were in a situation where I could stop a child rapist, I would. That's the difference between me and your god."[9]

The Last Battle: Chapter 2

"Great, the king murders people."
"He did seem to be itching to do it for a while."
"Let me guess, he's the *good guy*?"
"*Oh* yeah."

***

In past books our protagonists have always been children, extensions of the readers, who fall into Narnia and set about on an epic adventure. In this last book, however, there's a sense the great quests are behind us and Narnia sits stagnant waiting to be put down. Our new characters will be war heroes gearing up for their final fight.

---

[9] Available at: https://www.youtube.com/watch?v=WrfWs52Kjk0&feature=youtu.be

King Tirian is introduced as the "last of the Kings of Narnia" and although it's not clear just how many kings there have been, I can count the number of ruling queens on one hand; that is, if I bend my hand in the shape of a big fat zero. We've had queen subordinates—sisters or wives—but none that had power over royal men.

Tirian is White with blue eyes so we know he's a *good guy*. (Sarcasm, folks.) He also has an "honest face" whatever that means. (We know *exactly* what that means.) Tirian's description reads like a Tinder bio: early twenties, broad shoulders, strong arms, and hard muscles. (Lewis has a new crush.)

Tirian's best friend is Jewel the Unicorn, a "lordly beast." Bitsy was disappointed Jewel wasn't a girl, partly because that means there are no girls this time around and partly because *My Little Pony* didn't prepare her well for boy unicorns. Jewel is also described as having muscles upon muscles. The total emphasis on physical size and strength is to make it clear that these two are the best kind of heroes who have already seen blood, which is a bit disconcerting when we realize Tirian likely started killing while still a child. Aslan's wonderful Narnia has seemingly been soaked in violence the entire time it has existed. Part of the all-knowing plan or something.

This is the very end of Narnian history. It was around, what? Thousands of years? At least? And in all that time technology never once advanced. They spent all their time killing each other. Every tool is the same—no paved roads, no communication system, no Internet, no nothing—similar to the biblical end times that are described as if they would take place in the Iron Age they were written in. It's as if the Bible can't really see that far into the future.

Our muscle-y heroes are on vacation away from Cair Paravel and talking about all the rumors that Aslan has returned. They are waiting around for more news without so much as a simple telegraph to rely upon. Seriously, put a queen in charge and maybe there would be one less war and a single modern advancement!

At this point Aslan has been gone for ages and his sightings have all been rumors. The most convincing testimony of his return comes from a Calormene described as "that dark Man" which reads like someone's racist uncle writing about his "Black neighbor." (*Oh, are they Black?*) The Calormene's word is treated as a more reliable source than the rumors of the animal people because Aslan's return for Narnians is meaningful in the same way Jesus' return is for Christians so the animals would be more likely to experience a sighting as part of wishful thinking. Calormenes won't care though, so they have less reason to lie about it. Obviously, no one is expecting a donkey in a lion skin.

Christians have prophets to base their beliefs upon, whose words are written in their Scriptures, so what would be the Narnian equivalent? Centaurs! These centaurs read the stars and divine their meaning as if its holy writ. One such creature approaches to warn the king that Aslan is not coming. How can we trust this info? Well, "The stars never lie." So there we go.

The stars are certainly misleading, though, since Aslan is totally coming; we'll see him in just a few chapters. Regardless, this is their clue that the current Aslan running around is a fake. Upon hearing that Aslan's return is a lie, the king does something that will reveal his character: He put his hand on his sword hilt "without knowing it." I wonder if this guy is about to kill some folks? (Of course he is!)

Their conversation is cut short when a nymph of a beech tree, which is like an anthropomorphized soul of a living plant, comes out of nowhere wailing in pain. She tells them her people, the Dryads, are being murdered. Then she convulses multiple times as if an invisible axe is slicing through her body and dies. Turns out a very real axe is slicing through her tree body miles away.

Bedtime story is over! Sweet dreams, children!

No wait, the king and his pony have got to go kill some people in a rage first! Sword-happy Tirian has already drawn his blade for the task. They run ahead to the battle and send the centaur prophet back to Cair Paravel to get a small army together. The centaur gallops off, drunkenly I assume; he downed a giant bowl of strong wine "enough for six strong men" minutes before.

Our heroes, full of "just wrath" and murder-y muscles and probably barrels of wine, come to a river. Floating above the waters is a Narnian rat on a raft made of our dearly departed trees. The king demands to know who ordered this. The rat replies, "The Lion's orders, Sire. Aslan himself." At hearing that Aslan was the one who ordered the murder of the Dryads, our heroes IMMEDIATELY BEGIN JUSTIFYING IT.

Yeah, miss me with that.

Jewel wonders if the Dryads did something wrong. The king thinks this is plausible but can't understand why Aslan would then sell the wood to the Calormenes. Like, *that* was the bridge too far.

Jewel responds, "He's not a *tame* Lion." This is the phrase that has been repeated in awe and respect so many times in this series. Now it's seen for the rubbish it is, although I doubt the author had such awareness. The reader is supposed to know that this can't be Aslan because he's the good guy. He'd never do this to Narnians. Yet, when murder, violence, and all sorts of harm can be excused or even called *good* when it happens to the *other guys*, then how can it be called something else when it happens to them?

Even if the false Aslan ordered these things, the real one is omniscient and sovereign, like the Christian deity he's based on, so he either allowed the slaughter to happen or simply sat back and watched. Which is worse? (At least maybe he's sad about it?)

When the king comes upon the scene, he realizes with horror it's the same place Digory planted the magic tree, called the Tree of Protection, thousands of years ago. How symbolic that now everything is deforested. In the clearing are a large number of humans who were "not the fair-haired men of Narnia: they were dark, bearded men from Calormen, that great and cruel country." You know, *bad guys*. If the story didn't repeatedly reference how un-fair and dark-skinned they all were, we might have forgotten!

One of the horses doing the work and being whipped by the men to go faster is a Talking Horse. Realizing this, our heroes fly into a rage and immediately attack without warning. King hand-always-unconsciously-on-weapon Tirian beheaded one man while Jewel, the lordly *My Little Brony*, gores the chest of the other with his freaking horn.

That brings us to the question: Can godly heroes be murderers? Sure! Moses did the exact same thing under very similar circumstances in his Bible story.[10] In both cases the murdered men had been forcing a good guy into labor and either beating or whipping them. They were also of different nationalities than our heroes which justified the murder. It seems murder is only *big-consequences* wrong when it happens to God's guys, but it's completely forgivable when it happens to the *other* guys who probably had it coming.

The chapter ends with two men lying dead on the ground, one without a head and one with a bloody hole in his chest. Little Bit was staring at me with wide eyes from her bed as if to say, "You're seriously sending me off to sleep with those images?" It was past bedtime and well past wine-o'clock but we read something else to transition to sleep.

Things are bad, but they are about to get much worse.

---

[10] Exodus 2:11-12

The Last Battle: Chapter 3

"Aslan and Tash are the same guy? That makes so much sense!"

"No, he's lying."

"Really?"

"Yep."

"But *really*? I mean, it makes sense."

"In this book it's not Aslan doing all these things. It's the ape and donkey pretending to be him."

"Aslan did plenty of bad things already in all the other books. They're obviously both bad."

***

What do these heroes do after killing some folks without warning? Run away of course! It's okay, though, they'll feel bad about it. The running away that is, not the murdering.

Tirian and Jewel get some distance before talking about how unsporting it was to kill unarmed people without warning. They also discuss how they were wrong to try to prevent harm to the sapient forest since its destruction was at Aslan's order. At least they agree what Aslan is doing is "dreadful," but they justify it because he is Aslan. The king realizes the "right" thing to do in this situation is to give himself up to be killed:

"Do you think I care if Aslan dooms me to death?"

Bitsy and I just want to shake him. Shake them both, really. Both characters realize they have been worshiping a guy who is cruel and unjust (been there) and conclude life is now not worth living. This is horrible reasoning, but it might ring true for those of us who only saw our worth in the eyes of a heavenly master.

"Would it not be better to be dead than to have this horrible fear that Aslan has come and is not like the Aslan we have believed in and longed for?"

"You are in the right, Sire. This is the end of all things. [...] If you are dead and if Aslan is not Aslan, what life is left for me?"

Statements like these scare me. I've heard similar from those I care about: *God is the only reason I keep going. Without Jesus I'd have no hope. If I weren't a Christian my life would be meaningless.* It leaves those who deconstruct their faith terrified of the existential dread that certainly must await them. Outside the church *there be dragons*. It's even worse when I hear these messages taught to children who are raised to believe that their only hope is in an unsubstantiated belief system and their identity depends upon it being true. It is the cruelest cruel. Life is so much *more*.

As a small child I was encouraged to go into missions and forced to read books about missionaries dying for the sake of the gospel. My heroes were Paul the apostle (martyr), the disciples of Jesus (martyrs), and the people who burned and were beheaded for Jesus (*Foxe's Book of Martyrs*). The glorification of death is pounded into young readers in *The Last Battle* the same way.

Life is precious. Life is amazing all on its own without angels, miracles, and heavenly gates. It's priceless and real. I feel a greater sense of purpose and responsibility when I know all outcomes rest on our shoulders rather than spiritual forces. When circumstances are outside our control and random ills befall us, it makes more sense that there is no sadist being orchestrating it to teach us cruel lessons. I don't have to worry that I didn't pray hard enough or that I was too sinful for a real god to intervene. I prefer the truth, no matter how hard to accept, and following it led to finally having that inner peace I only tasted for brief moments inside of Christianity.

***

Jewel and Tirian go back to give themselves up to Aslan. Here's the very next sentence:

> Then the dark men came around them in a thick crowd, smelling of garlic and onions, their white eyes flashing dreadfully in their brown faces.

I don't think this communicates to children just how dark-skinned these men were. Allow me to fix it:

> Then the very dark men with dark skin and faces, and dark, like, everything probably, came up to them smelling like every stereotypical middle eastern thing because they are foreign and weird and dark and all. They used their white eyes to see out of, but that's just sclera, not, like, the whiteness we care about, and that sclera was surrounded by brown, y'all. BROWN. And they went about being dark and having dark skin and being unnecessarily brown.

The Calormenes tied up these two instead of killing them. That's rather sporting of them in this kill-your-enemies world, but it won't be considered a mercy since the colored men are doing it. The focus will instead be on them taking Tirian's crown off as if that is the worst sin of the day.

The two murderers are taken before Shift, who is working as the mouthpiece of Aslan. He's described as even more ugly than before since he was wearing jewels and a scarlet jacket—things for Dwarves and royal men, not those beneath them. Adding insult to insult, Lewis has the ape declare he is really a man, an incredibly old and wrinkled man. This claim will give him unwarranted authority over the others by adding not only humanity to his list of credentials, but also advanced years.

The ape has been *busy*, mostly ordering around the other animals, stealing all their food, and leaving them destitute. He's like a televangelist, manipulating the masses to give him their possessions while leveraging Aslan's favor to do it. It's the perfect scam to befall a place like Narnia.

Today Shift will be informing the cowering crowd that Aslan is giving them as slaves to their "dark-faced friends." (*Wait, what color are they?*) The animals are horrified. The ape assures them that it's not really slavery if the church, er, I mean Aslan's treasury gets the money. He says the money will be used to purchase things like prisons and whips (*heh*), but also roads, big cities, and schools... wait what? Technological advancement! EDUCATION?! Help!

"But we don't want all those things."

But we don't want those things? What? One queen. Just one! And they'd maybe already have a road. What *do* they actually want?

"We want to be free."

Narnians are a free people who are slaves of Aslan. If that doesn't sound like freedom, it's not; it is a Christian doctrine that considers true freedom slavery to Christ.[11] Paul tells believers they are freed from doing what they want so they can instead be "slaves to righteousness."[12] In other words, they are freed from their freedom. This is a theology of *control*. Aslan's ownership of the animals comes up immediately when they argue for their freedom.

"We belong to Aslan. They belong to Tash."

Why would Narnians be given in servitude to a people who worship a different god? There are serious religious differences here. How could the two systems work together? No worries, confirms the ape,

---

[11] 1 Peter 2:16; 1 Corinthians 7:22
[12] Romans 6:18

Tash and Aslan are just two names for the same thing! What's worse than slavery, education, and societal advancement? You guessed it: UNIVERSALISM.

How did the crowd react to this? With a deep depression and immense sadness:

> Every tail was down, every whisker drooped. It would have broken your heart with very pity to see their faces.

Not Tirian, though. Our boy lost his ever-lovin' mind:

> "Ape," he cried with a great voice, "you lie. You lie damnably. You lie like a Calormene. You lie like an Ape."

It must all be lies because Tirian can think of one pretty big difference between the two gods: Tash feeds on blood, i.e. receives sacrifices, and Aslan is "the good Lion by whose blood all Narnia was saved."

I can think of three human sacrifices offered to God in the Bible that were all considered righteous acts: Abraham's son (prevented at the last minute), Jephthah's daughter, and the more obvious, Yahweh's son. That's just off the top of my head! Reepicheep, who was being prepared for this when he was still a child, is my only ready example of a direct sacrifice to Aslan, and that was bloodless. Yet there are lesser examples, like those sent by Aslan to the wars. Heck, Tirian himself is only there in the first place to be killed by Aslan. Hwen asked to be eaten by the darn deity who has admitted to swallowing boys and girls in the past. I really don't think *receiving sacrifices* was the big difference between deities Tirian thought it was.

Tirian's head gets pounded by the baddies and he falls unconscious. He is about to have a bad night and a weird out of body experience that is of course not at all related to brain damage. This concussed dream will take him all the way to 1950s London. We may even meet quite a few familiar characters to join us on this adventure.

Unless everyone is dead. Which would be weird. Forget I said that.

271

The Last Battle: Chapters 4-5

"And that, honey, is why wearing black face is wrong."
"Why did the book put it in there? They could have done something
else as a disguise. Like a magic spell."
"Or hoods, or animal costumes, or capes. That's a good point. An
author is only limited by imagination. A responsible author would
avoid elements that hurt others."
"Okay let's get back to the story! I can't wait to see how this blows
up in their faces."
"No, it actually works out for them."
"What?!"

***

Lewis has gotten rather good at describing someone experiencing torture. I'm starting to feel Tirian's bruises and dizziness as I read about
him tied to a tree bleeding from a blow to the face. He is becoming
increasingly thirsty, hungry, cold, and sore as well. As I went through
the scene aloud it triggered some unpleasant memories of my evangelical childhood. Mostly of all the times I sat on my bed wondering how
I would be tortured and killed for Jesus when I grew up.

I assumed without question that I would die in some brutal way. I
was force-fed lots of examples, real and imagined, of people doing this
until it felt normal to expect. The Bible promised that I'd be perse-
cuted[13] and suffer for Jesus[14] in a world that hated me[15] in order to receive my super special persecution blessings.[16] I was not about to do
Christianity halfway.

---

[13] 2 Timothy 3:12
[14] 1 Peter 4:12
[15] John 15:19
[16] Matthew 5:10

***

Folks walked past their young king feeling sorry for him, but there was little they could do. The awful thing is that these passersby would have been rewarded for ignoring his suffering, or even adding to it, if the real Aslan had ordered it. A quick and imperfect example of this is when Aslan's people laughed at the suffering of the Calormene prince in *The Horse and His Boy*. Or maybe a better example would be when Aslan tore through towns in *Prince Caspian* and changed little boys into pigs for ignoring him while his posse danced and jeered. It was okay to join in the bullying since Aslan was doing it.

In my experience, when Christians do horrible things to people in the name of God—often in an attempt to follow biblical passages—others pipe up with, "Hey! That's not *real* Christianity!" I just find this response utterly dishonest in a weird way only a former fundamentalist can truly feel. For us literalists, the biblical Jesus is no peacenik. He lied about things like attending a party,[17] compared a woman to a dog,[18] snubbed his mother,[19] was xenophobic,[20] invented the idea of eternal torture that didn't exist in Abrahamic faiths until this point,[21] advocated violence to one's family if they didn't follow him,[22] preached giving up money and clothing since the world was ending in his disciples' lifetimes,[23] failed to stand up to the immorality of his day that stemmed from the sexist laws he backed,[24] made women into sexual objects and suggested self-mutilation for looking at them,[25]

---

[17] John 7:8, 10
[18] Mark 7:27; Matthew 15:26
[19] Matthew 12:48
[20] Matthew 10:5-6; 15:24
[21] Luke 16:19-31; Mark 9:43; Matthew 10:28
[22] Luke 12:51-53; Matthew 10:34-36
[23] Matthew 6:19-34; 16:27-28
[24] Matthew 5:17-18
[25] Matthew 5:28-29

and is prophesied in the last book of the Bible to come back and kill multitudes of people until he's literally covered in their blood.[26] Obviously, he did some good things too, but holding him up as the ultimate model of goodness is ethical peril.

Despite the full picture of Christ, Christians are some of the loveliest people. This brooks no argument. They comprise some of the best, brightest, most generous people in the world. There were members of my church who picked the kindest of holy passages to live by. My Gram went to her grave with a heart full of mercy because that's what the Judeo-Christian god was to her. More power to her.

I watched many kind believers in my church struggle with guilt when they lent a hand to someone the Bible did not like. My pastor preached that we should not eat at the same table as a "homosexual" or a girl engaged in premarital sex because when it came to sexual sins, the New Testament was specific about the command to "hand them over to Satan" by shunning them. [27] Our moral pull to do otherwise with our neighbors or our children was described as weakness, or worse, disobedience. Try telling a Baptist mom not to make a casserole for someone in need. It's a hard sell.

***

The residents of Narnia felt a moral pull to help Tirian, despite Aslan's rules, so they snuck back over to help him.

"I suppose what we're doing now may be wrong."

They feed him, alleviate his thirst with wine, and wash the blood off his face. They wanted to untie him, but they couldn't since "Aslan might be angry."

---

[26] Revelation 19:15
[27] 1 Corinthians 5

This offering of wine may have been reminiscent of Jesus being offered wine and gall while also bound to a thing made of wood. Scripture tells Christians to endure or "take up" a cross. Not literally, but by suffering in the world. My guess is this imagery is significant to solidify Tirian's holiness. The text says they had water with them, but they never offered him that to drink.

After "some more wine" they assured him:

> "If it were only the Ape and the Calormenes who were against you, we would have fought till we were cut into pieces before we'd have let them tie you up. We would, we would indeed. But we can't go against Aslan."

Lewis must make it clear that these animals are violent enough to be good guys. They are only allowing this injustice for the *right* reasons. They would have fought for their king otherwise.

One sad thing about all this is that the animals believe that they deserve the punishments the ape is doling out on them.

> "We must all have done something dreadfully wrong without knowing it. He must be punishing us for something."

I felt so much empathy for these little creatures. Victim blaming didn't start or end with the Bible, but it thrives there. This false Aslan resembles the biblical god closely enough by lashing out at his own people in anger.

> "He seems to have come back very angry this time."

The deity of The Book of Revelation is angry, violent, and sociopathic. He enacts terror and calls it justice. He releases disease and calls it mercy. He condemns not only his many enemies, but regular people—the kindly grandmas and ignorant foreigners who didn't accept salvation in time—and condemns them to eternal torture. God may be said to be "unwilling that any should perish"[28] but he drowns babies on his bad days.[29]

In the distance Tirian sees a bonfire and a very stiff Aslan lookalike emerging from the stable. The ape pretends to get instructions from the lion while the animals all wail: *"Aslan! Aslan! Aslan! [...] Be angry with us no more."* Tirian cries out to *"Aslan! Aslan! Aslan!"* as well but being at the top of the hierarchy comes with the privilege of actually being heard.

> "Let me be killed," cried the King, "I ask nothing for myself. But come and save all Narnia."

Aw the magic words of self-abasement and sacrifice! Aslan eats that up!

Tirian then asks rather specifically that the children who have come and helped save Narnia in ancient times would once again show up. Granting his request, Aslan triggers an out of body experience. All of a sudden Tirian finds himself standing in front of a group of familiar people sitting around a dining table in London. Every child—some grown up—who has ever been to Narnia, minus Susan, are there. Peter exclaims in surprise, "You have a Narnian look about you." (Wonder what all *that* implied.) Unfortunately, Tirian found he could not speak and simply faded away from their sight. He woke up still tied to the tree, but no longer alone. In front of him were two well-known children named Eustace and Jill.

They untie the king and flee. Eustace explains how Digory and Polly had invited all the seven friends of Narnia to dinner in London and it was at that dinner the king appeared in their midst. This was the catalyst for a series of events that would lead the entire group meeting up on a train where Aslan would warp two of them to Narnia. The

---

[28] 2 Peter 3:9
[29] Genesis 6:6-7

other five are still on the train, which will be important later. Eustace and Jill came alone because the others had been told by Aslan that they would not be returning to Narnia in their lifetimes. He prefers them young.

As a side note, the number seven is considered a godly number in Biblical Numerology. This was my mother's favorite number for exactly this reason. Seven represents perfection and completion. Eight does not, however, so Susan had to go. Just like Judas, Susan walked alongside Aslan, learned to follow him, and was still not meant for entering Aslan's Country. The Bible teaches that God predestines some people for eternal torture before they are even born or have done anything wrong[30] and hates others without any reason[31] so we have justification for a beloved character being rejected by Aslan.

As Eustace told Tirian the story of how they got there—Jill doesn't get to speak if a boy is around—he must stop several times to explain trains and telecommunication and all sorts of modern devices. *One queen in charge, Narnia!*

The three heroes make their way to an outpost where they can get weapons and put on black face. Yeah. They did that:

> "And look on this stone bottle. In this there is a juice which, when we have rubbed it on our hands and faces, will make us brown as Calormenes."
>
> "Oh hurrah!" said Jill. "Disguises! I love disguises."
>
> "Nothing but oil and ashes will make us white Narnians again."

Our heroes end their day by moaning the fact they have no wine. Because of course they would.

---

[30] Romans 9:22
[31] Romans 9:10-13

The Last Battle: Chapter 6

"Wow, Jill is super great at stuff now."

"Probably because she's dead."

"Wait, what?"

"Christians have this belief that after you die you get a new body."

"No, stop. This makes no sense. When did she die?"

"At the train station. She's been dead this whole time."

"You go to Narnia when you die? And fight wars and kill bunnies to eat?"

"I mean, the Bible's afterlife has battles and feasts with meat so I imagine bunnies die unless it is some sort of delicious magically conjured flesh being consumed."

"I'm so confused."

***

Our heroes set out to free Jewel. They are still in EFFING BLACK FACE, so I don't expect this to make it into the Hollywood version. Jill is the navigator for their trek through the forest and she's very skilled at the task. She leads them right to the stable where the unicorn is being kept in the dark. We've come a long way from the days Jill couldn't tell she was traveling west when the sun was in her eyes. Now Jill is this badass who can pinpoint their location by looking at the stars. A confident, capable, and skilled female character is probably a hint that something is *off*.

Tirian is surprised at how the children seemed to be "much stronger and bigger and more grown-up than they had been when he first met them a few hours before." There may be a reason for the children's enhancements that has less to do with "Narnia magic" and more to do with the Christian idea of glorified bodies—the physical bodies believers get after they die. Previously the children told Tirian that they were sent to Narnia by Aslan without the help of the magic rings, straight from the train station where their entire party was gathered. How did Aslan send them? We'll find out later he killed them. Or, to be much more disingenuous, Aslan *allowed them* to be tragically and violently killed by a train he both knew was coming and sovereignly sent.

Now here is where the Christian view of the afterlife comes into play, or I should say the *biblical* view, as the Christian one varies depending on the sect. After followers of Christ die, or are involved in a rapture event in which the dead bodily rise into the air,[32] they receive new physical bodies[33] that require food to eat.[34] The act of killing our food most likely continues as Heavenly feasts include meat as well as all the same cultural significances as the ones in ancient Jerusalem.

One feast, a marriage feast, is featured prominently in The Book of Revelation between Jesus and his saints, and is called The Marriage Supper of the Lamb.[35] This wedding is preceded by burning a "whore"[36] who was unworthy of Jesus. Guests at the heavenly wedding don't just witness the prostitute burning, they *celebrate it* as the "smoke from her goes up forever and ever."[37] Women and sex are never seen as positive. Then Jesus, the groom, goes out and "makes war" on folks while wearing a robe soaked in blood and "in righteousness" since he's Jesus. He strikes people down with a sword that comes out of his

---

[32] 1 Thessalonians 4:16-17
[33] Philippians 3:21; 1 Corinthians 15:42-44
[34] Revelation 19:9
[35] Remember how Aslan appeared as a lamb in *The Dawn Treader*?
[36] This is the English word my Bible uses (Revelation 19:2) and not my personal label. Some believers claim she was a metaphor for Babylon who cheated on the biblical god with other gods. For an ancient culture lousy with sex workers, they didn't respect them much.
[37] Revelation 19:2-3

mouth and rules them "with an iron rod."[38] (I don't want to know where *that* comes from!) After the slaughter, an angel tells birds to eat the carcasses of the enemy kings and their slaves. Also, their horses. (Don't tell Bitsy.) Others get thrown into a lake of fire and sulfur, a lovely landmark in Heaven apparently. The rest of the prisoners of war get slain by Jesus' flesh sword; he leaves no prisoners and the birds become gorged. The biblical last battle is how Jesus spends his honeymoon.

This is why Narnia will end in blood and violence. When Aslan implies that this is all normal for the afterlife, as well as planned, we see the clear biblical influence. This is a heavenly battle after all. What? Was anyone expecting harps?

***

Part of the plan to free Jewel is for Tirian to imitate a Calormene by talking "like a curst, cruel, proud lord of Calormen." He approaches a lazy guard asleep at his post and puts a knife to the man's back. In any other children's book, the kids might sneak around a sleeping guard. Not this one! Inside the barn, Tirian has Jewel threaten to kill the guard with his horn while Tirian unties him. I got to explain what "rive him to the heart" meant to my daughter. This has got to be the nastiest depiction of unicorns she's ever encountered.

While Tirian is getting Jewel, Jill sneaks into Aslan's stable. She drew her knife on the imposter because she's now much more violent and therefore *improved* by this book's standards, but it was an unnecessary threat since Puzzle, who was still in the lion skin, was ready to leave with them. *More than ready* since the Calormenes weren't giving him water. If Jill had left the false Aslan alone, their strategy would

---

[38] Revelation 19:11, 15

surely have failed; the animals would never have backed Tirian without permission from their deity. Jill saved the day! This causes Eustace to be quite impressed. He says if she "was a boy" she'd likely have been knighted for this act. Yet we know girls can't be knighted nor can they be held accountable for their actions. Tirian says that *if* Jill was a boy, he would have whipped her for disobeying orders. *Whipped her.* Huh.

This view of girls and women as second-class citizens is horrible, but it is also precisely why we have girls in this series. Girls can make mistakes, break the rules, and get emotional. They aren't considered anything more than dependent children, even when they grow up, and they don't have the same expectations of leadership, maturity, authority, or stoic detachment that male characters must have. When boys can't be emotional because that's considered a yucky female trait, it gets harder to communicate danger, tragedy, or excitement with them driving the story. This handicaps our author. The first version of Lewis' grand tale started with a small boy protagonist finding his way to Narnia through a wardrobe. It didn't work out. In her book, Miller explains:

> Writing about Narnia released something free, lyrical, and tender in Lewis, and none of those qualities fit within the limitations of what he would have viewed as an acceptable boy character. [...] Lewis is not the only storyteller to find that his own investment in conventional masculinity makes a female protagonist the most appealing choice. [...] Lucy can do and feel much more than a traditional boy character.[39]

Lucy got to cry and rely on others. Jill got to grieve loss and be terrified. Yet our boys will try not to cry and will be constantly holding it together rather than showing hints of human feelings. A girl must always be around to carry the emotional labor—both for the male

---

[39] Laura Miller, 2008. *The Magician's Book: A Skeptic's Adventures in Narnia*, (New York, NY; Back Bay Books), pp. 70-71.

characters and for the reader. The only time we need fewer girls around is when there is nothing of character left to develop and the world is ending in blood.

As awful as it is for girls to be seen as *less than* due to expressing emotion, boys don't benefit from a social structure that demands detachment. It leads to boys having to prove themselves to be above sensibilities in a violent way as we will soon see with Eustace who is about to taste his first kill in the next chapter. It will be considered a good deed since the life he ends will be a Calormene.

Upon seeing Puzzle in the lion skin, Tirian quickly unsheathed his sword to murder the sentient donkey. When asked what the heck he's doing, he admits he intends to "smite off the head of the accursed Ass." Jill defends the donkey in the meekest and gentlest way, but still gets lectured for being "the most malapert and disobedient" and told to stand clear. She has one female job, here, so she should submit already! She is seen as an emotional *girl* who doesn't know any better or whose feminine delicateness cannot stomach capital punishment. She must rely on the male characters, whom the king will hear out, to step up and explain that the donkey is innocent and dumb and it's the ape who is the real villain. Tirian responds by saying he will kill the ape by public hanging instead. Puzzle doesn't seem to mind talk of killing his friend. He's content to follow whoever is in charge.

In the distance they heard Dwarves approaching. The king tells the others these are probably "treacherous Dwarfs, enemies, as likely as not." I wondered why he would think this of his own subjects before even meeting them, but apparently it was foreshadowing for their eventual turn from Aslan. In truth, these Dwarves are largely bystanders and victims at this point, but by Lewis' standards, they will be something far worse. They'll be *unbelievers*.

The Last Battle: Chapter 7

"Slavery is good?"
"Under certain circumstances, by Narnian logic."
"But the Calormenes have slaves! And everyone keeps saying that's
why they're the bad guys!"
"Silly as it seems, Aslan gets special rules."
"No one should have slaves, Mom."

***

The large group of Dwarves who were approaching in the last chapter finally came within eyeshot of our party; they were being taken as slaves to the Calormene mines to benefit Aslan's treasury. Two Calormenes were leading them with two additional guards following behind. It didn't take many men to keep the group in line since they were so despondent.

Our blue-eyed king, still in black face, tricks everyone into thinking he's a Tarkaan. He then asks the Dwarves why they were going so willingly "to die in the salt-pits," making it clear to the reader that this kind of slavery was death by labor. Their response was heartbreaking:

"Aslan's orders. He's sold us. What can we do against him?"

The "sold us" line hit me unexpectedly hard, like a sucker punch. I knew people obeyed Aslan, but here I realized anew that Aslan *owns* people. This is something I just took for granted as a child, but now it unbalances me to see it mentioned so nonchalantly. This "God owns you" idea is often slipped into storylines or Bible readings unnoticed. Now it stands out badly like a third eye.

It might not feel like a big deal to be owned by a deity who is loving, silent, invisible, and dare I say, imaginary. If only deities didn't have *enforcers*—real humans, historically men, with rules for pleasing these gods. I was used for unpaid labor in my church when I was little and I was sent on mission trips starting at sixteen. My Christian primary school expected I do unpaid work for them and my Christian college once required I do a special day-long service project or risk not getting my diploma. I was bused down to Mexico and painted a church in the sun until I almost passed out.

Not just me, but my mom did so much unpaid labor for our church and religious school that it was a hardship on our family. Thankfully good Christians, not that we could associate with anyone else,[40] provided our clothes, shoes, and bread to make up for it.

We would not have wanted to be saved from this labor. I loved my family and church and believed deeply that my love had to be shown in service. One of my absolute favorite songs as a teen was "Use Me Here."[41] Service under compulsion doesn't have to be overly traumatic to be wrong.

My obedience required not only my body, but my mind—literally my every thought.[42] One prayer I said repeatedly was, "Please give me the ability to unplug my brain like a television." For many years I had a small TV set on a narrow nightstand at the end of my bed. I became jealous of the way it would snap off with the push of a button. I reasoned if I could petition God for that ability, to flip a switch and suddenly be a mindless puddle, I could serve him better by not having to battle myself near-constantly over every train of forbidden thought. Worrying about the future, imagining bullies getting their comeuppance, examining the biblical contradictions too closely, and contemplating my wedding night were all hovering over the boarder of sin territory. Lustful thoughts were especially upsetting to my heavenly

---

[40] 1 Corinthians 15:33

[41] The song literally says to give up our "plans" and "dreams" to be used of God despite "what the future holds." Album: Seized by the Power of a Great Affection. Artist: Everybodyduck, 1999.

[42] 2 Corinthians 10:5

master. After puberty, I was convinced I was the most evil and dirty person alive for having COMPLETELY NORMAL urges and drives. These thoughts were disrespectful of my future husband who would be given ownership over my body under God's direction. Again, it came down to ownership: My husband owned me, my father owned me, God (presented as a male deity) owned me; I would never be allowed to own myself.[43]

Aslan owns the Dwarves, despite Narnians being called *free* people. Recall being "free in the Lord" is exactly the same as being a "slave in Christ."[44] Paul's[45] New Testament letters taught slaves to obey their masters,[46] fear their masters,[47] and to work hard without complaining.[48] Paul's equally horrible advice to women, whom he considered slaves to their husbands,[49] was to be silent,[50] not ask questions or learn from anyone who was not their master,[51] cover their heads to show their subservient position,[52] not have authority over men,[53] and be "saved" from God's wrath by giving their owners children.[54] This biblical author would find a friend in Lewis who once wrote:

> "Some of us most dread for our own species […] the dominance of the female."[55]

---

[43] 1 Corinthians 6

[44] 1 Corinthians 7:22

[45] Or whichever author was claiming to write for Paul at the time. I realize scholars do not think he wrote every biblical letter attributed to him. Often letters pushing reforms on churches were given his name to lend them authority.

[46] Colossians 3:22

[47] Ephesians 6:5

[48] Philippians 2:14-16

[49] Ephesians 5:22; Titus 2:5

[50] 1 Corinthians 14:34

[51] 1 Corinthians 14:35

[52] 1 Corinthians 11:6

[53] 1 Timothy 2:12

[54] 1 Timothy 2:15

[55] When expressing his fears of women leading men: C. S. Lewis, 1955. *Surprised by Joy: The Shape of my Early Life*, (London; Geoffrey Bles).

After Tirian showed the Dwarves that their Aslan was a donkey in a lion skin, the Calormenes realized the jig was up. They drew their swords, but it was too late. Tirian quickly killed one, Eustace killed the other, and the Dwarves themselves took care of the last two. Keep in mind Eustace is a child and just killed a person. This should come with a bit of shock, horror, or disgust. Yet Tirian happily pats the boy on the shoulder and Jill becomes downright hot for him. She was "very impressed" and felt "almost shy." *Oh Eustace, do you have a bit of grey matter on your shirt? Some small intestine in your hair? You sexy beast, you.*

Tirian then turned to the Dwarves to give them their marching orders. He *is* Aslan's rightful mouthpiece after all. They *are* slaves of Aslan, are they not?

Maybe the Dwarves never really thought about Aslan's dominance over them before, but after Tirian used the Socratic method to get them to think about their situation, perhaps for the first time, they fail to stop thinking things through after their master switched hands. Could it be that true freedom meant not belonging to *anyone*?

A Black Dwarf (because of course he's Black!) who is described as "not-very-nice-looking" finally speaks up:

> "I don't know how all you chaps feel, but I feel I've heard as much about Aslan as I want to for the rest of my life."

A free-thinking Dwarf? No! That's awful! You're supposed to go back to happily serving the other Aslan! You're not supposed to figure out the game is rigged!

The narrator notes that Tirian was not pale when he was slaughtering the Calormene, for that was *nothing*, but he becomes pale now at the thought of someone not following Aslan. (Pale *under* the black face of course.) He starts practically shouting at the former slaves. The Dwarves simply respond:

> "We've been taken in once and now you expect us to be taken in again the next minute. We've no more use for stories about Aslan, see!"

I like how they now sound like old-timey gangsters.

Jill was so "disgusted with the Dwarfs" that she considered them worse than the Calormenes. Tirian tries to say the real Aslan, who does not speak for himself naturally, is the boss of Narnia and is on their side. Our main Dwarf is not having it:

> "And you've got a better imitation, I suppose! [...] No thanks. We've been fooled once and we're not going to be fooled again."

Tirian is spitting mad now and insists angrily, "I serve the real Aslan." They respond, "Where's he? Who's he? Show him to us!" Tirian calls them fools—the comeback of a man standing solidly on an empty argument. The king then messes up big time. He tells them that Aslan won't come show himself as he's "not a tame lion." This was the same exact phrase the ape kept using to convince the Dwarves that Aslan was selling them into slavery. This was obviously the very worst thing to say.

Realizing the huge need for evidence, Jill tries to play witness by assuring the Dwarves that she's seen Aslan herself, um, hundreds and hundreds of years ago... by *magic*. She is just baffled why they would then need evidence to back up that claim. I mean, maybe it's because outlandish claims without evidence led them directly into slavery in the first place? Yeah, their doubt is a *complete and total* mystery, girl-friend.

Eustace calls the Dwarves "little beasts" and yells at them for not saying thank you for the rescue.

> "You wanted to make use of us, that's why you rescued us."

Technically yes, the king would require the Dwarves to work for him, to pay him tribute, and to serve the humans in the hierarchy. In fact, the very next section shows how depressed Tirian is because the Dwarves won't be ~~getting killed~~ helping in the upcoming fight with the Calormenes, which he had planned to lead them to "the next night." Despite this, we are supposed to be just as frustrated as our heroes that the stupid Dwarves have not jumped into service to the real Aslan.

The Bible speaks of there being believers from every tongue, tribe, and nation who will join Jesus, which is why missionaries travel to get converts. I couldn't help but notice during my New Tribes missionary training that there were plenty of language groups that died out before Christians could reach them. There were also all sorts of tribes and nations that existed before Christianity was invented. I was told it would only take one person to bravely accept Jesus to make that verse true. Incredibly, this one person could even be a *great great great* descendant of that long-forgotten group who had nothing to do with the original culture. The myth of the "lone believer" became a kind of urban legend permeating the stories I heard at my Christian school, Vacation Bible School, and church family camp. It also was spread during Missions Week talks, AWANA Council Time meetings, and Sunday School lessons. I immediately recognized this familiar trope when one lonely Dwarf comes running after our group, validating their belief in Aslan. Later we'll have a lonely Calormene join in. Although that would be one VERY WHITE and VERY NON-DWARFIAN Heaven for these poor guys.

Tirian and the others surround the single Dwarf, pat him on the back, and give him the weapon he requested to fight alongside them. This exact Dwarf also happened to have overheard a conversation between the ape, a Calormene, and a clever cat who is in on the fake Aslan ruse about how there was really no such thing as Tash or Aslan.

That's right! They were dreaded atheists! They're multiplying! They're everywhere! Nothing is sacred or good!

Truly this is the end of the world.

The Last Battle: Chapter 8

"What are demons again?"
"They're like bad invisible spirit creatures."
"Invisible? Do they exist?"
"What do you think?"
"What's the evidence for them?"
"Oh, that's a smart question!"

***

One aspect of my religion that I had real trouble explaining away was my Bible's dearth of knowledge; it didn't seem to know anything outside the time and place it was written. It wasn't just the lack of prophesies about technological advancements that was a problem, there was also a clear lack of understanding about how the world worked. Surely God should have known certain things before modern science. For example, not once do we get a single hint by any biblical book that germs exist. Imagine the countless lives one verse about handwashing could have saved! The closest we get is ceremonial washings in germ-infested mikvahs, or later, dips in stagnant baptismal fonts. With a bit more knowledge, maybe these practices could have been traded in for healthier alternatives, like streams of running water or water poured from a jug over people.

I once visited the Jordan River in Israel since it was the setting for Jesus' baptism. I had plans to get baptized there. That changed after putting a few fingers in the disgusting water. If God can magically clean baptismal water in holy sites, he's not.[56] He's too busy getting rid of the real cause of illness: invisible demons!

Jesus spends a large chunk of his ministry defeating demons in order to heal people. Illness and demons go together in Scripture like peanut butter and jelly.[57] Demons are even presented as specific conditions such as muteness,[58] deafness,[59] blindness,[60] seizures,[61] paralysis or inability to ambulate properly,[62] and, the more obvious, mental illness.[63] This whole or partial misattribution of physical ailments and conditions to the supernatural not only contradicts scientific findings, it subverts efforts to look for evidence-based explanations in the first place!

The New Testament writers had no excuse for this. Ancient Greeks had already been busy studying disease, disability, and the human body. They had started out just like their Jewish and Christian neighbors by believing illness was divine punishment, yet they had advanced well beyond these explanations by the time the Scriptures were being written. The Greeks used reason to apply their theories to their patients, checking which remedies affected which symptoms.[64] They had come up with a system of medical science that outpaced superstitious thinking. Unfortunately, we've already been over what the Bible thinks of all things "Greek."

---

[56] Since writing this, there has been a worldwide pandemic that temporarily shut down many churches. As a result, one Christian shrine in France, Our Lady of Lourdes, shut down its world-famous healing waters due to risk of Covid-19 transmission. The religious leaders correctly chose the health and safety of their pilgrims over their belief in the waters' healing powers over illness.

[57] Luke 9:1-2; 13:31-32; Acts 5:15-16

[58] Mark 9:17

[59] Mark 9:25

[60] Matthew 12:22

[61] Luke 9:39

[62] Acts 8:7

[63] Luke 8:27-28

[64] Mark Cartwright, 2013. "Ancient Greek Medicine," World History Encyclopedia. Available at: https://www.worldhistory.org/Greek_Medicine/

Apologists have claimed that Jesus is speaking metaphorically or that his biblical stories are allegorical. One argument I heard was that maybe he thought of germs as *tiny demons*. That he then *talked to* like a lunatic. Sorry, germs don't have conversations with people and can't be gotten rid of with magic thoughts.

Narnia also has demons. Word is spreading through Narnia that Aslan and Tash are one and the same, and they have started calling this divine creature Tashlan. Lewis cannot let children take any time to consider this, so no sooner does our new Dwarf friend mention overhearing a belief that Tash is not real than the demon itself flies past our group of heroes!

"It seems, then, that there is a real Tash, after all."

Belief in demons is alive and well today. As a newly married teenager, my mom once saw a demon in her apartment hallway when she was in a semiconscious state. Her pastor confirmed it had to be one and encouraged her to get rid of it by burning my dad's records that contained worldly music. Goodbye *Journey*, *Pink Floyd*, and *demons*!

It's hard to grow up hearing about evil spirits and not be affected by that. I once thought I saw a demon in the dark window of my childhood home on Halloween night—a night I was repeatedly told was especially wicked. Thoughts of demons kept me up a lot as a scared child. When my cat would stare at a wall for no discernible reason, I got worried there was a demon in the room! As a teen, I had to write a paper for my Christian school about how my religion was right and all the others were wrong. I interviewed my pastor for some money quotes I would use to support my thesis, but when he noticed the library books I had checked out for this project, he warned me that demons hunted at libraries and could enter me through those books. Evil spirits were more likely to be drawn to these specific books because they taught about other religions, which we knew were all invented by Satan. He specifically instructed me not to hold one so close to my body. It was the kind of thing that would give Frank Peretti a wet dream. In the end, I got an A for a research paper claiming my religion was true and my only two allowable sources were a Bible and my pastor.

All of this is really embarrassing, too bad there's so much more. As a young adult I prayed demons out of a building in Northern Ireland with a church group. During a missionary trip to Africa, I avoided part of the open market because they were selling carved images that could be considered idols and I had been taught idols attracted demons. During my missionary training in Papua New Guinea, I even learned how to pray against demons who lived in the tribes we were trying to win for Christ. Another time, while I was in the Middle East, a pastor shared his testimony with a group of us Bible students that included descriptions of the demons he claimed to have seen in his ceiling. He blamed the demons for keeping him from his holy calling for so long by causing him to make all sorts of bad decisions he never took responsibility for. I recently listened to the interview of a Christian church leader who claimed a demon was responsible for him murdering people.[65] It seemed the man's beliefs stopped him from getting help and allowed him to scapegoat his behavior.

Tash, our Narnian demon, had four arms, twenty curved fingernails, and the head of a bird of prey. This description of Tash is different than my mother's hallway demon, my Halloween window demon, and the pastor's ceiling demon, but they are all scary in some way the person describing them finds horrible. Demons are grotesque because they are products of fear. Tash, however, is funny to me since the Bible doesn't physically describe demons even once, but it does

---

[65] "Snapped: Notorious the BTK Serial Killer." Oxygen Media. Aired September 2, 2018.

describe **angels** who have multiple eyes,[66] six wings,[67] and the faces of eagles,[68] making Tash a lot closer to one of God's heavenly spirits than Satan's!

***

Our heroes have a new friend—one lonely Dwarf away from all the "treacherous" ones. To prove he is good, he speaks wisdom to the group:

> "People shouldn't call for demons unless they really mean what they say."

If unbelievers can call on demons unaware, then they are the worst kind of dangerous. This explains so much fear-based hatred and mistrust of people like me. (I pretty much summon demons daily with my haircut alone.) Yet even believers could inadvertently summon demons according to my pastors. Exactly how one avoided demon possession was nebulous—not following the rules, not praying for protection, Trick-or-Treating, having sex, or apparently by holding library books; one must stay deep within the church's authority to remain safe.

Our unicorn then makes a curious remark that I didn't catch until a second reading. He wonders if Tash will be visible to the ape. Not once does it say that Tash can turn invisible, but our heroes seem to intuitively know this can happen when unbelievers are looking. The Christian God supposedly blinds the minds of unbelievers from seeing these things so there can be no outside (read: Greek) validation of insider religious claims.[69]

---

[66] Ezekiel 10:12
[67] Isaiah 6:2
[68] Ezekiel 1:10
[69] 2 Corinthians 4:4

After Tash has gone, our party decides to head back to Cair Paravel. They like the idea of leaving the demon to haunt the ape and Calormenes for a while. They assume Tash will bother them subtly like how demons bother nonbelievers. That is why atheists and people in non-Christian religions are all depressed all the time—an affliction Christians *never* have.

The Last Battle: Chapters 9-11

"People actually believe they'll have to kill other people when they die?"

"Beliefs aren't anchored to reality. You can believe anything."

"So bad people who want to kill others have those beliefs?"

"Maybe. It's more complicated with people who have been indoctrinated. I didn't want anyone to suffer after they died, but I was taught it was right if God ordered it."

"I'm glad you didn't ever *doctorate* me."

"I have attempted it in others ways."

"What?"

"I taught you a love for *Star Trek* and *Doctor Who*. Oh, and your bedtime song is actually the theme to *Firefly*."

"Sneaky!"

***

By this point Tirian and the children have FINALLY removed their black faces since they "didn't want to be mistaken for Calormenes and perhaps attacked by any loyal Narnians." Why would the good guys just attack people for being Black? (Hmmmmm.) After becoming White again Tirian says, "I feel a true man again." *Groan.*

The last chapter closed with our party reminiscing about the history of Narnia. In pure Lewis fashion, they will speak of the good old days; it was never as good as it was before then. The picture of all those happy years, all the thousands of them, piled up in Jill's mind.

"Oh, Jewel—wouldn't it be lovely if Narnia just went on and on—like what you said it has been?"
"Nay, sister, [...] all worlds draw to an end, except Aslan's own country."

This is some major foreshadowing that the world is ending. A talking eagle flying overhead, who they threaten to shoot with an arrow, spots them and reports that Cair Paravel has fallen to Calormen:

"Narnia is no more."

A fight with the Calormenes is inevitable, but in every likelihood, they will be slaughtered in the ensuing battle they refer to as "the adventure that Aslan sends." Eustace asks what Jill thinks will happen when they die in Narnia—whether their dead bodies will appear back in London or not. Jill says she doesn't know but she would rather die for Aslan in Narnia than live a long life back home. (Ew.) Eustace strangely responds that dying in battle would be better than dying "smashed up by British Railways!" He explains that the "awful jerk" they experienced when coming to Narnia felt like the beginning of a railway accident. (Spoiler: It was.)

The party sneaks behind the stable where Puzzle had been presented in the lion skin every night. The ape, clearly hungover, comes out to address the crowd. He tells them that a donkey has been dressing up like Aslan and due to this sacrilege, the real Aslan won't be coming out tonight. This enrages the other animals. Our heroes are horrified that their plan is now ruined as the ape beat them to the reveal and used it to his advantage.

The Black Dwarf from the slavery rescue speaks to the crown, telling everyone Aslan was the same donkey the entire time. This Dwarf must be magical because he was marching off in the opposite direction last we knew and is now suddenly here before them with the speed of Yzma and Kronk. Unfortunately, no one listens to him. The Dwarf demands the ape show the crowd what exactly is in the stable since "seeing is believing." Readers are supposed to recognize this as bad advice since it goes against biblical wisdom that *not* seeing counts as evidence if you believe hard enough.[70]

The ape says the crowd is welcome to see Tashlan, who is totally in the stable (wink), but whoever wants to go in must do so alone, one at a time, behind closed doors. The Dwarf points out that this shady set up allows Calormenes with swords to lie in wait to kill whoever walks in. Ignoring this, the ape asks for a volunteer from the audience to go in and report what they see. A plant in the audience, the atheist cat, volunteers. It's all like a bad magic act.

One thing I want to specifically mention is Lewis' repeated use of the slur "Darkie" in this part of the story. I found it hard to read aloud to my daughter and explained that it was a racist sentiment and not to use it. In this context, it's the closest thing to the N-word. I think if we all look at our Narnia racism bingo cards, all the boxes are now full.

The cat goes into the stable to see Tashlan and comes out terrified. It loses the ability to speak and it is never seen again. We get the idea that something is not going according to plan. Even so, the effect on the crowd is the desired one with the animal people begging the ape to speak all Moses-like to Aslan on their behalf.

Next a young Calormene named Emeth asks to go into the stable. Since Aslan and Tash are one and the same, Emeth is eager to meet

---

[70] Hebrews 11:1

the god he has served all his life. He is so brave that Jewel tells Tirian this young man is "worthy of a better god than Tash." Emeth goes into the door of the stable and a few brief moments later a dead man falls out of the same door. The captain announces that Emeth has died after looking upon Tash. Before we think too badly of Tash, this whole *seeing-equals-dying* thing is originally a brutality of the god of the Bible.[71] Our heroes behind the stable, however, see that the dead man isn't Emeth at all, but some other Calormene.

In a move that made no sense whatsoever, the ape then volunteers a talking boar to come next to meet his death in the stable. The implication is that all the Narnians are going to be killed one by one. Why would he do this when he already has the crowd cowering and obedient? It seems like lazy writing just so Tirian will finally have enough motivation to step out from his hidey spot and start attacking folks. (As if murder boy needs much prodding.) Tirian picked up the ape and threw him in the stable. A weird greenish-blue light appeared and a "clucking and screaming as if it was the hoarse voice of some monstrous bird" was heard from inside. The ape was gone forever.

Tirian then addresses the crowd and asks all Narnians to join the fight. The dogs who are loyal by nature join up immediately as well as a few small woodland creatures, but most of the crowd is too afraid of Tashlan's wrath.

Tirian orders the woodland creatures to go to where the talking horses have been tied up by the Calormenes and ask them if they are going to fight to the death for him. If they agree to do it, the creatures are to gnaw the ropes and free them. Can't let them out of their unlawful bondage if they aren't willing to go die for the king, though. (Seriously, this is messed up.) This ends with the horses arriving just in time to be slaughtered immediately by the Dwarves! They are killing

---

71 Exodus 33:20

people with absolutely no motivation due to just being evil unbelievers.

The battle rages and several animals die. Little Bitsy had major problems with this section of the story. When the doggies died it was sad, but it was somehow worse when they were severely injured and whimpering. The saddest of all was when the bear, who has always been described as a gentle giant, died:

> The Bear lay on the ground, moving feebly. Then it mumbled in its throaty voice, bewildered to the last, "I—I don't——understand," laid its big head down on the grass as quietly as a child going to sleep, and never moved again.

Eustace gets a lecture about not acting like a "kitchen-girl" and to keep killing more folks. Jill has now killed a human as well as a Narnian wolf with her arrows, and she's done this while shaking. She'll later start crying and have to be careful not to get her bowstring wet. I am thankful that she is portrayed as very capable, but she is not allowed to be unfazed like the boys. Conversely, boys are not allowed to be emotional or nonviolent without being compared to girls, which the text implies is the *very worst thing to be.*

When it's clear our team is losing, Tirian calls them to retreat and all but one run a safe distance away. They turned to see who was missing. It was Eustace. He was thrown into the stable with Tash just as the ape had been.

The Last Battle: Chapter 12-13

"I thought you'd have more of a problem with what happens to the Dwarves."
"Remind me again who killed the horses? Yeah, those Dwarves can suffer."
"Dang kid, you're super scary right now."

***

Eustace has already been thrown into the stable, and Jill follows, thrown in by her hair. Lastly Tirian is cornered by the captain of the Calormenes and they fight right into the doorway of the stable. When it's clear he will be overpowered, Tirian grabs the captain and takes the man with him through the wooden door. It's over. The door of the stable has eaten them all. None of our main characters is left alive.

***

When Tirian recovered enough to remember who he was, he noticed he was outdoors surrounded by bright sunlight and grass. Standing before him were past kings and queens of Narnia.

The Calormene captain was also there but had no time to enjoy himself since his demon god, Tash, had come for him. The book mentions how terrified the captain was when he began to suspect that the demon was real. It was too late for this unbeliever. Tash even gets this dopey line—speaking with his beak mouth I guess—about having been called there. I expected some demon screams or something, but we get the queen's English, doubtless to drive home the lesson that people call demons with their actions.

Tash scoops the captain up to take him away and no one tries to stop him. Instead we hear Peter say:

"Begone, Monster, and take your lawful prey to your own place: in the name of Aslan and Aslan's great Father, the Emperor-over-sea."

I add a friendly reminder to Bitsy between finishing this chapter and brushing her teeth that gods don't get to own or eat people. Okay, goodnight sweetie!

When I was her age, I was taught that something similar would happen to my unbelieving relatives as they were thrown into fire and I happily played with Jesus. Now I realize it would be pretty psychotic to not only allow my loved ones to be dragged off to be tortured forever, but to be happy and cheerful about it since, according to the Bible, there's "no sorrow" and "no concern" in Heaven.[72] The same biblical book talks about people being thrown into a fiery lake of burning sulfur literally four verses after assuring believers they will be happy and concern-free. That puts a dark spin on things.

The kings and queens present include Dead Peter, Dead Edmund, Dead Lucy, Dead Jill, Dead Eustace, Dead Digory, and Dead Polly— the gang from the dining table that Tirian once visited as a ghostly apparition. They were dressed in royal clothes with crowns and we're told Polly's beauty was restored. I imagine Digory's was as well, but since he's fully human (read: male) and not some object that always has to be pretty (read: female) it doesn't get emphasized. Both older folks get equally unstiffened and made younger.

Dead Tirian realizes that his own attire has changed and his blood and sweat has disappeared. He greets everyone and asks where Susan is:

> "My sister Susan," answered Peter shortly and gravely, "is no longer a friend of Narnia."

Damn.

Then several of the royal party start in with trash-talking her. Eustace says Susan never wants to come to their Narnia meetings anymore. Jill says Susan is only interested in "nylons and lipstick and invitations" and is "too keen on being grown-up." Um, so? Then Polly chimes in that Susan loves being mature and couldn't wait to become

---

[72] Revelation 21:4

a young adult and now wants to enjoy it for as long as possible. As if that is a bad thing!

Yep the girl totally deserves rejection by Aslan. What an evil woman! Keep in mind that the thing Susan missed out on was dying violently in a train crash! Peter must step in to prevent this petty dog-pile and get them all to talk about something else. Gossip and judgement will be a major thing in the Narnian afterlife, apparently.

In Christian theology it is sin that keeps a person from God.[73] So what sin did Lewis imply Susan committed? It seems she grew up. Worse, though. She grew up *into a woman*. Lewis once wrote to a child reader about Susan's fate that it was due to her being a "silly, conceited young woman"[74] but he added that there's "plenty of time for her to mend, and perhaps she will get to Aslan's country in the end." Mend what exactly? The sin of silliness? What even is that? The sin of being female? Or is it the sin of acting in a way Lewis doesn't prefer while female? (My personal life goal.)

Philip Pullman noticed the sexism in Susan's story:

> Where are the nice women of childbearing age? [...] There was a level on which of course [Susan] doesn't get to heaven because she's just like the witches, and they wear dresses and they're pretty."[75]

My daughter recently saw a cartoon with Poison Ivy in it and declared with no small amount of reverence, "One of her powers is kissing people *to death*!" Before I could react, she asked, "Can I wear lipstick to school?" Her excitement about wearing something that would make her feel powerful was palpable. What could I say? Deny my child a *killer* look? (Heh.) We have no rules against adding color to hair,

[73] Isaiah 59:2; 2 Thessalonians 1:9
[74] Letter to Kilmer family, dated 22 January 1957. Printed in "C. S. Lewis: Letters to Children." Edited by Lyle W. Dorsett and Marjorie Lamp Mead, 1985. (Touchstone).
[75] Laura Miller, 2008. *The Magician's Book: A Skeptic's Adventures in Narnia*, (New York, NY; Back Bay Books).

body, or clothing, which applies to all genders in my home, so I agreed. It was Little Bit's first time wearing purple lipstick. When she got to school, one of her girlfriends responded in a tone of pure judgment, "You're wearing lipstick? Really?" To this young girl, lipstick was forbidden for kids her age since her parents had taught her it was sexual. It couldn't be colorful or fun or anything else. Like the male creators of Poison Ivy, female lips were dangerous. And female sexuality? Now that's just darn right scary!

In "The Problem of Susan," a short story by Neil Gaiman which I consider Narnia canon, we see how life was for Susan after the events of *The Last Battle*. She is an older woman now, haunted by dreams of "bodies on the grass," throats being slit, and flies on corpses from the war with the White Witch Aslan had the children fight. Gaiman gives these battles the gritty reality they deserve instead of presenting them as a thrilling adventure.

Susan is now a retired professor. An eager young journalist is interviewing her about her life's work in literature. Gaiman answers Lewis' absurd charge of vanity when he has Susan tell her interviewer there was no "opportunity for nylons and lipsticks" when she found herself destitute without caretakers. (Spoiler: The Pevensie parents also died on another train at the same moment.) She went on to talk about another hard aspect to finding herself the sole survivor: identifying her family's bodies. When the interviewer gets a bit flippant about the experience, Susan responds:

> "There were a lot of people dead in that crash. I was taken to a nearby school, it was the first day of term, and they had taken the bodies there. My older brother looked okay. Like he was asleep. The other two were a bit messier. [...] I remember thinking what a great deal of

damage a train can do, when it hits another train, to the people who were travelling. I suppose you've never had to identify a body, dear?"[76]

When the journalist says no, Susan continues:

"My younger brother was decapitated, you know. A god who would punish me for liking nylons and parties by making me walk through that school dining room, with the flies, to identify Ed, well... he's enjoying himself a bit too much, isn't he? Like a cat, getting the last ounce of enjoyment out of a mouse."

I love the gruesome details laid out in an otherwise pedestrian conversation. Gaiman does not glorify the gore as the Narnia tales do, nor does he skip over the aftermath that such violence brings about. He makes it real. When this side of the story is told, the idea that Susan's sexuality should have been so harshly punished seems farcical. Sexuality is not evil, and Gaiman embraces it by having Susan happily recall her first sexual encounter or dream about a centaur's penis.

Defenders of C. S. Lewis have said that it was vanity, not female sexuality, that condemned Susan. However, Miller points out the inconsistency in such an argument:

Bree's vanity is a minor flaw in an otherwise good character, and Uncle Andrew's pride runs much deeper than just a preoccupation with appearances. Although Susan is not yet damned and still has a chance to 'mend,' the implication, in both Lewis's novel and the letter to his child reader, is that if she keeps on as she has been, preoccupied with feminine nonsense, this alone will be enough to bring her to a bad end. And that prompts a question: Why does Lewis consider an interest in lipstick, nylons, and invitations such an especially pernicious form of silliness? What makes these amusements so much worse than pipes and beer and 'bawdy' with your buddies at the pub? Why is feminine triviality so much worse than its masculine counterpart?

---

[76] Neil Gaiman; edited by: Al Sarrantonio, 2004. "The Problem of Susan," *Flights: Extreme Visions of Fantasy*, (New York; New American Library), pp. 393-402.

Miller's question is a solid one since Lewis was known to enjoy pipes, beer, and bawdy, which is explicit sexual talk. He obviously didn't feel he must "mend" his ways to achieve the perfect deathly destination.

The women in Narnia of "childbearing age" as Pullman puts it, are boring, and often unnamed. They *have to* be boring; almost everything else is considered a sin. Also, female sin means missing out on a Heaven filled with men. By the numbers, there are more men than women and boys than girls in the Narnia stories, and that also applies to the Narnian afterlife. Having one less woman there is rather like salt in the wound.

Maybe the trick is to commit as many female sins as possible (like talking, teaching, or thinking) to avoid dying in a horrific accident orchestrated by a sadist deity and going to a heaven populated by religious men and judgmental gossips? #LifeGoals

***

The door to the stable Tirian had come through stood alone in a field, unattached to a structure; the dead king could even walk completely around it! Yet a glimpse through the crack in the wood showed the nighttime stars and the Calormenes soldiers still standing around a bonfire. It was surely the same stable door, but, as Dead Digory explained, "Its inside is bigger than its outside."

Seven years after *The Last Battle* was published, a TV series produced in the same country would introduce us to a Time Lord with a time-traveling TARDIS that was "bigger on the inside." Coincidence? Or do we owe Lewis some credit for inspiring a major aspect of the longest-running television series of all time?

The "bigger than its outside" line will be followed up with Dead Queen Lucy saying:

"In our world too, a Stable once had something inside it that was bigger than our whole world."

Then everyone gagged on the blatant Jesus preaching. (Or maybe just me.) Bitsy was confused by this line and kept waiting for it to be explained. It never was. I asked if she knew what it meant after the chapter was over. "I just figured everything is going to be weird now," she shrugged.

Spoiler: *Everything is going to be weird now.*

***

The Calormenes then threw the Dwarves into the magic stable one by one. Instead of a sunny grassland, or even the harsh claws of Tash, these guys fall into an actual stable. Our kings and queens can see the Dwarves huddled together, only instead of the inside of a stable, it looks like they are sitting in a lovely field. Even when the Dwarves tell them plainly that they are experiencing a stable—its smells, its darkness, the feel of it—our royal lot cannot get their collective heads around the idea that maybe just maybe the Dwarves can't see the sun and sky. Lucy calls them stupid, and even puts "filthy stable-litter" in one's face that look like beautiful flowers from her perspective. That's an easy enough mistake, but her continued failure to understand that Dwarf's reaction to her and her failure to listen to him as he repeatedly tells her about his reality seems deliberate on her part. (Why listen to unbelievers, I guess, when God has blinded them?)

Tirian takes ignorance-bordering-on-idiocy one step further by adding violence to the mix! After making a big point of telling the Dwarves that he is their lawful king (dude, let it go), he angrily grabs one Dwarf and throws him hard away from the others. This action smashes the Dwarf's face into the stable wall! Now the Dwarf is in pain, but no one blames Tirian for this. **They blame the Dwarf** for still believing he's in the stable!

Then Aslan growls at the Dwarves to scare them. Oh, surprise, it's Aslan! It is the afterlife after all, and this is our Jesus. When he appears, the kings and queens immediately start groveling at his feet and worshipping him. Tirian gets told "Well done" by the lion, which is the biblical equivalence to getting the ultimate pat on the head. Lucy begs Aslan to please help the Dwarves, so Aslan makes a meal magically appear in front of them. This food looks like a feast to the kings and queens, but turns out to be hay, trough water, and a raw cabbage leaf in the Dwarves' world. This causes the Dwarves to randomly start beating each other up over the food. Thanks for nothing, Aslan.

Our Jesus lion then explains that the Dwarves are stuck in the stable because they are clever unbelievers. He launches into the most ridiculous explanation for it:

> "They have chosen cunning instead of belief. Their prison is only in their own minds, yet they are in that prison; and so afraid of being taken in that they cannot be taken out. But come, children. I have other work to do."

Being clever is apparently bad! (Being taken in: good!) Also, who cares about these people because we have other stuff to do! Instantly Lucy, who earlier could think of nothing else, stops caring about the Dwarves when Aslan is done with them. Moving right along!

Aslan is powerless against unbelief just as the Christian god seems to be. Aslan can do little for the Dwarves in a God-created-a-rock-so-big-even-he-can't-lift-it scenario. I once asked my Sunday School teacher if God could simply save people without them believing, specifically after they had been sent to Hell. The answer was a firm "no." The "all-powerful" Yahweh's hands were tied when it came to his own rules. (And iron chariots,[77] randomly.) If God could just forgive or eliminate all humans of sin then there'd be no reason for Jesus to be brutally killed to atone for it! Clearly God can't change his mind or change the rules. (Except when he totally does that all the time.[78]) Therefore the system is our god now since God is a slave of the system.

A problem I have with Aslan's logic in this case is if it truly is the Dwarves' inability to accept the idea of a different reality that keeps them locked in their current one, then their sin is only rigidity of thinking. How then is it different than our main characters' inability to accept the Dwarves' reality? That's also a rigidity of thinking. It makes me wonder if there's not some other dimension where a version of Lucy, Peter, Tirian, Jill and the rest are sitting huddled in a dank stable as the Dwarf version of Aslan pities their attachment to fantasy worlds. He won't help them since he has other, more important Dwarf god work to do. Meanwhile the children see nothing but grassy fields as they rack up concussions from bumping into stable walls.

Aslan will leave the Dwarves there permanently for all eternity, huddled together in a kind of hellish purgatory in their own heads.

Not *all* Dwarves were locked in the eternal torture stable thanks to the lone believer myth! Dead Eustace spots a Dwarf who had helped shoot the horses standing there in Heaven! He started to wonder about how that was right when "a great joy put everything else out of his head." Little Bit did not like this part. I mean, this Dwarf murdered PONIES! Like talking pony, people! (Not that that distinction matters for Bitsy.) Why was he rewarded for it?

It was not the evil actions of the Dwarves that condemned them, but the evil unbelief that kept them from paradise. Christianity must present doubt over its claims as coming from "an evil heart of

---

[77] Judges 1:19
[78] Exodus 32:14

307

unbelief"[79] in order to justify its doctrine that salvation is through faith alone.[80] If not wanting to be "taken in" is truly evil, then the Bible can justify Yahweh ordering the death penalty for it.[81] If belief is the only thing that gets a person a ticket to Heaven, as my denomination believed, then we can have one of the Dwarves enter Heaven no matter how immoral he was or how heinous his actions. He must have secretly believed *not so deep down*.

***

After Little Bit goes to bed at night, I stay up and think over what we have read together. After chapter thirteen, there are several things not sitting right with me—all of which come from High King Peter's mouth. None of these things particularly offended or even grabbed Bitsy's attention. With something like the Dwarves storyline, Bits talked back to the book and said, "Hey! That's wrong!" Yet when Peter implies his sister is a bad person for being too girly or he brushes off abuses of others, it would often not elicit the same reaction. It's like how the smell of a full kitty litter box is inarguably bad but smelling cat pee very faintly elsewhere in the house is worse because while the smell isn't as bad, it's likely done more damage. These small things are sneaky as they can pile up and influence our opinion of what is acceptable.

When Peter is catching Tirian up on what has happened since he saw them around the dining room table in London, he describes dying—the noise and the jolt of it—and then arriving in this beautiful place with fruit so tasty Lewis takes great pains *not* to describe it, only to compare it negatively with anything in the real world. Then he says:

---

[79] Hebrews 3:12
[80] Titus 3:5
[81] 2 Chronicles 15:13

"Well, for a long time (at least I suppose it was a long time) nothing happened."

Being in a place where you can never die or age, and having *nothing* happen, has got to be one of my top ten nightmares. White torture is a form of psychological abuse that involves sensory deprivation and isolation. People cannot tell how much time is passing which makes their imprisonment feel extraordinarily longer. Peter knows Tirian arrived "five minutes ago," so he is still aware of time passing. Yet when he speaks of nothing happening "for a long time," we get the idea that a long, concrete amount of time did pass while they were stuck on pause in this post-death existence. It's just hard to consider the possibilities, especially when we realize Lewis believed this state they find themselves in now will last for *all eternity*.

Oh and Peter is *smiling*. He just saw a terrifying monster grab a man "five minutes ago" and he's already smiling! Is Peter a sociopath? Maybe. Maybe they all are. When Lucy next opened her mouth there was a "thrill in her voice" because she had been "too happy to speak" up to this point. FIVE MINUTES AFTER SEEING A MOTHER-EFFING DEMON GRAB A DUDE.

While eternal boredom was something I fretted over as a kid, it was this emotional castration I worried about as a young adult. According to my childhood theology, many people I loved would go, along with the demons, into Hell. I couldn't stomach this thought. How would I enjoy Heaven knowing people were actively being tortured? How could Heaven be all smiles? This meant it would necessarily have to be a place that steals a person's humanity, binds their mind, and gives them an abnormal, almost mentally ill response to the pain of others. How else do you survive living in a place with a lake of literal fire in your backyard[82] and the sounds of "weeping and gnashing of teeth" nearby?![83]

My mom once told me that I'd be "too busy looking at the face of Jesus" to worry about anything else. This thinking is mirrored in Eustace's great joy that "put everything else out of his head." It's like a lobotomy that takes out all the human parts that would make a person rightly horrified by Aslan's actions and leaves them happy and brainless.

In an episode of *Doctor Who* called "The God Complex," a monster calls people to worship him by giving them feelings of spiritual bliss. This causes the devoted to happily sacrifice themselves to the monster. The only warning they get that a member of the group is about to be eaten is when that person starts reverently saying, "Praise Him." In a memorable scene, a character named Rita feels the spiritual pull and knows she's going to her death. She says goodbye via a monitor and her words still haunt me.

> "Doctor, I can feel the rapture approaching me like a wave. I don't want you to witness this. I want you to remember me the way I was."[84]

You can watch her fear turn to bliss in this heart-rending scene right before she's torn apart.

Here is where Lewis loses his sense of our characters. They are no longer compelling, no longer understandable. I would argue they are no longer human, and by that I do not mean they have become something *better*, but instead some integral part of them is missing. This world no longer clicks. These people and their reactions no longer work. They may be blissful, but they are *wrong*. Off. Twisted. Their lion could tear them apart and it would be bliss.

---

[82] Revelation 21:8

[83] Luke 13:28

[84] "The God Complex." *Doctor Who*, written by Toby Whithouse, directed by Nick Hurran, BBC. 2011.

Narnia's afterlife loses all the aspects of Narnia proper that gave it its depth and richness. Taking out the darker parts means the image loses its dimensions, like taking the shading out of a painting. Even the fruit of Heaven is not described by what it is, but simply as better than what we know. This description is empty and meaningless. It also turns the simple pleasures of Narnia we have experienced so fully to this point—drinking, smoking, eating, dancing, adventuring—and labels it all *less than*.

I was born into a group of people who longed for Heaven. I watched this longing for precious everyday joys and experiences. There was an anticipation of some future thing, always nebulous, that would be unimaginably better than what was. And *unimaginable* it must be! Giving it shape makes all its flaws and unfitting parts stand out badly like hearing all those details in my friend's 3x5 card read out in an anthropology class.

In Narnia's version of the hereafter, Aslan doesn't care if you're a good person, nor does his Heaven make you one. That is, unless we have a *very* different definition of goodness. For example, Eustace says he hopes "Tash ate the Dwarfs" and calls them "little swine." Lucy chides him for being "horrid." Saying horrid things, being judgmental, wishing violence on people, and gossiping about a person must not count as sin since all of it is tolerated in Aslan's Country. I mean, we all know the real sin is *nylons*.

With perfect holiness, as Heaven is supposed to be, how can one be horrid? They can't be. Yet how can Lewis write a good story with compelling characters if some are not, at least occasionally, honestly horrid? What about glum? What happens to our favorite Marsh-wiggle when he finds himself in the afterlife with everyone? He is struck mute! Lewis does not give him a single line of dialog! What could Puddleglum be allowed to say? Everything that made up his character was, well, *glum*. When that is not allowed, who exactly is he? It's not like we get a happier version of the character; the words that defined both himself and his culture are struck from his mouth. Whatever he has become, he's no longer Puddleglum.

Aslan's "other work to do" was way more important than alleviating the suffering of Dwarves, so he's about to get to it.

He's got a Narnia to destroy.

The Last Battle: Chapter 14

"Where is Aslan sending the people he doesn't like?"
"Are you familiar with what the New Testament says happens to non-Christians after they die?"
"*Ooooooooh.* Um, Mom? Do all Christians think something like that will happen to me when I die?"
"No, not all of them."
"But isn't that why I got pulled aside at that family event and they wouldn't let me go until I lied and said I believed in Jesus?"
"That shouldn't have happened to you. I'm sorry."
"I still feel weird about it."
"That's because of the Holy Spirit inside you. You're a Christian forever now!"
"What?! *MOM!*"
"Hahahaha!"

***

Aslan starts to destroy Narnia by waking up Father Time. He was mentioned briefly in *The Silver Chair* when Jill and Eustace saw him sleeping under the earth. Well, he's up now and blowing a horn of "deadly beauty." Aslan says that while Father Time is sleeping his name is "Time" but now he needs a new name. This is another hint that this new life will be lived in eternity, and that time will cease to exist. (More nightmares for me.)

Next all the stars crash down onto the planet. This causes a "spreading blackness" that creates "some terror" in the children's minds. (Death, darkness, and terror! Much better than harps!) The stars that are falling turn out to be people—people with spears. They had been trapped in the sky and were now free. What a wonderful imagination Lewis has. So original. Oh wait, this is all taken directly from Scripture.[85]

One popular astrophysicist has said of these prophecies:

> "You know, one of the signs of the Second Coming is that the stars will fall out of the sky and land on earth. To even write that means you don't know what those things are. You have no concept of what the actual universe is. So everybody who tried to make proclamations about the physical universe based on Bible passages got the answer wrong."[86]

While I can no longer base my astronomy (or eschatology) on the Bible, I still get a chill when I read Lewis' words about the sky being "starless for ever." It really does feel like the end of everything. The star people land next to Aslan and create an "enormous and very terrible" shadow. Aslan's shadow is rather clearly the entrance to Hell.

For whatever reason these glorified bodies our characters have only seem to erase sweat and blood and project beautiful clothing, but they don't protect them physically as we'll see later when Peter's hand goes numb from cold. Their new glorified minds are also unpredictable. They keep our saints from experiencing the horror of watching people snatched by terrifying demons or sentenced to shadow hell in the next

---

[85] Revelation 12:4

[86] Many people will recognize these are the words of Neil DeGrasse Tyson. His name has been moved to the footnotes in respect to readers his alleged sexual misconduct has affected. Available at: http://loltheists.com/?p=4062

scene, but they can still experience terror when watching the sky fall. The *happy happy* here is not super consistent.

Aslan sends dragons, giant lizards, and featherless birds with bat wings (so just *bats* then) to literally eat Narnia's landscapes. The Book of Revelation includes this same removing of mountains and islands[87] but without the dragons, making Lewis' version officially superior. Without land masses, the oceans flood all of Narnia. When the destruction is done, all the dragons and lizards and giant bats shrivel up and become bones before the children's eyes like Walter Donovan in *Indiana Jones and the Last Crusade* after drinking from the wrong grail.

What happens to the people living on the planet getting destroyed? They die. If not by a dragon's bite, then in the flood. Wait, drowning babies in a flood? What kind of monster would cause that? (*cough*)

Wailing is heard as millions and millions of (probably newly drowned) people are forced before Aslan while our dead heroes watch from behind the stable door.

It's Judgement Day, bitches!

Each person is made to look Aslan in the eye. Lewis, in his narrator hat, says, "I don't think they had any choice about that." He's unusually passive in these pages. As if saying, "The children never saw them again," and "I don't know what became of them," distances himself in the least from the words he's actively writing about their demise. It's clear that the ones Aslan didn't like—you know, the unbelievers and Black people—are sent into Aslan's "huge black shadow." Since Lewis publicly believed in eternal torture in Hell, it's no secret where the shadow leads.

---

[87] Revelation 6:14

Are we still smiling? Yes! There was "laughter in Aslan's eyes." What did people have to do to be spared from this psycho's shadow? They had to love him:

> But the others looked in the face of Aslan and loved him, though some of them were very frightened at the same time. And all these came in at the Door, in on Aslan's right.

Being frightened of someone you love is super healthy. That way they don't hurt you. Ask any abuser.

Little Bit listened to this whole scene silently without any of her usual interruptions. She kept waiting to hear if all this madness was some kind of dream sequence or if there'd be a better explanation. Without a Sunday School background this section doesn't make a lot of sense. Honestly, it's all truly ugly without religious whitewashing.

After Judgement Day was over, Aslan ordered what was left of Narnia to die. The sun started to swell and caused a deep red glow to reflect upon the moon. This red reflection looked "like blood" to match the prophecy out of the Old Testament that says the final day of judgement and destruction of Earth will have a dark sun and a moon that turns into blood.[88] The New Testament also mentions this prophecy.[89] Instead of literal blood, Lewis simply has the moon reflecting a dying sun, which is rather poetic.

Father Time—still named this since Aslan was too lazy to rename him after obliterating time—is ordered to smash the sun into the moon. (Because these two things are totally the same size and distance.) With this act, the world dies in an icy blast. I assume, but it's not clear, that this action also kills Father Time in a Sampson-murders-a-temple-full-of-people-for-God-and-also-gets-crushed-to-death way.[90] If not, he's stuck all alone for all eternity on a cold, dead planet.

---

[88] Joel 2:31
[89] Acts 2:20
[90] Judges 16:28-31

And that's it for Narnia.

"I saw it begin," said the Lord Digory. "I did not think I would live to see it die."

With nothing more than death on the other side, Aslan has Peter close the stable door forever. (This hurts his hand.) While no one mourns for the *people* eaten by Aslan's shadow, they do mourn for Narnia. For those curious about how this works with the whole "no tears in Heaven" thing, Lucy informs our readers that she's sure Aslan would not stop their mourning. Tirian even says it would be discourteous not to cry for "mother," as he called Narnia. There is no virtue in withholding tears. He's not wrong. Lewis departs from Scripture here for the best of reasons. He stops just short of making his beloved characters total and complete zombies. Well, all except for Peter.

Peter, Lewis' version of the perfect man, chides his sister.

"What, Lucy! You're not crying? With Aslan ahead, and all of us here?"

First off, crying is not a bad thing. It's actually super weird that Peter is *not* grieving the death of all those people and his whole beloved world. The implication is that "with Aslan ahead" they should not be sad. Ever. No matter what Aslan has allowed or is doing to other people.

Second, *all of them* are there? Aren't we forgetting someone? YOUR OWN SISTER, YOU HEARTLESS POTATO NUGGET! Screw Susan, right? Out of sight out of mind. (This is your brain on Aslan.) Peter is supposed to be our role model to emulate. To Lewis, Peter is the mature one handling things correctly, controlling his emotions *like a man should*, and who is exactly in the right headspace. In other words, he's the worst kind of apathetic, emotionally stunted brute. The other children should be learning from his example. Well, I keep calling them children, as they technically are, but I'm not sure

I can use that label and remain true to the text. Heaven has robbed them of childhood, just as it has taken the physical years from the body of Polly. Each character is in a state of in-between—their bodies maturing or reversing to that same developmental age Susan is condemned for desiring.

So far, Heaven has been incredibly underwhelming or downright disturbing. Yet it is supposed to be these aspects that make it a real adventure. Narnia was only as good as its imperfect anchor to the corporeal. What *is* the richest fruit, but one that alleviates hunger? How is the sweetest drink satisfying if all our drinks are sweet? What is a good rest without its connection to a stressful reprieve? Laura Miller sums this disconnect up perfectly:

> Lewis, reaching for celestial beauty, attains only a hallucinatory hyperrealism that unstitches Narnia from the humble, medieval details that made it live.

Miller found *The Last Battle* to be the least favorite of every single author and expert she interviewed for her compendium on Narnia. It left her, as it left me, empty and gloomy. There's no doubt as to why. Lewis killed off a beloved world only to attempt to upsell us on some heavenly one. I couldn't help but notice the analogy between this and the trade-in Christianity offers: give up your life for a presumed eternity no one has seen or touched or tasted or known. It's just *better*. Take our word for it.

The only thing left for our group to do is turn their backs on the Narnia they have known, believing the lie that it was somehow inferior to where they find themselves now, and head into this blinding necrocountry before them.

Further up, and further in.

The Last Battle: Chapters 15-16

"Yay! Our bodies crumpled up and we died! Woohoo! We're so happy!"
"Yeah, they did have a weird reaction to that."
"I hope someone saves them from all this."
"From all what?"
"This weird place that makes their heads funny."
"You mean Heaven?"
"I guess?"

***

Aslan calls everyone he hasn't sentenced to Shadow Hell to follow him further into Narnia Heaven. Our party starts walking along while talking fondly about past wars, among other things, because this is how we remember the late, blood-soaked Narnia. All the dogs are there because, obviously, woofies go to Heaven. After a short period of time, arguing breaks out amongst the dogs since they could swear they smelled a Calormene.

A dark-skinned person in Heaven? What! How is that even possible?

Tirian wonders if they will meet the Calormene "in peace or war." You'd think war would stay out of Heaven. Not Tirian's Heaven, and certainly not the biblical one. The smell does turn out to be a Calormene. There's a possible implication here that Calormenes smell bad, or at least different than what Lewis would think of as the typical person. Also, this smell is **rare** here. He may be the only man of color in Heaven. He turns out to be Emeth from the bonfire scene who went willingly into the stable. If this seems like it happened a million years ago, it might have! Time no longer exists. (*internally screaming*)

Everyone immediately demands an explanation for what the hell (no pun intended) Emeth is doing there. We can't let him just be here without explaining himself. It's like when police officers find a person of color walking through their own neighborhood, especially when it's a *nice* neighborhood.

Emeth greets the men first, calling them "Warlike Kings," and then next, "Ladies whose beauty illuminates the universe." (That about sums up men and women. Nothing lazy, missing, or unnecessary about that description in the least.) Then he launches into his tale. This guy was a true believer in Tash, so when he figured out his masters were atheists, it created all sorts of rage feelings inside him. He knew they had "called on [Tash] without knowledge or belief" and now Tash was about to get some vengeance on their unbelieving asses.

When Emeth went through the stable door he ran into a Calormene guard sent there to kill anyone who entered. Emeth killed that guy instead and dumped his body outside. Afterwards, he went to explore this sunshine and grass world on the other side of the door and that's when he ran into Aslan. (Insert a lot of lavish praise here for the terrible lion in his story.) Aslan was particularly pleased with Emeth's gross willingness to be happily killed by him:

"[B]etter to see the Lion and die than to be Tisroc of the world and live and not to have seen him."

Aslan calls Emeth a son and welcomes him to Heaven. When he asks why he gets to be here, Aslan says:

"Child, all the service thou hast done to Tash, I account as service done to me."

What? Have we forgotten that Tash required human sacrifices? Human sacrifices! Better *that* than being an unbeliever?

Aslan then explains how belief is so very important—how even if a person believed in a deity, but it happened to be the wrong deity, it at least counted as earnest seeking through faith, and faith always gets rewarded. Therefore, all Emeth's deeds in service of Tash now count as service to Aslan. Lewis gets this idea from Hebrews 11:6 and Matthew 7:7-8. Now before half the Christian denominations can protest, these ideas are also directly contradicted by Revelation 9:20 and Hosea 4:6. (It's almost like the Bible is a hot mess.)

Emeth finishes his story with joyful self-abasement:

"[Aslan] called me Beloved, me who am but as a dog."

This immediately offends the dogs present. I imagine it would offend the other Brown people, too, but where'd they all go? Welcome to White Heaven, you poor lonely bastard!

In the biblical tales, when Jesus calls the Canaanite woman a dog, after initially straight up ignoring her, she responds by agreeing with him! She had to mollify him so that he would heal her daughter who was "suffering terribly."[91] Just try getting Christians to admit this is bad behavior from their favorite biblical character. *Good luck.* According to Divine Command Theory, refusing to alleviate terrible suffering until a woman (whole other issue) agrees she's a "dog" (Jesus' word) must also qualify as good if Jesus does it.

After Emeth finished justifying his presence in Heaven, a fat donkey approached timidly. It was Puzzle!

I like the idea of fat heavenly bodies. Fat isn't bad, doesn't make him run slower according to the text, and is just another beautiful difference. I don't want to know Lewis' motivation for making him fat since it might be a punishment for his deeds when alive. I'd love to pretend Lewis is fat-friendly, but even if he were, it's only when a *guy* is fat. Women certainly aren't allowed to be.

Let's recall that Puzzle had a direct hand in bringing about the fall of Narnia which led to the suffering and death of many creatures. It's

---

[91] Matthew 15

okay, though, BECAUSE HE'S NOT A SILLY GIRL LIKE SUSAN. (One ticket to heaven please!)

Puzzle was suffering from extreme shame over his part in the end of the world and everyone reassured him it would be okay. Later when our group meets up with Aslan again, Puzzle will be the first called before him. It's a great honor. Puzzle has the most tragic of self-views and often calls himself stupid. Aslan loves that!

At some point they all start running together towards Aslan. Emeth isn't mentioned again so he's either silent after this or left behind. (Hey, we don't socialize with the Calormene just 'cause he's here!) They realize they do not get "hot or tired or out of breath." They must still have had to breathe as evidenced by the dogs getting water in their noses that caused them to start "spluttering and sneezing." The physical rules here are always changing, and so are the emotional ones. It's during this run that Lucy realizes she is incapable of feeling afraid. "Try it," she dares the others. Eustace takes her up on the challenge and he finds he cannot achieve that emotion. What they *could* feel, however, was some sort of hesitation or worry, even shame in Puzzle's case. When they arrived at the garden where Digory first took the magic fruit from the magic tree, they dared not enter as "none of them was bold enough." Reepicheep must personally welcome them inside before they'll go in.

Yes, our favorite murderous mouse is here! He's wearing a sword for killing folks, too! Actually, everyone is here![92] Tirian's father greets our party. He's no longer weak from the battle he died in, but young and healthy. Fledge, formerly Strawberry, is also there, as well as every main character: Rilian "and his mother, the Star's daughter"—who even in the afterlife has no name—who comes out with Caspian. There's also our silenced Puddleglum, Trumpkin, Bree, Hwin, Cor,

---

[92] Minus silly girls and most women of childbearing age and people of color and foreigners from other countries and certain animal species.

Aravis who is referred to as Cor's wife even though no married man is listed as someone's husband, the Beavers, Tumnus, etc. The brutal Corin even gets a place in Heaven, valued far and above the gentle Susan.

Lewis explains that this world is like the real Narnia, but better in some indescribable way. Lewis tries his best to explain what he means by "better" and compares it to seeing a beautiful bit of nature reflected in a mirror. The reflection is mysteriously "deeper, more wonderful, more like places in a story." That mirror world is Narnia Heaven. Little Bit says she would have reversed the analogy and made the mirror reflection the poorer one, and the real thing the better one. It reminds me of what Neil Gaiman said in that same interview with Laura Miller:

> "As a kid, you edit out The Last Battle in a way because it's not true."[93]

Our friends find there's an entire other Narnia inside of the garden they were initially worried about entering. The gate of the garden is similar to the stable door as it's also bigger on the inside. Somewhere inside this garden is another entire version of Narnia. There may be countless Narnias resting inside each other.

Across some distant divide, England is there, and with it, the dead Pevensie parents. They had been waiting for their children who are no longer quite children. They are happy, smiling, and waving. No one misses the child who is not there—the one left home to identify the bodies.

> "You do not yet look so happy as I mean you to be."

Something is still wrong, and Aslan notices the group's mood. Lucy informs him that they were "so afraid" of enjoying themselves fully since they didn't know when they'd be sent away. (Flashback to Lucy

---

[93] Miller, *The Magician's Book: A Skeptic's Adventures in Narnia.*

daring anyone to be afraid. "Try it," she had recently said.) Here, at the very end, Aslan reveals they are all dead—brutally killed in the railway accident along with their parents who were in a different train. (*Surprise! I orchestrated your deaths!*) At hearing this, "Their hearts leapt, and a wild hope rose within them." Then the book ends with everyone thrilled they don't ever have to go home again.

Bitsy rolled her eyes. I agreed with her that that wasn't a normal reaction, but it is the Christian expectation.

Honestly, it's all very, dreadfully *Christian*.

9
Where Do We Go From Here?

"That's the end of the very last book."
"Cool. Can we read something else?"
"…"

***

This is the way the Narnia series ends, not with applause but with a shrug.

As we put the large volume back on the shelf for the final time, I couldn't help feeling sad. Bitsy moved on from the series so quickly with hardly a look back. I wanted to sit with it a while, grieve the ending, and memorialize the story. Bitsy was already suggesting other titles, *rather callously during my fragile state I might add.*

Bits has yet to reference the series since its ending. Well, except for once when filling out the "hobbies and interests" section on her baseball player bio card. The announcer uses the players' cards to talk about them when they are up to bat. (It's as adorable as it sounds.) A parent of another player wearing a cross around her neck came up to Little Bit after a game and got in her face with that loud, overly-friendly high-pitched voice some people affect around kids with disabilities: *"You read Narnia? I loved those books! I'm so glad you enjoyed them. Aren't they great? I loved Aslan!"*

Bitsy smiled politely and quietly dropped the Narnia reference from her card before the next game.

My kid enjoyed our talks about Narnia, but not the story itself, at least not how I enjoyed it at her age. This baffled and disappointed me in a way I didn't expect. Even Narnia's worst critics acknowledge the magic of the series. To Bitsy, the harmful elements ruined the magic. She enjoyed the conversation much more.

I feel honored and overjoyed that my daughter loves our talks and continuously seeks out discussion with me on various topics. Pushing back against the harmful ideas in the Narnia series was something she excelled at as a naturally empathetic person. It was easy sport for her to pick apart the rubbish from Lewis' worldview. Yet it was this constant alertness—seeking out any trappings of elitism, racism, sexism, and religious bias—that made getting lost in the fantasy harder for her.

Bitsy has read many books whose writings pale in comparison to Lewis' Narnia, yet which gave her a great deal more pleasure. Modern books are superior in this regard, or perhaps they are simply more insidious when it comes to their moral failings. In either case, children's novels these days speak Little Bit's language and avoid the obviousness of 1950s' prejudices. They are safer vehicles in which to sit back, relax, escape.

I can't help feeling that when attempting to add these stories to my daughter's imagination toolbox, I put too much emphasis on all the rust. This is pure egotism on my part since what I found rich and fulfilling in my childhood will not be what my child finds so. For her, Harry Potter is a much better story. I must respect that she is her own person, and while I may never try to push her into the family business, or live vicariously through her sports or academic life, I have indeed had expectations when it came to literature. *I brought you into this world, daughter, and you will be enamored of magic wardrobes!*

I take perverse comfort in the thought of Bitsy reading J. K. Rowling to her own children someday, and them picking apart the lack of diversity, the gender binary language of witch and wizard, and other things not even on my radar yet. Her own daughter will say, "Didn't this author say some transphobic things about our friends? Why are we reading this again? Why is Grandma grinning so devilishly right now?"

I needn't worry. Little Bit has a multitude of books from our shelves, her school, and our oft-visited library to outpace and outstrip what constituted my meager offerings at her age. My literary world resembled the ruins of Charn; if it wasn't "inspired by God" or written by certain Christian evangelicals, it was discouraged. Narnia was so different with its mysteries, magic, and subversion of my safe Baptist bubble that it will always mean a great deal to me. Despite its faults, it gave me something not too foreign but not too safe—a pagan-inspired Christian-fueled steppingstone out of fundamentalism and into the blinding grassland of the world of literature.

I hope Bits will come back to these stories one day, without Mom around to impress or a bedtime to stall with questions, and she will allow herself to drink deeply and drown in these stories.

Yet, let's be real, Narnia is problematic AF.

So back around we circle to the question that inspired this entire literary endeavor: "Is Aslan evil?"

He kills. He hurts for his pleasure. He takes. He controls. He tortures. He is, from all accounts, a slave master and sadist. If that is evil, then he is thoroughly bathed in the definition. The heartache inherent in this revelation is that *The Chronicles of Narnia* has often been referred to as "Aslan's story." If so, it is lessened by the association.

I want to believe Narnia is more than this, just as the Bible has more literary value than simply teaching about a brutal ancient god. It is amazing to me that a man such as Clive Staples "Jack" Lewis, mired as he was to his oppressive preconceptions, could draw readers, then and now, to Mr. Tumnus' door, up the giant steps to Harfang castle, down the tunnels of Underland, through portals disguised as pools, and finally into an endless playground hidden forever in the one before it. Narnia inspires our imaginations despite the constraints that dogma placed around it like a vice.

Narnia is not for everyone. Maybe it will never be fully embraced by Little Bit's generation who, much better than we, cannot help but to kick loudly at the parts that cause harm to those they love. However, for that evangelical Christian girl forced to abstain from worldly life and education, who is imprisoned in a religion that treats her as chattel—these books are for her. Just like they were for me.

Escape, all you Little Bits who are less fortunate, into a world of life, dancing, imagination, talking beasts, witches, wild rides, and magic.

Don't worry, your church won't mind.

Acknowledgments

I would like to profusely thank Karen Garst who gave me a voice and a platform. Without her encouragement, this book would not exist. We've now both appeared in each others' acknowledgment pages. (*high five*)

Also a huge thanks to the not-so-little-anymore Bitsy who let me capture her ten-year-old intellect and bottle it into these pages. Your thoughts and insights made this possible.

And a special thank you to my husband who was hugely supportive while writing and editing took me away from our evenings together. Thanks for saving *The Good Place* episodes for me and sorry for gushing about Queen Jadis so much.

Lastly, a shout out to Microsoft Word's oft-ignored suggestion of, "Consider using precise language." You were… ever present.

About the Author

As a child, Alexis was forced to memorize scripture before she could even read. She memorized six books of the Bible and hundreds of other verses before turning 12.

Alexis earned an interdisciplinary degree in biblical studies and psychology from San Diego Christian College where she graduated valedictorian, then devoted the first thirty years of her life to Bible study, foreign missions, and church service. The birth of her daughter ignited her faith deconstruction. Today Alexis serves as the executive director of Sunday Assembly San Diego, an inclusive, non-religious community. She lives in San Diego with her spouse and two children.

www.ingramcontent.com/pod-product-compliance
Lightning Source LLC
Chambersburg PA
CBHW031125090426
42738CB00008B/972